JavaScript™ For Dummies® 3rd Edition

Cheat Sheet

W9-BNR-089

Why Doesn't Anything Work?!

Stuck? Clueless? *Nothing* works and no idea where to start? Not to worry; take a look at the following suggestions (scanning them in order will work best).

✔ Is your Web browser installed and configured correctly, including your communications stuff? (See Chapter 1.)

✔ Is JavaScript enabled?

From Navigator:
   Choose Edit➪Preferences➪Advanced➪ Enable JavaScript in Navigator

From Internet Explorer:
   Choose Tools➪Internet Options and click the Security tab

   Click the Custom Level button

Scroll down until the Scripting category appears

Click Enable for these options: Active Scripting; Allow Paste Operations Via Script; and Scripting of Java Applets

✔ Are all your JavaScript statements between <SCRIPT> . . . </SCRIPT> tags (except JavaScript statements attached to event handlers, which don't have to be in these tags)?

✔ Does your HTML file work as it should by itself if you delete your JavaScript statements?

✔ Do the names of your JavaScript variables all start with an alphabetic character (or an underscore)?

Helpful Hints

To Do This . . .	Do This . . .
Load a JavaScript-enabled Web page	
In Navigator:	Double-click on the Navigator icon of a file on your machine; or File➪Open Page
In Internet Explorer:	File➪Open
Look at someone else's JavaScript code	
In Navigator:	View➪Page Source
In Internet Explorer:	View➪Source
Copy and paste someone else's JavaScript code	Ctrl+C to copy; Ctrl+V to paste
Find a JavaScript-related news group	
In Navigator:	Communicator➪Collabra Discussions➪Join Groups
In Internet Explorer:	Tools➪Mail and News➪Read News
Create a hyperlink	<A> . . . </A>
Create an HTML form	<FORM> . . . </FORM>

For Dummies®: Bestselling Book Series for Beginners

JavaScript™ For Dummies,® 3rd Edition

Cheat Sheet

Netscape Navigator's Document Object Model

The following document object hierarchy lists the built-in objects you can work with in client-side JavaScript, along with their relationships to each other.

Object	JavaScript syntax
window	window (optional)
document	document
applet	document.applets[0]
anchor	document.*someAnchor*
area	document.*someArea*
image	document.*someImage*
form	document.*someForm*
button	document.*someForm.someButton*
checkbox	document.*someForm.someCheckbox*
fileUpload	document.*someForm.someFileElement*
hidden	document.*someForm.someHidden*
password	document.*someForm.somePassword*
radio	document.*someForm.someRadio*
reset	document.*someForm.someReset*
select	document.*someForm.someSelect*
submit	document.*someForm.someSubmit*
text	document.*someForm.someText*
textarea	document.*someForm.someTextarea*
link	document.*someLink*
object	document.*someObject*
plugin	docment.embeds[0]
frame, parent, self, top	frame, parent, self, top (all of these are also synonyms for window)
history	history
location	location
locationbar	locationbar
menubar	menubar
navigator	navigator
personalbar	personalbar
scrollbar	scrollbar
statusbar	statusbar
toolbar	toolbar

Hungry Minds™

Hungry Minds, the Hungry Minds logo, For Dummies, the For Dummies Bestselling Book Series logo and all related trade dress are trademarks or registered trademarks of Hungry Minds, Inc. All other trademarks are the property of their respective owners.

For Dummies®: Bestselling Book Series for Beginners

TM

BESTSELLING BOOK SERIES

References for the Rest of Us! ®

Are you intimidated and confused by computers? Do you find that traditional manuals are overloaded with technical details you'll never use? Do your friends and family always call you to fix simple problems on their PCs? Then the For Dummies® computer book series from Hungry Minds, Inc. is for you.

For Dummies books are written for those frustrated computer users who know they aren't really dumb but find that PC hardware, software, and indeed the unique vocabulary of computing make them feel helpless. For Dummies books use a lighthearted approach, a down-to-earth style, and even cartoons and humorous icons to dispel computer novices' fears and build their confidence. Lighthearted but not lightweight, these books are a perfect survival guide for anyone forced to use a computer.

Already, millions of satisfied readers agree. They have made For Dummies books the #1 introductory level computer book series and have written asking for more. So, if you're looking for the most fun and easy way to learn about computers, look to For Dummies books to give you a helping hand.

Hungry Minds™

1/01

JavaScript™

FOR

DUMMIES®

3RD EDITION

JavaScript™
FOR
DUMMIES®
3RD EDITION

by Emily A. Vander Veer

Hungry Minds™

Best-Selling Books • Digital Downloads • e-Books • Answer Networks • e-Newsletters • Branded Web Sites • e-Learning

New York, NY ◆ Cleveland, OH ◆ Indianapolis, IN

JavaScript™ For Dummies¸ 3rd Edition

Published by
Hungry Minds, Inc.
909 Third Avenue
New York, NY 10022
www.hungryminds.com
www.dummies.com (Dummies Press Web Site)

Library of Congress Control Number: 00-106297

ISBN: 0-7645-0633-1

Printed in the United States of America

10 9 8 7 6 5

3B/QU/QT/QS/IN

Distributed in the United States by Hungry Minds, Inc.

Distributed by CDG Books Canada Inc. for Canada; by Transworld Publishers Limited in the United Kingdom; by IDG Norge Books for Norway; by IDG Sweden Books for Sweden; by IDG Books Australia Publishing Corporation Pty. Ltd. for Australia and New Zealand; by TransQuest Publishers Pte Ltd. for Singapore, Malaysia, Thailand, Indonesia, and Hong Kong; by Gotop Information Inc. for Taiwan; by ICG Muse, Inc. for Japan; by Intersoft for South Africa; by Eyrolles for France; by International Thomson Publishing for Germany, Austria and Switzerland; by Distribuidora Cuspide for Argentina; by LR International for Brazil; by Galileo Libros for Chile; by Ediciones ZETA S.C.R. Ltda. for Peru; by WS Computer Publishing Corporation, Inc., for the Philippines; by Contemporanea de Ediciones for Venezuela; by Express Computer Distributors for the Caribbean and West Indies; by Micronesia Media Distributor, Inc. for Micronesia; by Chips Computadoras S.A. de C.V. for Mexico; by Editorial Norma de Panama S.A. for Panama; by American Bookshops for Finland.

For general information on Hungry Minds' products and services please contact our Customer Care Department within the U.S. at 800-762-2974, outside the U.S. at 317-572-3993 or fax 317-572-4002.

For sales inquiries and reseller information, including discounts, premium and bulk quantity sales, and foreign-language translations, please contact our Customer Care Department at 800-434-3422, fax 317-572-4002, or write to Hungry Minds, Inc., Attn: Customer Care Department, 10475 Crosspoint Boulevard, Indianapolis, IN 46256.

For information on licensing foreign or domestic rights, please contact our Sub-Rights Customer Care Department at 212-884-5000.

For information on using Hungry Minds' products and services in the classroom or for ordering examination copies, please contact our Educational Sales Department at 800-434-2086 or fax 317-572-4005.

For press review copies, author interviews, or other publicity information, please contact our Public Relations Department at 317-572-3168 or fax 317-572-4168.

For authorization to photocopy items for corporate, personal, or educational use, please contact Copyright Clearance Center, 222 Rosewood Drive, Danvers, MA 01923, or fax 978-750-4470.

 Hungry Minds‎ is a trademark of Hungry Minds, Inc.

About the Author

Freelance author and Web guru **Emily A. Vander Veer** has penned several books and countless articles on Internet-related technologies and trends. You can visit her online at `http://www.emilyv.com`.

Dedication

To CMM, the ultimate buddy.

Author's Acknowledgments

Many thanks to Gareth Hancock for giving me the opportunity to write the very first edition of this book; to my project editor, Marla Reece-Hall, for her wise counsel in reshaping this new and improved edition; to programming expert Colin Banfield, who reviewed this book for technical accuracy; and to all of the other tireless professionals at IDG Books Worldwide, without whom this book wouldn't have been possible.

Publisher's Acknowledgments

We're proud of this book; please send us your comments through our Online Registration Form located at www.dummies.com.

Some of the people who helped bring this book to market include the following:

Acquisitions, Editorial, and Media Development

Project Editor: Marla Reece-Hall

Acquisitions Editor: Debra Williams Cauley

Proof Editor: Teresa Artman

Technical Editor: Colin Banfield

Permissions Editor: Carmen Krikorian

Associate Media Development Specialist: Megan Decraene

Editorial Manager: Constance Carlisle

Media Development Manager: Heather Heath Dismore

Editorial Assistants: Candace Nicholson, Sarah Shupert

Production

Project Coordinator: Nancee Reeves

Layout and Graphics: Beth Brooks, Jason Guy, Gabrielle McCann, Tracy K. Oliver, Kristin Pickett, Brent Savage, Jacque Schneider, Brian Torwelle, Jeremey Unger

Proofreaders: Laura Albert, Corey Bowen, John Greenough, Susan Moritz, York Production Services, Inc.

Indexer: York Production Services, Inc.

General and Administrative

Hungry Minds Technology Publishing Group: Richard Swadley, Vice President and Executive Group Publisher; Bob Ipsen, Vice President and Group Publisher; Joseph Wikert, Vice President and Publisher; Barry Pruett, Vice President and Publisher; Mary Bednarek, Editorial Director; Mary C. Corder, Editorial Director; Andy Cummings, Editorial Director

Hungry Minds Manufacturing: Ivor Parker, Vice President, Manufacturing

Hungry Minds Marketing: John Helmus, Assistant Vice President, Director of Marketing

Hungry Minds Production for Branded Press: Debbie Stailey, Production Director

Hungry Minds Sales: Michael Violano, Vice President, International Sales and Sub Rights

Contents at a Glance

Introduction 1

Part I: Building Killer Web Pages for Fun and Profit 7
Chapter 1: All You Ever Wanted to Know about JavaScript
(But Were Afraid to Ask!) 9
Chapter 2: Writing Your Very First Script 21
Chapter 3: JavaScript Programming Concepts 43

Part II: Adding Intelligence to Your Web Pages 83
Chapter 4: I Spy! Detecting Your Users' Browser Environment 85
Chapter 5: Making Every Date Count 109
Chapter 6: That's How the Cookie Crumbles 123

Part III: Making Your Web Pages Interactive 141
Chapter 7: Button Up! 143
Chapter 8: Picture Perfect 161
Chapter 9: Roll Over, Boy! Good Mouse! 179
Chapter 10: Hunting and Gathering (And Validating) User Input 195
Chapter 11: Framed Again! 219

Part IV: Automating Your Web Site 233
Chapter 12: DHTML Dyn-o-mite! 235
Chapter 13: Timing Is Everything 249
Chapter 14: JavaScript Tricks 259

Part V: The Part of Tens 281
Chapter 15: Top Ten (Or So) Online JavaScript Resources 283
Chapter 16: Ten (Or So) Most Common JavaScript Mistakes
(And How to Avoid Them) 289
Chapter 17: Ten (Or So) Tips for Debugging Your Scripts 299

Part VI: Appendixes 313
Appendix A: JavaScript Reserved Words 315
Appendix B: JavaScript Color Values 317
Appendix C: Document Object Model Reference 321
Appendix D: Special Characters 347
Appendix E: About the CD 353

Index 359
Hungry Minds End-User License Agreement 382
Installation Instructions 384

Cartoons at a Glance

By Rich Tennant

page 7

page 83

page 233

page 141

page 281

page 313

Fax: 978-546-7747
E-mail: richtennant@the5thwave.com
World Wide Web: www.the5thwave.com

Table of Contents

Introduction 1
  System Requirements 1
  About This Book 2
  Conventions Used in This Book 2
  What You're Not to Read 3
  Foolish Assumptions 4
  How This Book Is Organized 4
    Part I: Building Killer Web Pages for Fun and Profit 4
    Part II: Adding Intelligence to Your Web Pages 4
    Part III: Making Your Web Pages Interactive 5
    Part IV: Automating Your Web Site 5
    Part V: The Part of Tens 5
    Part VI: Appendixes 5
  Icons Used in This Book 5
  Where to Go from Here 6

Part I: Building Killer Web Pages for Fun and Profit 7

**Chapter 1: All You Ever Wanted to Know about JavaScript
(But Were Afraid to Ask!)** 9
  What Is JavaScript? (Hint: It's Not the Same Thing as Java!) ... 10
    It's easy! (sort of) 11
    It's speedy! 13
    Everybody's doing it! (Okay, almost everybody!) 13
  JavaScript and HTML 14
  JavaScript and Your Web Browser 15
  What Can I Do with JavaScript That I Can't Do with HTML? ... 15
    Add Intelligence To Your Pages 16
    Interact with users 16
    Create cool animations 17
    Customize Your Pages 17
  What Do I Need to Get Started? 17
    Hardware 18
    Software 18
    Documentation 19

Chapter 2: Writing Your Very First Script 21

From Idea to Working JavaScript Application 21
Ideas?! I got a million of 'em! 22
Part I: Creating an HTML file 22
Part II: Creating and attaching the script 26
Testing the script 29
Cast of Script Characters (In Order of Appearance) 31
Shoehorning JavaScript into HTML with the <SCRIPT> tag 31
Shhh! I'm hiding from a non-JavaScript-enabled browser! 32
Fully functioning 35
Comments, please! 36
If this, then that 37
The virtues of being method-ical 38
Those daring event handlers 40

Chapter 3: JavaScript Programming Concepts 43

JavaScript Syntax 43
Express Yourself 44
var (That's variable to you, Bud!) 55
Why, I declare! (Functions, that is) 57
Operators are standing by 59
Leftovers again? 65
Object Models Always Pose Nude 66
Object-ivity 68
For sale by owner: Object properties 69
There's a method to this madness! 71
How do you handle a hungry event? Event Handlers! 73
Company functions 74
Netscape Navigator's Object Model 77
JavaScript data types 78
Microsoft Internet Explorer's Object Model 81

Part II: Adding Intelligence to Your Web Pages 83

Chapter 4: I Spy! Detecting Your Users' Browser Environment 85

JavaScript: The Non-standard Standard 85
Can't we all just get along? The ECMA Standard 86
Whacking your way through the browser maze 87
The Browser Detective Script 88
Order in the court! 94
Variables: Think global, act local 97
String manipulation (Don't worry, it's ethical!) 101
Talkin' about my JavaScript generation 106

Chapter 5: Making Every Date Count 109

How About a Date? 109
Not Your Ordinary Date 115
    Finding time: The time formatting script 116
    Spelling it out: The date formatting script 118

Chapter 6: That's How the Cookie Crumbles 123

The Cookie Sampler 123
    Why use cookies? 124
    Cookie security issues 124
    Tasting cookies 125
The Repeat Visitor Script 130
    Mixing a master cookie recipe 136

Part III: Making Your Web Pages Interactive 141

Chapter 7: Button Up! 143

Pick A Button — Any Button! 143
    Handling the big events on page and screen! 145
    Custom tailored buttons: The button and radio elements 147
    Off-the-rack buttons: The reset and submit elements 151
The Order Form Script 154

Chapter 8: Picture Perfect 161

A Picture by Any Other Name 161
The Splash Page Script 164
    onDonner, onDasher, onPrancer, onClick 166
    The mouse detective I: onMouseOver 166
    The mouse detective II: onMouseOut 167
Splash Page Redux 168
The Best Navigation Bar None 172
    Creating image links 172
    Linking to e-mail 176

Chapter 9: Roll Over, Boy! Good Mouse! 179

What's a Rollover? 179
Adding Living Color to Perk Up a Navigation Bar 182
    Pre-loading images 182
    Setting up the swap meet 184
    The whole enchilada 187
    Toolin' around 193

Chapter 10: Hunting and Gathering (And Validating) User Input **195**

   Forming Opinions (And Other Data) 195
      Scrub-a-dub-dub: Scrubbing user input 196
      Puttin' on the feedback 199
   Creating the Order Form Script 200
      Wow! Exist-ential, dude! 201
      Running numbers 203
      I think I see a pattern here! 205
      Pulling it all together with form-level validation 208

Chapter 11: Framed Again! **219**

   One Page at a Time 220
      Constructing frames 221
      Adding the wiring 224
   Creating Collapsible Indexes 227
      Checkin' out the library 227
      Calling all code 229

Part IV: Automating Your Web Site **233**

Chapter 12: DHTML Dyn-o-mite! **235**

   Animation Sensation 236
   Tickets to a Slide Show 240
   Now You See It . . . Now You Don't! 244
   You're Really Stylin' Now! 247

Chapter 13: Timing Is Everything **249**

   Ready, Set, Go! Keeping Track of Time In JavaScript 249
   The Stopwatch Script 250
   The Pause That Refreshes (Content, That Is!) 253

Chapter 14: JavaScript Tricks **259**

   Dated for Freshness 260
   Applet-y Good 262
   Psst! Pass It Along! 265
   Window of Opportunity 268
   Are Your Users Plugged In? 270
   Just Scrollin' Along 276
   Different Strokes for Different Folks 277

Part V: The Part of Tens 281

Chapter 15: Top Ten (Or So) Online JavaScript Resources 283
Ten Web Sites to Check Out 283
    Netscape 284
    Microsoft 284
    CNET 284
    ZDNet 284
    Project Cool's JavaScript Zone 284
    Gamelan 285
    About.com 285
    Netscape's DevEdge FAQ 285
    WebReference.com 285
    ScriptSearch.com 285
Not-to-Be-Missed Newsgroups 286

Chapter 16: Ten (Or So) Most Common JavaScript Mistakes (And How to Avoid Them) 289
Typing-In-a-Hurry Errors 289
Breaking Up a Happy Pair 291
    Lonely angle brackets 291
    Lonely tags 291
    Lonely parentheses 292
    Lonely quotes 292
Putting Scripting Statements in the Wrong Places 293
Nesting Quotes Incorrectly 294
Treating Numbers as Strings 294
Treating Strings as Numbers 296
Missing the Point: Logic Errors 297
Neglecting Browser Incompatibility 297

Chapter 17: Ten (Or So) Tips for Debugging Your Scripts 299
JavaScript Reads Your Code, Not Your Mind! 300
Isolating the Bug 301
Consulting the Documentation 302
Displaying Variable Values 302
Breaking Large Blocks of Statements into Smaller Functions 305
Honing the Process of Elimination 305
    Debugging browser problems 306
    Tracking HTML bugs 306
    Checking the JavaScript code 307
Taking Advantage of Others' Experience 307
Exercising the Time-Honored Trial-and-Error Approach 308
Just Try and Catch Me Exception Handling! 308

Part VI: Appendixes *313*

Appendix A: JavaScript Reserved Words .... .315

Appendix B: JavaScript Color Values .... .317

Appendix C: Document Object Model Reference .... .321

The Document Object Model .... .321
    Anchor .... .322
    Applet .... .322
    Area .... .323
    arguments .... .323
    Array .... .323
    Boolean .... .324
    Button .... .324
    Checkbox .... .324
    clientInformation .... .325
    crypto .... .325
    Date .... .326
    document .... .326
    elements[] .... .327
    event .... .327
    FileUpload .... .328
    Form .... .328
    Frame .... .328
    Function .... .329
    Hidden .... .329
    History .... .329
    Image .... .330
    java .... .330
    JavaArray .... .330
    JavaClass .... .331
    JavaObject .... .331
    JavaPackage .... .331
    Link .... .332
    Location .... .332
    Math .... .332
    MimeType .... .333
    navigator .... .333
    netscape .... .334
    Number .... .334
    Object .... .334
    Option .... .335
    Packages .... .335
    Password .... .335
    Plugin .... .336

   Radio 336
   RegExp 336
   Reset 337
   screen 338
   Select 338
   String 338
   Style 339
   Submit 340
   sun 340
   Text 341
   Textarea 341
   window 341
  Global Properties 342
  Built-in JavaScript Functions 343
   escape() 343
   eval() 343
   isFinite() 343
   isNaN() 344
   Number() 344
   parseFloat() 344
   parseInt() 344
   String() 345
   taint() 345
   unescape() 345
   untaint() 345

Appendix D: Special Characters **347**

Appendix E: About the CD **353**
  Getting the Most from This CD 353
  System Requirements 354
  Using the CD with Microsoft Windows 354
  Using the CD with a Mac OS Computer 355
  JavaScript For Dummies Chapter Files 356
  What You'll Find 356
  If You Have Problems (Of the CD Kind) 357

Index..*359*

Hungry Minds End-User License Agreement *382*

Installation Instructions..*384*

Introduction

• •

Welcome to the wonderful world of Web programming with JavaScript. If you've worked with HTML before but want to add more flexibility and punch to your pages, or even if you've never written a stick of code in your life but are eager to hop on the Infobahn-wagon, this book's for you.

(Although I don't assume that you know HTML, much of what you want to do with JavaScript is interact with objects created using HTML — so you understand the examples in this book that much quicker if you have a good HTML reference handy. One to consider is *HTML For Dummies,* 3rd Edition, by Ed Tittel and Steve James (published by IDG Books Worldwide, Inc.).

I do my best to describe how JavaScript works by using real-world examples — and not a foo (bar) in sight. When explaining things in formal notation makes sense, I do that, but not without a recap in plain English. Most importantly, I include tons of sample programs that illustrate the kinds of things you may want to do in your own pages.

Along with this book comes a companion CD-ROM. This CD-ROM contains all the sample code listings covered in the text along with many other interesting scripts, examples, and development tools. From experience, I can tell you that the best way to get familiar with JavaScript is to load the scripts and interact with them as you read through each chapter. If it's feasible for you, I suggest installing the contents of the CD right away, before you dig into the chapters. Then, when you come across a listing in the book, all you have to do is double-click on the corresponding HTML file you've already installed. Doing so helps reinforce your understanding of each JavaScript concept described in this book. For more information and instructions on installing the CD-ROM, see the About the CD appendix in the back of this book.

System Requirements

Here's what you need to get the most out of this book and the enclosed CD-ROM:

- ✔ A computer with a CD-ROM drive and a modem
- ✔ A sound card (Okay, this one's strictly optional, but it's a lot of fun!)

- Windows 95, Windows NT, or Macintosh already installed with the following:

  - A Pentium or faster processor, at least 16MB of RAM, and at least 25MB of free disk space if you're running Windows 95/NT

  - A PowerPC or faster processor, at least 16MB of RAM, and at least 10MB of free disk space for Macintosh users

  - A copy of either Netscape Navigator 6.0 or Microsoft Internet Explorer 5.5 (Chapter 1 tells you how to get a copy, if you haven't already.)

About This Book

Think of this book as a good friend who started at the beginning, learned the ropes the hard way, and now wants to help you get up to speed. In this book, you can find everything from JavaScript basics and common pitfalls to answers to embarrassingly silly questions (and some really cool tricks, too), all explained from a first-time JavaScript programmer's point of view. While you don't find explanations of HTML in this book, you do find working examples on the companion CD complete with all the HTML you need to understand how JavaScript works.

Some sample topics you can find in this book are

- Creating interactive Web pages

- Validating user input with JavaScript

- Testing and debugging your JavaScript scripts

- Adapting your scripts for cross-browser issues

- Integrating JavaScript with other technologies, such as Java applets, Netscape plug-ins, and ActiveX components

Building intelligent Web pages with JavaScript can be overwhelming — if you let it. You can do so *much* with JavaScript! To keep the deluge to a minimum, this book concentrates on the practical considerations you need to get your interactive pages up and running in the least amount of time possible.

Conventions Used in This Book

The rules are pretty simple. All code appears in monospaced font, like this HTML line:

```
<TITLE>JavaScript For Dummies</TITLE>
```

Make sure you follow the examples' syntax exactly. Sometimes your scripts work if you add or delete spaces or type your keywords in a different case, but sometimes they don't — and you want to spend your time on more interesting bugs than those caused by spacing errors. (If you're like me, you cut and paste working code examples directly from the CD to cut down syntax errors even more!)

Type anything you see in `code font` letter for letter. These items are generally JavaScript keywords, and they need to be exact. Directives in *italics* are placeholders, and you can substitute other values for them. For example, in the following line of code, you can replace *state* and *confusion* and leave the equal sign out entirely, but you need to type `var` the way that it's shown.

```
var state = "confusion"
```

Due to the margins of this book, sometimes code examples are wrapped from one line to another. You can copy the code exactly the way it appears; JavaScript doesn't have a line continuation character. JavaScript has only one place where you can't break a line and still have the code work — between two quotes. For example, the following line is invalid:

```
. . .
var fullName = "George
Washington"
```

And, when you see ellipses in the code like this: . . .you know I've omitted either a part of the script to help you focus on just the part I'm talking about. Or, I've placed more code (like the HTML around the JavaScript) on the CD to save paper.

All the URLs listed in this book are accurate at the time of this writing. Because the Internet is such a dynamic medium, however, a few may be inaccessible by the time you get around to trying them. If so, try using a search engine, such as Yahoo! or Webcrawler, to help you find the slippery Web site you're looking for.

What You're Not to Read

Okay, you *can* read the text next to the Technical Stuff icons, but you don't have to to understand what's going on! Technical Stuff icons point out in-depth information that explains *why* things work as they do (interesting if you're in the mood, but not necessary to get the most out of the JavaScript examples I present).

Foolish Assumptions

Everybody's got to start somewhere, right? I'm starting out with the following assumptions about you, the reader:

- ✔ You know how to navigate through an application with a mouse and a keyboard.
- ✔ You want to build interactive Web pages for fun, for profit, or because building them is part of your job.
- ✔ You have, or can get, a working connection to the Internet.
- ✔ You have, or can get, a copy of Netscape Navigator 6.0 or Microsoft Internet Explorer 5.5.

How This Book Is Organized

This book contains five major parts. Each part contains several chapters, and each chapter contains several sections. You can read the book from start to finish if you like, or you can dive in whenever you need help on a particular topic. (If you're brand-new to JavaScript, however, skimming through Part I first sure couldn't hurt.) Here's a breakdown of what you can find in each of the five parts.

Part I: Building Killer Web Pages for Fun and Profit

This part explains how to turn JavaScript from an abstract concept to something happening on the screen in front of you. It takes you step-by-step through obtaining your choice of Netscape Navigator or Microsoft Internet Explorer, discovering how to access and modify the document object model, and writing and testing your first script. Part I also includes an overview of the JavaScript language itself.

Part II: Adding Intelligence to Your Web Pages

By the time you finish Part II, you'll have seen sample code for such common JavaScript applications as detecting your users' browsers on the fly, formatting and displaying times and dates, and storing information for repeat visitors using *cookies*.

Part III: Making Your Web Pages Interactive

The chapters in Part III are devoted to helping you create Web pages that visitors can interact with easily and efficiently. You find out how to use JavaScript's event model and function declaration support to create hot buttons, clickable images, mouse rollovers, and intelligent (automatically validated) HTML forms.

Part IV: Automating Your Web Site

JavaScript is evolving by leaps and bounds, and Part IV keeps you up-to-date with the latest and greatest feats you can accomplish with JavaScript, including brand-new support for dynamic HTML and cascading style sheets. In this part you also find a double handful of the most popular JavaScript effects, including password protection, plug-in detection, and much more.

Part V: The Part of Tens

The concluding part pulls together tidbits from the rest of the book, organized in lists of ten. The categories include great JavaScript-related online resources; common mistakes; and debugging tips.

Part VI: Appendixes

At the back of the book you find a handful of indispensable references, including JavaScript reserved words, color values, document objects, and special characters. There's also a nifty how-to section that describes all the cool tools you find on the companion CD.

Icons Used in This Book

Ever get in one of those moods when you're reading along and get really excited, and you just wish there was a way to cut to the chase and absorb an entire chapter all at once? Well, if so, you're in luck! Not only is this book organized in nice, easily digestible chunks, with real-life figures and code examples, but there's an extra added value, too: eye-catching icons to give you a heads-up on the most useful tidbits, categorized so that you can tell at a glance what's coming up.

Take just a second to become familiar with the kind of information you can expect from each icon:

This icon flags some of the cool stuff you can find on the CD-ROM included in the back of this book. Because all the JavaScript source code listings are on the CD (plus lots more), you can load up the scripts for each section and follow along while you read if you want.

This icon lets you know that some really nerdy technical information is coming your way. You can skip it if you want; reading through isn't absolutely necessary if you're after the bare-bones basics, but it does give you a little show-off material!

Next to the tip icon you'll find handy little tricks and techniques for getting the most bang out of your JavaScript buck.

These little gems can help you figure things out, so pay attention.

When you see this icon, a really cool Web site URL is coming up that you just don't want to miss.

Before you jump in and start applying the information in any given section, check out the text next to these babies — chances are they'll save you a lot of time and hassle!

The browser icon alerts you to an important difference between the way Netscape Navigator implements JavaScript, and the way Internet Explorer implements JavaScript.

Where to Go from Here

So what are you waiting for? Pick a topic, any topic, and dive in. Or, if you're like me, begin at the beginning and read until you get so excited you have to put the book down and try stuff out for yourself. And remember: From now on, your life will be divided into two major time periods — *before* you mastered JavaScript and *after* you mastered JavaScript. Enjoy!

Part I
Building Killer Web Pages for Fun and Profit

The 5th Wave   By Rich Tennant

IF BOB DYLAN HAD PURSUED A CAREER IN COMPUTERS

"He's a whiz at researching online, but thank goodness for email because I can't understand a word he says when he talks."

In this part . . .

*J*avaScript is one of the coolest Web tools around — and its use is spreading like wildfire. An extension to HyperText Markup Language (HTML), JavaScript enables you to access and manipulate all of the components that make up a Web page. With JavaScript, you can make what's known as *intelligent* Web pages: pages that verify input, calculate it, and make presentation decisions based on it. You can create all this, all on the client, without having to learn an industrial-strength language such as C or C++!

Part I introduces you to JavaScript, then walks you step-by-step through the process of creating your first script. Finally, this part acquaints you with basic JavaScript programming concepts — everything you need to know to create sophisticated custom scripts, from syntax to the document object model.

Chapter 1

All You Ever Wanted to Know about JavaScript (But Were Afraid to Ask!)

. . . .

In This Chapter

▶ Understanding a working definition of JavaScript

▶ Dispelling common JavaScript misconceptions

▶ Getting started with JavaScript tools

▶ Finding online information

. . . .

*E*ver surfed to a Web site that incorporates really cool features, such as

✔ Images that change when you move your mouse over them?

✔ Slide-show animations?

✔ Input forms with pop-up messages that help you fill in fields correctly?

✔ Customized messages that welcome repeat visitors?

Using JavaScript and the book you're reading right now, you can create all these effects and many more! The web page in Figure 1-1 shows you an example of the kinds of things you can look forward to creating for your own site.

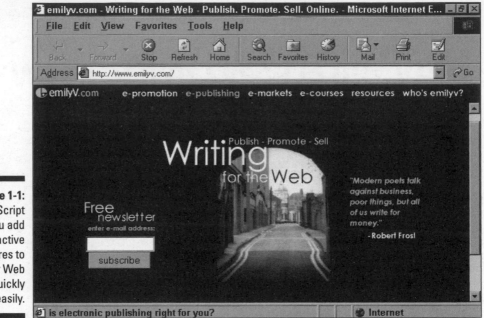

Figure 1-1:
JavaScript
lets you add
interactive
features to
your Web
site quickly
and easily.

A lot has changed since the previous edition of *JavaScript For Dummies*. For one thing, JavaScript has evolved from a relatively basic scripting language to a full-blown programming language in its own right.

The good news is that you can use JavaScript to create even more breathtakingly cool Web sites than ever before. The bad news is that the JavaScript language itself is a bit more complex than it was in its earlier incarnations — but that's where this new, improved, better-tasting edition of *JavaScript For Dummies* comes in! Even if you're not a crackerjack programmer, you can use the techniques and sample scripts in this book to create interactive, "intelligent" Web pages bursting with animated effects.

Before you hit the JavaScript code slopes, though, you might want to take a minute to familiarize yourself with the basics presented in this chapter. That way you'll have all the background you need to get started using JavaScript as quickly as possible!

What Is JavaScript? (Hint: It's Not the Same Thing as Java!)

JavaScript is a *scripting* language you can use — in conjunction with HTML — to create interactive Web pages. A scripting language is a programming language designed to give folks easy access to pre-built components. In the case of JavaScript, those pre-built components are the building blocks that make up a Web page (links, images, plug-ins, HTML form elements, browser configuration details, and so on).

You don't need to know anything about HTML to put this book to good use; I explain all the HTML you need to know to create and use the JavaScript examples you see in this book. If you're interested in learning more about HTML, I suggest checking out a good book devoted to the subject. One to try is *HTML For Dummies,* 3rd Edition, by Ed Tittel and Steve James (published by IDG Books Worldwide, Inc.).

It's easy! (sort of)

JavaScript has a reputation of being easy to use because:

- ✔ The bulk of the *document object model* (the portion of the language that defines what kind of components, or *objects,* you can manipulate in JavaScript) is pretty straightforward.

  For example, if you want to trigger some kind of event when a push button is clicked, you access the onClick event handler associated with the button object; if you want to trigger an event when an HTML form is submitted, you access the onSubmit event handler associated with the form object. (You become familiar with the JavaScript object model in this book by examining and experimenting with working scripts. You can also check out Appendix C, which lists all of the objects that make up the document object model.)

- ✔ When you load a cool Web page into your browser and wonder how the author created the effect in JavaScript, ninety-nine times out of a hundred all you have to do to satisfy your curiosity is click to view the source code (View⇨Page Source in Navigator, View⇨Source in Internet Explorer). (Chapter 3 describes the .js files that are responsible for that hundredth time.) This source code free-for-all, which is simply impossible with compiled programming languages such as Java, helps you decipher JavaScript programming by example.

Having said all that, becoming proficient in JavaScript isn't exactly a no-brainer, either. One of the biggest factors contributing to the language's growing complexity is the fact that the two major JavaScript-supporting browsers on the market (Netscape Navigator and Microsoft Internet Explorer) implement JavaScript differently. Netscape supports JavaScript directly — hardly a surprise, since Netscape was the one who came up with JavaScript in the first place! Internet Explorer, on the other hand, supports JavaScript indirectly by providing support for *JScript,* its very own JavaScript-compatible language.

And despite strident claims by both Netscape and Microsoft that JavaScript and JScript, respectively, are "open, standardized scripting languages," neither company offers explicit, comprehensive, all-in-one-place details describing

✔ Precisely which version of JavaScript (or JScript) is implemented in each of their many *interim* browser releases (an interim browser release contains a decimal point; for example, Navigator 4.6 and Internet Explorer 5.5 are interim browser releases)

✔ Precisely what programming features are included in each version of JavaScript/JScript

✔ How each version of JavaScript compares to each version of JScript (as you see in Chapter 4, JavaScript and JScript differ substantially)

The upshot is that creating cross-browser, JavaScript-enabled Web pages now falls somewhere around 6 on a difficulty scale of 1 to 10 (1 being the easiest technology in the world to master and 10 being the hardest).

Fear not, however. Armed with an understanding of HTML and the tips and sample scripts you'll find in this book, you'll be a JavaScript jockey in no time flat!

What's in a name?

A long time ago, JavaScript was called *LiveScript.* In a classic "if you can't dazzle them with brilliance, baffle them with marketing" move, Netscape changed the name to take advantage of the burgeoning interest in Java (another programming language that Netscape partner Sun Microsystems was developing at the time). By all accounts, the strategy worked; unfortunately, many newbies still mistake JavaScript for Java, and vice versa.

Here's the scoop: Java is similar to JavaScript in that they're both object-based languages developed for the Web. Without going into the nitty-gritty details of syntax, interpreters, variable typing, and just-in-time compilers, all you have to remember about the difference in usage between JavaScript and Java is this: on the gigantic client/server application that is the Web, JavaScript lets you access *Web clients* (otherwise known as *browsers*); Java lets you access *Web servers.*

This difference may seem esoteric, but it can be very useful in helping you determine which language to use to create the Web site of your dreams. If what you want to accomplish can be achieved inside the confines of a Web client (in other words, by interacting with HTML, browser plug-ins, and Java applets), JavaScript is your best bet. But if you want to do something fancier — say, interact with a server-side database — you'll need to look into Java or some other server-side alternative.

It's speedy!

Besides being relatively easy, JavaScript is also pretty speedy. Like most scripting languages, it's *interpreted* (as opposed to being *compiled).* When you program using a compiled language, such as C++, you must always reformat, or compile, your code file before you can run it. This interim step can take anywhere from a few seconds to several minutes or more.

The beauty of an interpreted language like JavaScript, on the other hand, is that when you make changes to your code — in this case, to your JavaScript *script* — you can test those changes immediately; you don't have to compile the script file first. Skipping the compile step saves a great deal of time during the debugging stage of Web page development.

Another great thing about using an interpreted language like JavaScript is that testing an interpreted script isn't an all-or-nothing proposition, the way it is with a compiled language. For example, if line 10 of a 20-line script contains a syntax error, the first half of your script still runs; you still get feedback immediately. The same error in a compiled program would prevent the program from running at all.

The downside of an interpreted language is that testing is on the honor system. Because there's no compiler to nag you, you might be tempted to leave your testing to the last minute or — worse yet — skip it altogether. But remember: whether the Web site you create is for business or pleasure, it's a reflection on *you* — and testing is essential if you want to look your very best to potential customers, associates, and friends. (A few years ago visitors to your site might have overlooked a buggy script or two, but frankly, standards out there are much higher these days.) Fortunately, Chapter 17 is chock-full of helpful debugging tips to help make testing your JavaScript code as painless as possible.

Everybody's doing it! (Okay, almost everybody!)

Two generally available Web browsers currently support JavaScript: Microsoft's *Internet Explorer* and Netscape/AOL's *Navigator.* (Beginning with version 4.0, *Navigator* became synonymous with *Communicator,* even though technically Netscape Communicator includes more components than just the Navigator Web browser.) Between them, these two browsers have virtually sewn up the browser market; almost everyone who surfs the Web is using one or the other (and thus has the ability to view and create JavaScript-enabled Web pages).

Web browsers aren't the only software tools that provide support for JavaScript, however; Netscape's Web servers support JavaScript, as well — albeit a special server-side version.

This book focuses on client-side JavaScript, the most popular and widespread form by far. Netscape did develop a special version of JavaScript that runs on certain Web servers instead of in Web browsers, however. For more information on server-side JavaScript, visit

```
http://developer.netscape.com/docs/manuals/ssjs/1_4/
                  contents.htm
```

JavaScript and HTML

You can think of JavaScript is an extension to HTML; an add-on, if you will.

Here's how it works. HTML tags create objects; JavaScript lets you manipulate those objects. For example, you use the HTML `<BODY> . . . </BODY>` tags to create a Web page *document.* Once that document is created, you use a special JavaScript construct called the `onLoad` *event handler* to trigger an action — play a little welcoming tune, perhaps — when the document is loaded into a Web browser. Examples of other HTML objects that you interact with using JavaScript include windows, text fields, images, and embedded Java applets.

Keep in mind that most of the examples in these printed pages focus on the JavaScript portion of the code (naturally!). But, I include the HTML you need to create the examples on the CD-ROM, so you don't have sweat recreating the web pages from scratch!

Because Web pages are not made of HTML alone, however, JavaScript provides access to more than just HTML objects; it also provides access to browser- and platform-specific objects. Browser plug-ins (such as RealAudio and Adobe Acrobat), the name and version of a particular viewer's browser, and the current date are all examples of non-HTML objects you can work with using JavaScript.

Together, all the objects that make up a Web site — HTML objects, browser- and platform-related objects, and special objects built right into the JavaScript language — are known as the *document object model* (*DOM* for short).

JavaScript and Your Web Browser

You need to use Netscape Navigator 4.0 (or higher) or Microsoft Internet Explorer 5.0 (or higher) to use the latest enhancements in JavaScript demonstrated in this book.

Not all browsers are created equal: Internet Explorer's support for JavaScript differs significantly from Navigator's. For details, check out Chapter 4, "JavaScript: The Non-Standard Standard."

Although you *can* create and view JavaScript scripts with an old version of one of these browsers, I recommend that you install the most current version of either Navigator or Internet Explorer. (What the heck — they're both free!) The latest versions of each product boast the very latest JavaScript features and bug fixes; they're also the version you see described in the figures and examples in this book.

You can use another browser, such as Opera or America Online (or even another Internet protocol, such as FTP) to download the latest version of either Navigator or Internet Explorer and try it out. "What Do I Need To Get Started?" later in this chapter, is devoted to the ins and outs of obtaining and installing a JavaScript-enabled browser. For now, suffice it to say that:

- ✔ You need Navigator or Internet Explorer to work with JavaScript, which means that you have to be running one of the client platforms that supports these browsers. (Macintosh and Windows both support Navigator and Internet Explorer.)
- ✔ You need to be aware that people may use other, non-JavaScript-enabled browsers to view your Web pages — or they may use JavaScript-enabled browsers with JavaScript support turned off. Either way, you have no way to guarantee that everyone who visits your page will be able to view your JavaScript handiwork. (Check out Chapter 4, "I Spy! Detecting Your Users' Browser Environment" for more information on this topic.)

What Can I Do with JavaScript That I Can't Do with HTML?

HTML lets you create static Web pages using tag building blocks, or *objects;* JavaScript lets you inspect and manipulate those objects to punch up static pages with intelligence, interactivity, and simple animations. (In other words, in order to use JavaScript, you need to use HTML.) Using JavaScript, you can even create a page that appears differently depending on who's viewing the page, what browser they're using to view it, and what time of day it is! Read on for details.

Add Intelligence To Your Pages

In software parlance, "intelligence" refers to any chunk of code that does anything snazzier than a simple input-output process. Accepting a user's zip code is an example of a simple input process; taking that zip code and using it to calculate sales tax is an example of software *intelligence*.

When it comes to adding intelligence to your Web pages with JavaScript, the only limiting factor (besides your imagination, of course!) is this: you're only allowed to work with client-side objects. In other words, you can use JavaScript to inspect any object in the browser DOM and to perform any calculations you like — but you *can't* use it to communicate with, say, an Oracle database sitting on a server somewhere.

Generally speaking, to access information outside the DOM — whether it's on your user's hard drive or on a machine somewhere else on the Internet — you need to use either Java or a *CGI* program. (CGI, or *Common Gateway Interface*, programs are stored on Web servers and are typically written in either Perl or C.)

In the Web's early years, the only way to add intelligence to Web pages was to create a CGI program — and you can still do so, if you choose. However, there are two drawbacks associated with using CGI. One, creating a CGI program is trickier than crafting a JavaScript script (if only because you have to have access to a Web server to test your CGI program). And two, accessing a CGI program from a Web page requires a trip to the server — a potential time suck (and an unnecessary one, if you can perform the same processing on the client using JavaScript).

Interact with users

The most common way to perk up your pages with JavaScript is to make them interactive: in other words, to do something useful when a user clicks a mouse or types a word. For example, you can use JavaScript to

- Load content into multiple frames when a user clicks a button
- Swap images when a user drags a mouse over a certain area of the screen (this effect is called a *mouse rollover*)
- Display helpful information when a user clicks or drags a mouse over a specified area of your page
- Inspect the data your users type in and pop up helpful suggestions if they've made an invalid entry
- Display a thank-you message after a user submits a form

In addition to user-initiated events such as clicking and dragging a mouse, JavaScript also recognizes *automatic* events — for example, loading a Web page into a browser. (Check out Chapter 4 for details, including sample scripts that run in response to automatic events.)

Create cool animations

Many folks assume you need Java to create animations for the Web, but that's just not so. While JavaScript certainly won't be mistaken for the most efficient way to create high-density animations, you *can* use JavaScript with layers (sometimes known as dynamic HTML, or DHTML) to create a variety of really neat animated effects. As a matter of fact, using JavaScript is the easiest way to implement common effects, such as rollovers, as you can see in Chapter 9.

Customize Your Pages

Everyone likes to feel special, and the folks who visit your Web site are no exception. Using JavaScript, you can tailor the way your pages look to different users based on criteria such as

- The specific kind and version of browser someone is using to view your page
- The current date or time
- Your users' behavior the last time they visited your page
- Your users' stated preferences
- Any other criterion you can imagine!

What Do I Need to Get Started?

I hope you're champing at the bit to get started on your first JavaScript-enabled Web page! First things first, though . . . You have an idea of what JavaScript can do for you, and by now you probably already have something specific in mind for your first attempt. Now's the time to dive into the preliminaries: what you need to get started and how to get what you need if you don't already have it. After you've dispensed with the setup, you can go on to the *really* fun stuff!

Hardware

For the purposes of this book, I assume that you're beginning your JavaScript adventure with either a personal computer or a Macintosh computer. Your machine (or *box,* to use the vernacular) should be a Pentium PC or better (unless it's a Power Mac) and should have at least 32MB of RAM and at least 25MB free disk space. If none of this makes sense, try asking your local hardware guru; every organization seems to have at least one. (I've found, through extensive trial and error, that most hardware gurus are fairly responsive to sugar-based snack foods.)

You also need hardware installed that lets you connect to the Internet. This hardware usually consists of a modem and a phone line. Depending on your computer, you may have an internal modem installed (many come complete with a built-in modem). If not, you can buy a modem at your local computer discount store. The differentiating factor among modems is line speed: the faster, the better. (Most computers these days come with a 56.6 Kbps model pre-installed, but 14.4 or 28.8 will work just fine.) If you don't already have a modem and need to purchase one, consider buying the fastest modem in your price range; you'll be very glad you did when you try to look at spiffy Web pages with many graphics, each of which takes a loooong time to load (because graphics files are typically so large).

Software

For the purposes of this book, I assume that you have either a Macintosh computer, or a personal computer loaded with Windows 95, Windows NT, Windows 98, Windows 2000, or Linux. (Currently, only Netscape Navigator is available for use with Linux.)

I also assume that you have some way to create text files. (Most operating systems come packaged with a variety of text editors and word processors, any of which will work just fine for creating JavaScript scripts.)

On the CD included with this book you'll find some great text editing utilities designed specifically for creating JavaScript files.

JavaScript-specific software

You also need a Web browser. Navigator (Netscape Communication's commercial Web browser) and Microsoft's Internet Explorer are the only generally available browsers that support JavaScript at the time of this writing. So, the first thing to do is to get a copy of Navigator or Internet Explorer.

(The examples you see in this book are demonstrated using both Netscape Navigator and Internet Explorer running on Windows 95.)

Most personal computers come with Internet Explorer already installed. To find out if this is the case for your particular computer, select Start⇨Programs and look for Internet Explorer.

Netscape Navigator

Netscape Navigator version 6.x bundles the Navigator browser with messaging, Web construction, and other Internet-related goodies.

You can download a copy by visiting the following site (which offers step-by-step installation instructions)

```
http://www.netscape.com/download/index.html
```

Of course, I'm assuming that you already have a Web browser installed or that you have access to FTP. (FTP is short for *file transfer protocol,* which is an Internet application that enables you to nab files from other people's machines.) If you prefer, you can purchase a copy of Navigator on CD ROM for a nominal fee (details are available at Netscape's site).

Internet Explorer

If you're a Microsoft buff, you might want to download a copy of Internet Explorer. Download it for free (or order your copy on CD-ROM for a nominal fee) from the following site, which offers easy-to-follow installation instructions:

```
http://www.microsoft.com/windows/ie/default.htm
```

Documentation

For the latest Netscape Navigator and Microsoft Internet Explorer documentation and technical support, respectively, check out the following URLs:

```
http://help.netscape.com/products/client/communicator/index.
         html
http://www.microsoft.com/windows/ie/default.htm
```

To get a copy of the *JavaScript Authoring Guide,* the must-have tome from Netscape that explains JavaScript basics and language concepts (and includes an extensive reference section), visit the following Web page:

```
http://developer.netscape.com/docs/manuals/javascript.html
```

Chapter 2

Writing Your Very First Script

In This Chapter

▶ Designing your first JavaScript application

▶ Creating an HTML file

▶ Creating and attaching a script

▶ Running the JavaScript application

▶ Getting to know the most common scripting elements

*O*ne of the best ways to figure out the particulars of a new scripting language is to dive right in and create a script — and that's just what this chapter shows you how to do! Actually, this chapter shows you how to do more than just create a script; it shows you how to create a *JavaScript application*. JavaScript isn't much use all by itself, you see; it really needs to work in conjunction with HTML. So, a JavaScript application includes at least one script and at least one HTML file, as you soon will see.

Every single, solitary aspect of JavaScript development is covered here, from coming up with a useful idea to implementing, testing, and executing that idea. I don't assume any previous knowledge at all, so even if you're new to JavaScript or the Web, you should be able to follow along with the examples in this chapter. And because the example I use demonstrates most of the common JavaScript constructs — including statements, variables, operators, functions, and event handlers — you can apply the strategies and code shown here to your very own script creations.

So turn on your computer, roll up those sleeves, and get ready to have some fun!

From Idea to Working JavaScript Application

Like great art, great software doesn't just happen. Creating either one requires you to do a bit of planning first, then use a tool — along with some kind of logical process — to translate your plan into something concrete.

In this section, you become familiar with the basic tools you need to create a JavaScript application: a simple text editor, and a JavaScript-supporting Web browser. You also get a good look at the logical process, called the *development cycle* in programming circles, which you need follow to create a JavaScript application.

Ideas?! I got a million of 'em!

The first step in creating a knock-out JavaScript application is deciding exactly what you want your application to do. Provide some feedback to your visitors? Perform some calculations? Display requested information in a pop-up window?

Many of the things you want to do with JavaScript — from validating user input to creating mouse rollovers — are described in this book. For more ideas, check out ScriptSearch.com's JavaScript section at

```
http://www.scriptsearch.com/pages/14.shtml
```

Once you have a clear idea in mind, take a few minutes to jot your thoughts down on a piece of paper. This phase — clarifying in writing exactly what you want your application to accomplish — has a long history of success in professional software development. Formally dubbed the *requirements phase*, completing this step gives you the means to test your application at the end of the process. (Hey, you can't test something if you don't know exactly how it's *supposed* to work!)

Here are the requirements for the JavaScript proverb application described in this section:

I want to create a Web page that uses JavaScript to generate a proverb based on user input. First, I want to ask the user for a couple of words. Then, I want to use JavaScript to plug those words into a well-known proverb and display the result in a pop-up window.

Oh, yes. I also want to define some sort of default, just in case somebody tries to generate a proverb without having entered any words.

Notice that the requirements can be in your own words; you don't need to fill out a formal requirements document, or (gasp!) labor over a flow chart. A simple, concise description fills the bill nicely.

Part I: Creating an HTML file

Once you have your script requirements in hand, you're ready to hit the coding slopes!

First off, as described in the requirements above, you need to create a Web page. You do that by typing HTML code into a text editor and saving that code as a separate file on your computer's hard drive, as you see below.

Because this book is all about JavaScript — not HTML — I don't go into great detail about the HTML language. Instead, I demonstrate only as much HTML as I need in order to describe all the wonderful things you can do with JavaScript. If you need a good introduction to HTML, I suggest *HTML For Dummies,* 3rd Edition, by Ed Tittel and Steve James (published by IDG Books Worldwide, Inc.).

Throughout this book, I use the Notepad text editor. Why? Because it comes free with the Windows operating system! (It's also easy to use.) But if you have another text editing program installed on your machine that you'd rather use to create your scripts, by all means, use that program. (In fact, I introduce you to some cool text editors optimized for JavaScript in Chapter 15, which you can test out for yourself by loading the companion CD.) Just make sure that you use a text editor to create your scripts and HTML files and not a word processor. The difference is this: when you save a file using a word processor application such as Microsoft Word, the application adds special non-text characters to the saved file. Unfortunately, HTML and JavaScript interpreters can only interpret text; they can't interpret word processing files containing special characters.

One exception exists to the rule about not using word processors to create HTML or JavaScript files. Some word processors allow you to save files in HTML or plain text format. If your word processor offers the ability to save files in HTML or plain text format, then you can use that word processor to create HTML and script files. Otherwise, you need to use a text editor such as Notepad.

Many word processing applications offer a way for you to save files in plain text format. To save a file in plain text format using Microsoft Windows, for example, you simply click File⇨Save As and select Text Only (.txt) from the Save as type: option.

Here are the steps you need to follow to create a file using Notepad:

1. **Click Start⇨Programs⇨Accessories⇨Notepad to pull up the Notepad editing window, as shown in Figure 2-1.**

2. **When the Notepad editing window appears, type in your HTML and JavaScript code.**

3. **When you're finished typing, save the file by clicking File⇨Save.**

   If you're creating an HTML file containing embedded JavaScript statements — such as the one described in this chapter — make sure the name you give your file contains the .HTM or .HTML extension.

The script demonstrated in this chapter is embedded in an HTML file, which is the most common way to implement JavaScript scripts. You can also implement a script as a separate file, however, using the .JS extension, and then reference that JavaScript file explicitly from an HTML file. You see an example of this technique in Chapter 14.

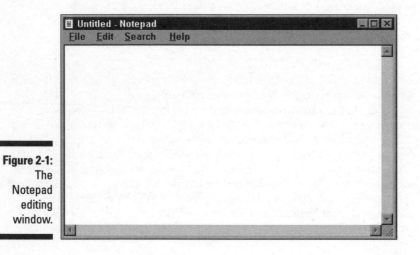

Figure 2-1:
The
Notepad
editing
window.

Listing 2-1 shows you what the HTML code for the proverb generator application looks like.

To see how the code in Listing 2-1 behaves in a Web browser, load the file list0201.htm — which you find on the companion CD — into either Netscape Navigator or Internet Explorer.

Listing 2-1:   The HTML Code for the Proverb Generator Application

```
<HTML>
<HEAD>
<TITLE>The JavaScript Proverb Generator (from JavaScript For
          Dummies, 3rd edition)</TITLE>
</HEAD>
<BODY>
<CENTER><H1>The JavaScript Proverb Generator</H1></CENTER>
To generate a proverb, enter a noun and an adjective; then
          push the "Click here for a proverb" button you see
          below.
```

```
<P>
If you make a mistake, or just want to start over, push the
          "Clear" button.
<P>
<FORM NAME="proverbForm">
Noun:
<INPUT NAME="userNoun" SIZE="25">
<P>
Adjective:
<INPUT NAME="userAdjective" SIZE="25">
<P>
<BR>
<P>
<INPUT TYPE="button" NAME="proverbButton" VALUE="Click here
          for a proverb">
<INPUT TYPE="reset" VALUE="Clear the form">
</FORM>
</BODY>
</HTML>
```

If you're familiar with HTML, you may notice that the code in Listing 2-1 displays:

- **A bit of text.** The text describes the purpose of the proverb generator, along with simple instructions for users to follow.

- **Two input fields.** These are the input fields into which users can type their own words.

- **A button.** Users can click this button when they're ready to generate a customized proverb.

- **A reset button.** Users can click this button to clear the input fields and start over.

Here's how the HTML code in Listing 2-1 appears in the Netscape 6.0 Web browser:

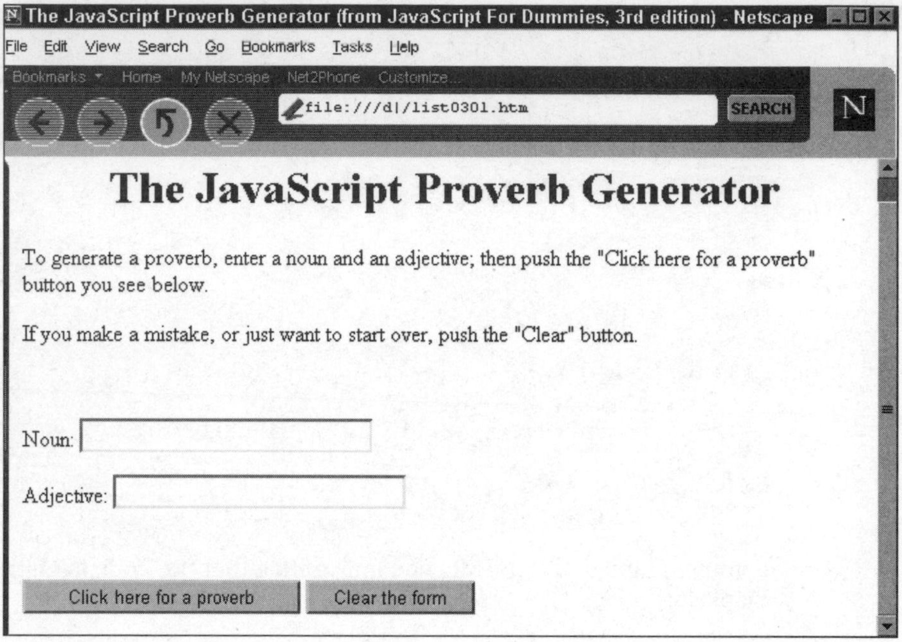

Figure 2-2:
The HTML
portion
of the
Interactive
Proverb
Generator
application.

Even though the Web page in Figure 2-2 looks nice, it's only half done: as you can see from reading through the code in Listing 2-1, nothing happens when a user clicks the button marked "Click here for a proverb."

That's where JavaScript comes in. You need a script to make something happen in response to a button click! You find out all you need to know to create and attach a JavaScript script to this HTML code in the next section.

Part II: Creating and attaching the script

Once you have a working HTML file, such as the one shown in Figure 2-2, you can begin creating your script.

For the proverb generator described in "Ideas?! I got a million of 'em!" earlier in this chapter, you need to create a script that:

✔ Uses whatever a user types into the two input fields to generate and display a customized proverb when the user clicks on the "Click here for a proverb" button

✔ Furnishes two default words (in case the user forgets to type in one or more words)

The JavaScript code required to do all this, as shown in Listing 2-2 below, is simpler than you might think! In "Cast of Script Characters (In Order of Appearance)," later in this book, you get to examine each and every line of JavaScript code in detail. For now, just take a gander at Listing 2-2 and try to get a feel for how JavaScript interacts with HTML.

(You may notice that the JavaScript script is embedded directly into the HTML code you see in Listing 2-1, earlier in this chapter.)

If you want to load the code in Listing 2-2 into your own Web browser and experiment with it, take a look at list0202.htm on the companion CD.

**Listing 2-2:   The HTML Code *and* Embedded JavaScript Code
                  for the Proverb Generator Application**

```
<HTML>
<HEAD>
<TITLE>The JavaScript Proverb Generator (from JavaScript For
        Dummies, 3rd edition)</TITLE>

// Begin JavaScript script

<SCRIPT LANGUAGE="JavaScript">


<!-- Hide this file from non-JavaScript-supporting browsers!

function displayProverb(noun, adjective) {

/* ===================================
        The purpose of this function is to construct
        a customized proverb by plugging user-supplied
        words into a proverb "template".  This function
        accepts two arguments and does not return a
        value. EAV 05/00
        ===================================*/

    // If the user didn't enter a noun, enter "iron" as a
        default.
    if (!noun) {
        noun = "iron"
    }

    // If the user didn't enter an adjective, enter "hot" as
        a default.
    if (!adjective) {
        adjective = "hot"
    }
```

(continued)

Listing 2-2 *(continued)*

```
        // Construct and display the proverb using an alert box
        window.alert("Strike while the "
                + noun
                + " is "
                + adjective
                + "!")
    }

    // stop the hiding -->

    // end JavaScript script

</SCRIPT>


</HEAD>

<BODY onLoad="document.proverbForm.userNoun.select()">
<CENTER><H1>The JavaScript Proverb Generator</H1></CENTER>
To generate a proverb, enter a noun and an adjective; then
            push the "Click here for a proverb" button you see
            below.</H3>
<P>
If you make a mistake, or just want to start over, push the
            "Clear" button.
<P>
<FORM NAME="proverbForm">
Noun:
<INPUT NAME="userNoun" SIZE="25">
<P>
Adjective:
<INPUT NAME="userAdjective" SIZE="25">
<P>
<BR>
<P>
<INPUT TYPE="button" NAME="proverbButton"
VALUE="Click here for a proverb"
            onClick="displayProverb(document.proverbForm.userN
            oun.value,
            document.proverbForm.userAdjective.value)">

<INPUT TYPE="reset" VALUE="Clear the form">
</FORM>
</BODY>
</HTML>
```

A step-by-step blow of all the JavaScript statements you see in Listing 2-2 is provided later in this chapter, in "Cast of Script Characters (In Order of Appearance)." For now, as you glance over Listing 2-2, just notice that:

- **The `onClick` event handler associated with the button named `proverbButton` calls the `displayProverb()` function.** You see this action near the bottom of the listing (see the JavaScript statement that begins `onClick="displayProverb ?`).

  What this JavaScript statement does is this: at runtime, when a user clicks the button marked Click Here for a Proverb, the JavaScript interpreter sends two pieces of information to the `displayProverb()` function: the noun and the adjective the user typed in.

- **The `displayProverb()` function defined at the top of the file generates and displays the customized proverb.** The `displayProverb()` JavaScript function is defined near the top of Listing 2-2, beginning with the statement `function displayProverb(noun, adjective) {`.

  The `displayProverb()` function does this: When the JavaScript interpreter calls this function and presents it with two bits of information — the noun and the adjective the user typed in — this function constructs the customized proverb and displays it on the screen.

Testing the script

Once you have an HTML file that contains embedded JavaScript code, as shown in Listing 2-2, you're reading to test out your JavaScript application! (This is the really fun part.)

To test a JavaScript application, all you need to do is load the JavaScript-containing HTML file into a JavaScript-supporting Web browser. Figure 2-3 shows you how the code in Listing 2-3 looks when it's loaded into the Netscape 6 browser.

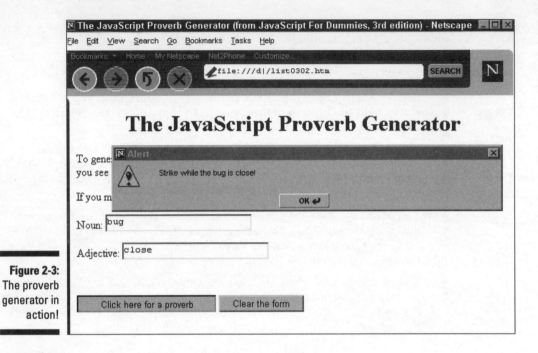

Figure 2-3:
The proverb
generator in
action!

Both Netscape Navigator and Microsoft Internet Explorer provide a way to "turn off" JavaScript support. When you turn off JavaScript support in your browser and then load a JavaScript-containing Web page, your browser ignores all the JavaScript code. It's as if it didn't exist!

If you load list0202.htm from the companion CD, click the Click Here for a Proverb button, and don't see a customized proverb similar to the one shown in Figure 2-3, try the following:

- ✔ If you're using Netscape Navigator 6.x, click Edit⇨Preferences⇨ Advanced and make sure the box next to "Enable JavaScript In Navigator" is checked.

- ✔ If you're using Internet Explorer 5.x, click Tools⇨Internet Options⇨ Security. Then select the Internet Web Content Zone, click Custom Level, and scroll down until you find the Active Scripting category. Finally, ensure that the radio button next to Enable (right under Active Scripting) is checked.

Cast of Script Characters (In Order of Appearance)

This is the section where you get up-close and personal with JavaScript. Specifically, you examine the JavaScript statements that create the proverb generator application shown in Listing 2-2 earlier in this chapter.

By the time you finish this chapter, you know exactly why the proverb generator script works the way it does. Not only that, but you see how to apply all the basic JavaScript language concepts and constructs to your own scripting efforts, as well!

Shoehorning JavaScript into HTML with the <SCRIPT> tag

HTML is a tag language, and one of the tag pairs it supports is the <SCRIPT> . . . </SCRIPT> tag pair.

The <SCRIPT> . . . </SCRIPT> tags let you insert scripts — whether written in JavaScript or some other scripting language, such as VBScript — into an HTML document.

You can insert a script into either the head or the body of an HTML document by placing both the beginning script tag (<SCRIPT>) and the ending script tag (</SCRIPT>) between the beginning and ending <HEAD> and <BODY> tags, respectively.

 Inserting a script into the head of an HTML document causes the script to run right away, even before the browser gets around to displaying the body of the HTML document! This technique lets you use JavaScript to manipulate the body of a Web page, as you see in Chapter 5.

Listing 2-3 below shows how the script tag looked in the proverb generation example.

Listing 2-3:   Inserting a JavaScript Script into the Head of an HTML Document

```
<HTML>
<HEAD>
  . . .
```

(continued)

Listing 2-3 *(continued)*

```
<SCRIPT LANGUAGE="JavaScript">
      . . .
</SCRIPT>
</HEAD>
    . . .
```

And here's the full syntax for the script tag:

```
<SCRIPT>
LANGUAGE="nameOfLanguage"
TYPE="mimeType"
SRC="sourceFileName"
CHARSET="isoCharSet"
</SCRIPT>
```

Where:

nameOfLanguage is *JavaScript* or some other text string denoting a valid scripting language.

mimeType is *text/JavaScript*, or some other string denoting a valid MIME type. (*MIME* stands for *Multipurpose Internet Mail Extension*, in case you're curious! MIME types are also sometimes referred to as *content* types or *media* types.)

You must specify a value for either *nameOfLanguage* or *mimeType*.

sourceFileName (OPTIONAL) is the name of an external script source file; myFile.js, for example. (Note: when you use the *SRC="sourceFileName"*, all of the other statements between the <SCRIPT> . . . </SCRIPT> tags are ignored. See Chapter 14 for details.)

isoCharSet (OPTIONAL) is the name of the character set you want the browser to use when interpreting your scripting statements. (ISO-8859 is used by default if you don't specify a value for the CHARSET attribute.)

Shhh! I'm hiding from a non-JavaScript-enabled browser!

Hard as it may be to believe, not all Web browsers support JavaScript. Sure, most versions of Microsoft Internet Explorer and Netscape Navigator still in circulation do — and together, these two browsers account for the lion's share of the browser market. But there are dozens of other, less widely used browsers out there, some of which can't recognize the tag.

Number crunching

Some JavaScript developers set the `LANGUAGE` attribute of the `<SCRIPT>` tag equal to a value of `JavaScript1.1`, `JavaScript1.2`, or `JavaScript1.3` (as opposed to plain old `JavaScript`) if their script takes advantage of version-specific JavaScript code. For example, you can use any of these three options:

```
<SCRIPT LANGUAGE="JavaScript">
   . . . (basic JavaScript 1.0
   code)
</SCRIPT>


<SCRIPT
   LANGUAGE="JavaScript1.2">
   . . . (some JavaScript code
   that was introduced in
   JavaScript version 1.2)
</SCRIPT>


<SCRIPT
   LANGUAGE="JavaScript1.3">
   . . . (some JavaScript code
   that was introduced in
   JavaScript version 1.3)
</SCRIPT>
```

The trouble with that approach is simply this: keeping track of JavaScript support in the many different versions of both Navigator and Internet Explorer is enough to keep a full-time accountant busy! Take a look at the following and you see what I mean:

✔ Navigator 2.0 and Internet Explorer 3.0 support JavaScript 1.0

✔ Navigator 3.0*x* and Internet Explorer 3.0*x* and 4.0x support JavaScript 1.1.

✔ Navigator 4.0 through 4.05 supports JavaScript 1.2

✔ Navigator 4.06 through 4.5 supports JavaScript 1.3

✔ Navigator 6.0x supports JavaScript 1.5.

✔ Internet Explorer 5.x supports JScript 5.x (which is compatible with JavaScript 1.3, more or less)

Whew! Even if you *do* manage to identify which version of JavaScript or JScript first introduced support for which JavaScript constructs you're using, specifying a value of `JavaScript 1.3` (rather than JavaScript*)* for the `LANGUAGE` attribute doesn't provide any additional JavaScript support. It simply prevents browsers that don't support JavaScript version 1.3 from trying to interpret those JavaScript statements sandwiched between the `<SCRIPT LANGUAGE="JavaScript1.3">` . . . `</SCRIPT>` tags.

My advice? Stick with `LANGUAGE="JavaScript"`, use cutting-edge JavaScript constructs sparingly — and test your scripts in as many different browsers (and versions of browsers) as you possibly can.

Browsers that can't recognize the `<SCRIPT>` tag do something mighty unfriendly. When they load your JavaScript-containing Web page, they display your JavaScript code, right in the body of the Web page, for all to see.

Fortunately, you can prevent this embarrassing situation — simply and safely — by inserting a combination of HTML and JavaScript comments into your code.

Take a look at Listing 2-4 below to see how what I mean.

Listing 2-4:   Hiding JavaScript Statements from Non-JavaScript-Supporting Browsers

```
<HTML>
<HEAD>
<TITLE>The JavaScript Proverb Generator (from JavaScript For
        Dummies, 3rd edition)</TITLE>

<SCRIPT LANGUAGE="JavaScript">
<!-- Hide this file from non-JavaScript-supporting browsers!

    . . .

// stop hiding now -->
</SCRIPT>
```

If you're familiar with HTML, you may know that <!– marks the beginning of an HTML comment, and –> marks the ending of an HTML comment. So, in effect, every browser that supports HTML (which, by definition, is every browser in existence) ignores everything between these two symbols.

JavaScript-enabled browsers, however, understand that an HTML comment right after an opening tag signals a script coming up — and process your JavaScript code just fine, thank you very much.

The result? With just two lines of code — the <!-- and // --> symbols — you can hide your script statements from non-JavaScript-enabled browsers at the same time you make them visible to browsers that support JavaScript. Cool, huh?

Make sure you put the beginning and ending *hiding* symbols (<!-- and // --> respectively) on their own separate lines. Placing either on the same line as a JavaScript statement could cause a non-JavaScript-enabled browser to display your JavaScript code, just as though the hiding symbols didn't exist.

The double slash (//) in front of the closing HTML comment tag is the JavaScript comment operator. You find out all about JavaScript comments later in this chapter, in "Comments, Please!"

Fully functioning

Functions are the software equivalent of black boxes: they allow programmers to name a bunch of JavaScript statements and then reuse those statements, over and over again, simply by referring to, or *calling,* the function.

Here's a quick-and-dirty description of JavaScript functions:

- ✔ **Functions may (but don't have to) accept values.** In the proverb generator example in this chapter, as you can see in Listing 2-5 below, the displayProverb() function accepts two values: a noun, and adjective.

- ✔ **Functions do something useful.** Inside the body of a function, you can place whatever JavaScript statements you like. In the proverb generator example in this chapter, shown in Listing 2-5 , the displayProverb() function:

  - Checks to see if a noun was passed in; if not, the function assigns the default value "iron" to the variable named noun.

  - Checks to see if an adjective was passed in. If not, the function assigns the default value of "hot" to the variable named adjective.

  - Constructs and displays a customized proverb using the values for noun and adjective.

- ✔ **Functions may (but don't have to) return a value.** Often, the JavaScript statement that calls a function expects an answer in return — even if the answer it expects is just *true,* meaning that everything went smoothly during the number-crunching, or false (if it didn't). In the example in Listing 2-5, however, the displayProverb() doesn't return a value, and the onClick event handler calls the displayProverb() function doesn't expect one. (For an example of returning and accepting a return value from a function, check out Chapter 3.)

Listing 2-5:   Defining and Calling the displayProverb() **Function**

```
<HTML>
<HEAD>
<TITLE>The JavaScript Proverb Generator (from JavaScript For
        Dummies, 3rd edition)</TITLE>

<SCRIPT LANGUAGE="JavaScript">
<!-- Hide this file from non-JavaScript-supporting browsers!
    . . .
function displayProverb(noun, adjective) {

    // If the user didn't enter a noun, enter "iron" as a
        default.
```

(continued)

Listing 2-5 *(continued)*

```
    if (!noun) {
        noun = "iron"
    }

    // If the user didn't enter an adjective, enter "hot" as
            a default.
    if (!adjective) {
        adjective = "hot"
    }

    // Construct and display the proverb using an alert box
    window.alert("Strike while the "
            + noun
            + " is "
            + adjective
            + "!")

}

 . . .
<INPUT TYPE="button" NAME="proverbButton"
VALUE="Click here for a proverb"
            onClick="displayProverb(document.proverbForm.userN
            oun.value,
            document.proverbForm.userAdjective.value)">
```

Oh, and one other thing to keep in mind when you define your own custom JavaScript functions: make sure that you place all of your JavaScript statements inside the function's curly braces, like this (and as shown in Listing 2-5); if you don't, you get a JavaScript error at runtime.

```
function displayProverb(noun, adjective) {

    //  All the JavaScript statements that
    // make up the displayProverb()
    //  function go right here.

}
```

Even if you don't plan to reuse a bunch of related JavaScript statements, you still might want to consider organizing them as a function. Why? Because coming up with a descriptive function name helps you to clarify the actions you want your JavaScript statements to perform. It also makes reading your code easier (both for you, and for other programmers).

Comments, please!

Comments are explanations you add to your script to describe, in human terms, why you created your script, what it does, what limitations it has, and so on. Because comments aren't strictly necessary (the JavaScript interpreter ignores them), many programmers don't add them to their code — but they *should!* Comments are an essential component of any good script, because they help human beings understand the script and maintain it, if need be.

Listing 2-6 shows the comments found in the proverb generator example shown in this chapter.

Listing 2-6:   JavaScript Comments Help Human Readers Understand Code at a Glance

```javascript
function displayProverb(noun, adjective) {

    /* =====================================
        The purpose of this function is to construct
        a customized proverb by plugging user-supplied
        words into an proverb "template". This function
        accepts two arguments and does not return a
        value.  EAV 05/00
        =====================================*/

    // If the user didn't enter a noun, enter "iron" as a
            default.
    if (!noun) {
        noun = "iron"
    }

    // If the user didn't enter an adjective, enter "hot" as
            a
    // default.
    if (!adjective) {
        adjective = "hot"
    }

    // Construct and display the proverb using an alert box
    window.alert("Strike while the "
            + noun
            + " is "
            + adjective
            + "!")
}
```

If this, then that

The if . . . then statement is one of the most widely used and useful of all JavaScript conditional expressions. This statement lets you test a condition, then perform one set of JavaScript statements if the condition is true and another set of JavaScript statements (or nothing at all) if the condition is false.

Take a look at Listing 2-7 to see how the if . . . then statement appears in the proverb generator example described throughout this chapter.

Listing 2-7: **Using the** if **Statement Without Using the Corresponding** then

```
. . .
function displayProverb(noun, adjective) {
    . . .

    // If the user didn't enter a noun, enter "iron" as a
            default.
    if (!noun) {
        noun = "iron"
    }

    // If the user didn't enter an adjective, enter "hot" as
            a default.
    if (!adjective) {
        adjective = "hot"
    }

    . . .
}
```

At first glance, the condition for the first if statement shown in Listing 2-7 (!noun) might look a little odd. That's because it couples the logical *not* operator (!), which is described in Chapter 3, with the variable named noun. In English,

```
if (!noun) {
    noun = "iron"
}
```

translates to:

"If there is no value defined for the variable called noun, set the variable called *noun* equal to iron."

The virtues of being method-ical

A *method* is a special kind of function associated with a JavaScript object. You may want to glance through Chapter 3's discussion, where I cover methods in detail.

In the proverb generator example described throughout this chapter, you see one method in action: the window.alert() method. Take a peek at Listing 2-8 to see what the code looks like to call the built-in window.alert() method.

Listing 2-8: **Calling the Built-in** `alert()` **Method Associated with the** `window` **Object**

```
. . .
function displayProverb(noun, adjective) {
    . . .
    // Construct and display the proverb using an alert box
    window.alert("Strike while the "
          + noun
          + " is "
          + adjective
          + "!")
}
```

Two things are going on in the code snippet you see in Listing 2-8:

- A string is being constructed using

  Three separate bits of text (`Strike while the`, `is`, and `!`)

  Two variable values (the value of `noun` and `adjective`)

- The constructed string is being passed to the `alert()` method associated with the `window` object. The `alert()` method then displays the string on the screen for the user to see.

You call methods in JavaScript much the way you call plain old functions: The difference is that you refer to methods using their fully-qualified names.

A fully-qualified name specifies the object to which a method belongs, preceded by all the objects which contain *that* object. For example, the fully-qualified name of the `click()` method might be `document.myForm.myButton.click()`. Fully qualifying a name helps the JavaScript interpreter distinguish between identical methods on different objects. For example, fully qualifying lets you create an HTML form containing three buttons and call the `click()` method on each of the three buttons separately, like so:

```
document.myForm.buttonOne.click()
document.myForm.buttonTwo.click()
document.myForm.buttonThree.click()
```

The `alert()` method is one of the few exceptions in JavaScript to the "always fully qualify a method call" rule. Because the JavaScript interpreter knows that there is always one window at the top of the Web page hierarchy (called, not surprisingly, `window`, you don't have to specify `window.alert()`; plain old `alert()` does the job just fine. However, since it never hurts to be specific — especially when dealing with a stickler for semantics like the JavaScript interpreter — I suggest you always fully qualify method names.

That way, you don't have to remember which methods represent an exception and which follow the rule!

Those daring event handlers

Event handlers allow you to trigger a series of JavaScript statements whenever a predefined event occurs.

In the case of the proverb generator example I describe in this chapter, the JavaScript interpreter triggers the displayProverb() function every time a user clicks a push button (in other words, every time the click event associated with that button occurs). Take a look at the code in Listing 2-9 to see what I mean!

Listing 2-9:   Associating a Function Call with the onClick **Event Handler**

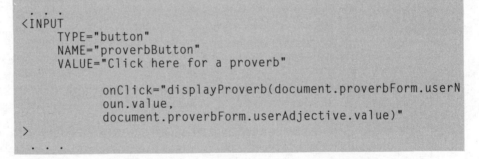

```
. . .
<INPUT
    TYPE="button"
    NAME="proverbButton"
    VALUE="Click here for a proverb"

        onClick="displayProverb(document.proverbForm.userN
        oun.value,
        document.proverbForm.userAdjective.value)"
>
. . .
```

See the last statement in Listing 2-9? The one that starts onClick=? This statement associates the onClick event handler with the HTML button named proverbButton. (Notice that both the NAME and onClick attributes are defined between the beginning HTML <INPUT tag and the ending >.

You provide actions for other event handlers inside the HTML tags for *their* associated objects. For example, the following code tells the JavaScript interpreter to call the doSomething() function whenever a document is loaded.

```
<BODY onLoad="doSomething()">
```

And the following code snippet triggers a JavaScript function called doSomethingElse() when the inputField element blurs.

```
<INPUT TYPE="select" NAME="inputField"
         onBlur="doSomething()">
```

Check out Appendix C for a complete list of the event handlers available in JavaScript.

When it comes to assigning a value to an event handler, you're not limited to a single JavaScript statement; you can specify as many JavaScript statements as you want — provided you separate them with semicolons, like this:

```
<INPUT
    TYPE="button"
    NAME="proverbButton"
    VALUE="Click here for a proverb"

        onClick="displayProverb(document.proverbForm.userN
        oun.value,
        document.proverbForm.userAdjective.value);
        calculateSomething(); printSomething();
        displaySomething()"
>
```

Chapter 3

JavaScript Programming Concepts

In This Chapter

▶ Taking a look at JavaScript syntax (expressions, functions, variables, and operators)

▶ Understanding how object models work

▶ Getting familiar with Netscape Navigator's object model

▶ Getting familiar with Internet Explorer's object model

Although JavaScript is an awfully powerful language, the way you use it can be boiled down to just two major concepts: 1) syntax, and 2) the JavaScript object model (also called the *document object model*).

Syntax refers to the rules you must follow to write JavaScript code. There aren't many syntax rules, but you do need to understand them — just as you need to understand and follow the rules of English syntax to write a sentence that English-speaking folks can understand.

The *document object model,* or *DOM,* refers to the Web page components, or *objects,* you can access and manipulate using JavaScript. In the same way that you need to master a vocabulary of English words before you can write a story in English, you need to be somewhat familiar with the DOM before you can write your own JavaScript scripts.

Once you've had a chance to glance through this chapter, you're armed with all the knowledge you need to write your own scripts!

JavaScript Syntax

The rules and regulations that govern how humans can communicate with the JavaScript interpreter is called the JavaScript *syntax*. Although you might feel a little overwhelmed (especially at first!) with all the technicalities of JavaScript syntax, you can focus on just these few things, which are the building blocks of your code:

✔ **Expressions:** You combine keywords with functions, variables, and operators to create the *expressions*, or meaningful directions, you want to pass along to the JavaScript interpreter. Every script is composed of one or more valid expressions.

✔ **Functions:** Functions are named groups of statements that you define once, then reuse to your heart's content.

✔ **Variables:** Variables are named placeholders that represent the bits of data you work with in your scripts.

✔ **Operators:** Operators are JavaScript's answer to conjunctions: the commas, periods, and other symbols you use to compare and assign values to variables, among other things.

Express Yourself

Defining an expression, like defining an English phrase, covers a pretty broad territory. In general, a JavaScript *expression* is made up of *operators* (operators, such as + and -, are covered in detail later in this chapter) and *operands* (variables and literals) that together can be evaluated by the JavaScript interpreter. For example, look at the following expressions:

```
new Date()
666 + (123 * 79) + (myAge)
document.myForm.mood.value + " to see you, " +
document.myForm.yourName.value
```

These three examples are each slightly different, but they all have one thing in common: They can all be evaluated to something. The first example evaluates to the current date; the second, to a number (and no, I'm not telling you what that number is!); the third, to a *string*. (A string is a group of characters you manipulate as a single block.) That's what an expression is: It's a combination of variables, operators, literals (non-varying values), and keywords that can be evaluated by the JavaScript interpreter.

Don't keep your comments to yourself

The JavaScript interpreter ignores *comments*. Comments do have value, though; they are very useful for explaining things to human readers of your script. (Include yourself in this category, by the way — after you've finished a script and put it aside for a few months, you may appreciate those comments yourself!)

You can write JavaScript comments in two different ways. Either type of comment can appear anywhere in your script and as many times as you like.

The first type of comment is a single-line comment. It begins with two forward slashes, and it's good for only one line. The second type of comment is a multiple-line comment. Because it spans multiple lines, you have to tell it where to start (you do this with a forward slash followed by an asterisk) and where to end (you do this with an asterisk and then a forward slash). For example:

```
// Single-line comments don't require an ending slash.
/* This comment can span multiple lines.  Always remember
to close it, though; if you forget, you'll get weird errors
when you try to display your script. */
```

Remember that JavaScript scripts are the lines of code that come between the `<SCRIPT>`...`</SCRIPT>` tags in an HTML file. You can't use HTML comment characters (`<!--` to begin a comment line and `-->` to end it) to create JavaScript comments, and you can't use JavaScript comment characters (`//` and `/* */`) to create HTML comments.

Don't overlap or nest multi-line comments in your JavaScript code. If you do, the JavaScript interpreter will generate an error.

Mint condition: if . . . else

The `if`...`else` (also called the _conditional_) expression is used to test a condition, which is often another expression (try saying _that_ three times fast!). If the condition is _true,_ the JavaScript interpreter executes all the statements that follow the `if` clause. If the condition is _false_, the JavaScript interpreter executes all the statements that follow the `else` clause (if the `else` clause exists). Here's the generic description of how to use `if`...`else`:

```
if (condition) {
    statements
}
[ else {
    statements
}]
```

The curly braces (`{` and `}`) combine statements into one big block. For example, if you follow an `if` condition with three JavaScript statements, all of which are surrounded by curly braces, the JavaScript interpreter will execute all three of those statements when the `if` condition is true.

The square brackets (`[` and `]`) mean that the entire `else` clause is optional. You don't actually put the square brackets in your JavaScript code; you just add the `else` clause if you want it, or leave it off if you don't.

Suppose you want to help the user make a case-sensitive entry. You can use JavaScript to test the user's preference and then make the input conform to upper or lower case letters accordingly. Your user won't have to worry about typing a BOb instead of BOB. Listing 3-1 shows `if`...`else` in action.

Listing 3-1: JavaScript if...else Example

```
// If the user selected uppercase,
if (caseSelection == "upper"){
    // change the values for first and last name to all
            uppercase

        document.form1.firstName.value =
            document.form1.firstName.value.toUpperCase()
    document.form1.lastName.value =
            document.form1.lastName.value.toUpperCase()
}
else {
    // otherwise, change the values for first and last name
            to all lowercase
document.form1.firstName.value =
            document.form1.firstName.value.toLowerCase()
    document.form1.lastName.value =
            document.form1.lastName.value.toLowerCase()
}
```

Some JavaScript programmers end each statement with a semicolon, like this:

```
if (a == b) { // if a is equal to b
    c = d;        // assign the value of d to the c variable,
    e = f;        // assign the value of f to the e variable,
                  // and assign the string "American Beauty"
                  // to the variable called favoriteMovie
    favoriteMovie = "American Beauty";
}
```

Semicolons are optional in JavaScript, with one exception. If you place more than one JavaScript statement on the same line, you <u>must</u> separate those statements with semicolons. For example:

```
c = d    e = f    favoriteMovie = "American Beauty"  // Wrong!
c= d; e = f; favoriteMovie = "AmericanBeauty";    // Right (if
        a bit hard to read)
```

The for loop: It's not just for breakfast anymore

The for loop lets you traverse a number of items quickly and easily. As an example, say you created a Web page that contained an HTML multiple-choice select element. At some point, you might want to find out which of the available options a user has selected.

You can do this easily using a for loop!

ch3_forloop.htm shows you an example of using the for loop to detect a selected element.

Unfortunately, the `for` loop looks a little geek-like until you play with it a bit. That's because it hails from the C language, which is known as much for its breathtaking brevity as for its power.

Here's a copy of the generic form:

```
for ([initial expression]; [condition]; [update expression])
        {
statements
}
```

The `for` loop introduces three terms that may be new to you: the *initial expression,* the *condition,* and the *update expression.* Here's how it all works:

1. **The JavaScript interpreter looks at the initial expression.**

   The initial expression is almost always a number (usually 0, because that's the number JavaScript arrays begin with) assigned to a variable, such as this: `var i==0`.

2. **The JavaScript interpreter then looks at the condition to see whether it is *true*.**

   (The condition compares the variable described in #1 to some programmer-defined constant; for example, `i<10`, `counter<length`, or `eachOne<=maximum`. If the value of i is indeed less than 10, for instance, then the "i<10" is true.)

3. **If the condition is *true*, the JavaScript interpreter performs all the statements in the body of the `for` loop, and then it evaluates the update expression.**

   The update expression typically increments the initial expression by one; for example, `i++` or `eachOne++`. (`++` looks kind of funny, but it's not a typo. It's an operator that adds one to the variable it's next to. Think of `eachOne++` as a shorthand way of typing `eachOne = eachOne + 1`.)

4. **Now that the variable has been bumped up, the whole thing starts over again. (That's why it's called a loop!) The JavaScript interpreter goes back to Step 2 to see whether the condition is *true*, and if it is. . . .**

   Of course, at some point the condition is no longer *true*. When that happens, the JavaScript interpreter hops out of the `for` loop and picks up again at the first statement after the loop.

It's possible to create a `for` loop condition that is always *true*. The easiest way to make this mistake is to specify an update condition that doesn't actually update the initial expression (for example, leaving off the "++" in the example code below.) Creating a loop condition that is always true and can never be changed or set to false is known as creating an *endless loop* because the JavaScript interpreter evaluates and performs the same statements in the body of the loop endlessly! (Okay, *never* is a long time; in practice, the interpreter will keep evaluating it until you kill the Web browser session. I've found that turning off the machine works nicely!)

Now here's an example of for in action:

```
for (var i = 1; i <= 10; i++) {
    document.writeln(i)
}
```

Here's what's going on:

1. var i = 1 **creates a variable called** i **and sets it to equal 1.**

2. i <= 10 **tests to see whether** i **is less than or equal to 10.**

3. **The first time through,** i **is 1, and 1 is less than 10, so the statement in the body of the** for **loop (**document.writeln(i)**) is performed (the value of** i **appears).**

4. i++ **adds one to** i.

5. i <= 10 **tests to see whether** i **is still less than or equal to 10.**

6. **The second time through,** i **is 2, and 2 is less than 10, so the statement in the body of the** for **loop (**document.writeln(i)**) is performed (the value of** i **appears).**

7. **Now the whole thing repeats from Step 3: 1 is added to** i, **the variable is tested to see whether it's still less than or equal to 10, and so on, for as many times as** i **satisfies the condition.**

Nothing is magical about the i variable name; you could just as easily have named your variable numberOfTimesToPrint, or numberOfPigs-Ordered, or Fred. i in for loops just happens to be a convention, nothing more.

As you may expect, the following appears on the screen when the for loop is executed:

```
1 2 3 4 5 6 7 8 9 10
```

Peeking inside objects with for...in

If you like for, you'll love for...in. for...in is used for looping, or *iterating*, through all properties of an object, like so:

```
for (var in object) {
    statements
}
```

Here's a useful function that you can use to loop through all properties of a given object and display each property's name and associated value:

```
function displayProperties(inputObject, inputObjectName){

    // Set result equal to a blank string
    var result = ""

    // For each property in the passed-in object

    for (var eachProperty in inputObject) {

                // Combine the name of the object, the name
                // of the property, and the property value
                // to the result variable.  (Adding strings
                // with + is called "string concatenation".)

            result += inputObjectName + "." + eachProperty +
        " = " + inputObject[eachProperty] + "<BR>"
        }

    // The result variable now contains a nice report
    // that displays the contents of all the properties in an
    // object.

    return result
}
```

Okay, this code is plug-ugly, but it's pretty straightforward after you understand what the `for...in` loop does. Here's how it works.

The code defines a function called `displayProperties()`. Here's one way to call this function:

```
document.writeln(displayProperties(document, "document"))
```

The JavaScript interpreter hops up to the `displayProperties()` definition, only this time it substitutes the `document` object for the argument `inputObject` and the string `"document"` for the argument `inputObjectName`.

Inside the `for...in` loop, the JavaScript interpreter loops through all properties of the `document` object. Each time it comes to a new property, it assigns it to the variable called `eachProperty`. Then it constructs a string and adds the string to the end of the variable called `result`. After the `for...in` loop has looped through all properties of `document`, the `result` variable holds a nice long string containing the names and values of all properties in the `document` object.

Displaying (or *dumping,* as it's called in programmer-ese) the property values of an object can be useful when you're trying to track down an error in your script. A function like this one enables you to know exactly what the interpreter thinks objects look like (which is sometimes quite different from the way *you* think they look).

Take a look at ch3_for_in.htm to see an example of the for...in loop.

While away the hours

The *while* loop's job is to do something — that is, to execute one or more JavaScript statements — while some programmer-defined condition is true.

Obviously, then, you want to make sure that one of the statements in the body of your while loop changes the while condition in some way so that it stops being *true* at some point.

```
while (condition) {
    statements
}
```

Here's an example of while in action:

```
var totalInventory=700, numberPurchased=200, numberSales=0

while (totalInventory > numberPurchased) {
    totalInventory=totalInventory - numberPurchased
    numberSales++
}
document.writeln("Our stock supply will support " +
numberSales + " of these bulk sales")
```

Step into the JavaScript interpreter's virtual shoes for a minute and take a look at how this all works! (Remember, you're the JavaScript interpreter now, so be serious.)

> While the total inventory is more than the number purchased. . . . Let's see, 700 is greater 200. Okay. Subtract the number purchased from the total inventory, and bump up the number of sales by one. Number of sales is now one. That's one loop down.

> While the total inventory is more than the number purchased. . . . Hmm. Total inventory is 500 now, and that's still greater than 200, so I'll subtract the number purchased from the total inventory and add another one to the number of sales. Number of sales is now two. Two loops down.

> While the total inventory is more than the number purchased. . . . Okay, total inventory is 300 now, which is still greater than 200. Subtract number purchased from total inventory, add one to the number of sales. Number of sales is now three. Three loops down.

> While the total inventory is more than the number purchased. . . . Hey! It's not! Total inventory is 100, and the number purchased is 200. I'm outta here.

Here's what I'll write to the screen: Our stock supply will support 3 of these bulk sales.

Nice to know how the other half thinks, isn't it?

Dooby dooby doo

The do while loop is mighty close to the while loop described in the preceding section. The main difference between the two loops is that unlike while, which may never be executed depending on whether or not the while condition is *true* when the loop begins to execute, the do-while loop always executes at least once. (In other words, whether or not you choose the do_while loop or the while loop is largely a matter of personal choice, since they both produce similar results.)

Take a look at the syntax for the do while loop:

```
do {
     statements
}
while (condition)
```

Here's a real-life example:

```
do {
     // The following line of code pops up a JavaScript
         prompt.
     // The "answer" variable is set to null if the user
         clicks
     // "Cancel"
     answer = prompt("Would you like to purchase " + article
             + " t-shirt? If so, enter the size.", "X-tra
         Large")

     // Change "a" to "ANOTHER" to make the display message
     // grammatically correct the second (and subsequent)
     // time around.
     article = "ANOTHER"
}
while (answer != null)
```

Load up ch3_dowhile.htm to see a working example of the do...while code shown above.

Never mind! Changing your mind with continue and break

Both continue and break are used inside loops to change how the loops behave. (break can be used also inside a switch statement, as the example later in this chapter demonstrates.) continue and break do slightly different things, as you'll see shortly, and they can be used in the same loop (although they don't have to be).

When the JavaScript interpreter encounters a `break` statement, the interpreter breaks out of the loop it's currently processing and starts interpreting again at the first line *following* the loop.

In contrast, `continue` also tells the JavaScript interpreter to stop what it's doing, but on a somewhat smaller scale. `continue` tells the interpreter to stop the loop it's currently processing and hop back up to the beginning of the loop again, to continue as normal.

`continue` and `break` are useful for exceptions to the rule. For example, you may want to process all items the same way except for two special cases. Just remember that `break` *breaks* out of a loop altogether, and `continue` stops iteration execution, but then *continues* the loop.

Here is an example of `break` used inside a `while` loop:

```
var totalInventory=700, numberPurchased=200, numberSales=0
while (totalInventory > numberPurchased) {
    totalInventory=totalInventory - numberPurchased
    numberSales++
    if (numberSales > 2) {
        break
    }
}
```

When the number of sales is greater than 2 (in other words, reaches 3), the `break` keyword causes the JavaScript interpreter to hop out of the `while` loop altogether.

And here's an example of `continue` used inside a `for` loop:

```
for (var i = 1; i <= 20; i++) {
    if (i == 13) {  // superstitious; don't print number 13
        continue
    }
    document.writeln(i)
}
```

In this code snippet, when the variable called `i` contains the value 13, the JavaScript interpreter stops what it's doing, without hitting the `writeln()` method, and continues on with the next iteration of the for loop (that is, it sets `i` equal to 14 and keeps going).

You can test this scrap of code for yourself. It should produce the following result:

```
1 2 3 4 5 6 7 8 9 10 11 12 14 15 16 17 18 19 20
```

Always check the label

The label statement gives you a way to label a group of other JavaScript statements in a way that lets you refer to them, en masse, from a break or continue statement. (The break and continue statements are described in the preceding section.)

In other words, say the JavaScript interpreter breaks out of a loop based on a break statement. Using label, you can redirect the interpreter to begin processing again at a group of labeled statements (rather than the default start-over place, which is the beginning of the broken loop).

Here's the syntax:

```
label :
    statements
```

To understand how labeled statements work, read through the following example, which uses a labeled statement with the break statement. The code contains two loops: an outer for loop, and inside that for loop, an inner while loop.

The label is called theOutsideLoop, and it describes (appropriately enough) the outer for loop.

When the interpreter encounters the line break theOutsideLoop, it breaks clean out of the labeled statement (the entire for loop). (In contrast, if you changed break theOutsideLoop to plain old break, the interpreter would break only out of the while loop and continue processing the rest of the for loop.)

```
theOutsideLoop :
for (var i=0; i<10;i++) {

    if (i > 3 && i < 6) {

        // here's the while loop
        while (i <5) {
            break theOutsideLoop
        }

    }
}
```

The old switcheroo

The switch statement provides an easy way to check an expression for a bunch of different values without resorting to a string of if statements.

Here's the syntax:

```
switch (expression) {
        case label :
            statement
            break
        case label :
            statement
            break

        ...

        default : statement
}
```

Suppose you want to examine a value and find out whether it matches one of the following strings: "S", "s", "M", "m", "L", "l". (Perhaps you're selling t-shirts and need to know what size a user has ordered.) Here's how you can go about it using the switch statement:

```
var answer
answer = prompt("What size t-shirt do you wear? (L, M, S)",
        "L")
switch (answer) {
    case "L" :
    case "l" :
        alert("Thanks for buying a large t-shirt")
        break
    case "M":
    case "m":
        alert("Thanks for buying a medium t-shirt")
        break
    case "S":
    case "s":
        alert("Thanks for buying a small t-shirt")
        break
    default: alert("I have no idea what size you want!")
    }
```

Note that if you forget to finish each case with a break statement (and it's easy to do), the interpreter will "fall through" and perform all the statements it finds until it either finds a break or detects the end of the switch statement. For instance, in the preceding code snippet, if we removed all the break statements, an answer value of "L" would cause the interpreter to call every last alert() method — all four of them!

Take a look at ch3_switch.htm to see a working example of the preceding JavaScript code.

The lazy typist's friend: with

with is a kind of shorthand that enables you to save keystrokes when you want to refer to several attributes of the same object. (You see all about objects in "Objects Defined" later in this chapter.) For example, if you want to display several attributes of the document object one after the other, instead of writing this:

```
document.writeln(document.lastModified)
document.writeln(document.location)
document.writeln(document.title)
```

you can write this:

```
with (document) {
    writeln(lastModified)
    writeln(location)
    writeln(title)
}
```

In this code scrap, JavaScript assumes that any property you reference inside the `with` clause belongs to the `document` object; you don't have to type in `document` explicitly for each property.

var (That's variable to you, Bud!)

A *variable* is a named placeholder for a value. Use the `var` keyword to construct an expression that first declares a variable and then (optionally) initializes its value. To declare a variable, you type something like this:

```
var myCat // variable names can be anything you want
```

This tells the JavaScript interpreter, "Yo, here comes a variable, and name it `myCat`, will you?"

Initializing a variable means setting a variable equal to some value, which you typically do at the same time you declare the variable. Here's how you might initialize the variable `myCat`:

```
var myCat = "Fluffy"
```

Technically, you can declare a variable in JavaScript without using the `var` keyword, like so: `myCat = "Fluffy"` However, using the `var` keyword to declare all your variables is a good idea; doing so helps the JavaScript interpreter properly scope variables with the same name.

After you declare a variable — whether you use the `var` keyword or no — you can reset its value later in the script by using the assignment operator (=). The name of the variable can be any legal identifier (you want to use letters and numbers, not special characters), and the value can be any legal expression. (A *legal expression* is any properly punctuated expression that you see represented in this chapter: an `if...else` expression, an assignment expression, and so on.)

A variable is valid only when it's *in scope*. When a variable is in scope that means it's been declared between the same curly brace boundaries as the statement that's trying to access it.

For example, if you define a variable named `firstName` inside a function called `displayReport()`, you can refer to the variable only inside the `displayReport()` function's curly braces. If you try to use it inside another function, you'll get an error. If you want to reuse a variable *among* functions (shudder — that way lies madness), you can declare it near the top of your script, before any functions are declared. That way, the variable's scope is the entire script, and all the functions get to "see" it. Take a look at the following code example:

```
...
function displayReport() {
    var firstName = document.myForm.givenName.value
    ...
    alert("Click OK to see the report for " + firstName)
    // Using firstName here is fine; it was declared
    // inside the same set of curly braces.
    ...
}
function displayGraph() {
    alert("Here's the graph for " + firstName) // Error!
    // firstName wasn't defined inside this
    // function's curly braces!
    ...
}
```

As you can see from the comments in the this code fragment, it's perfectly okay to use `firstName` inside the `displayReport()` function; `firstName` is in scope anywhere inside `displayReport()`. It's not okay, however, to use `firstName` inside `displayGraph()`. As far as `displayGraph()` is concerned, no such animal as `firstName` has been declared inside its scope!

Literally speaking

Sometimes you want to use a number, or a string, or some other value that you know for a fact will never change. For example, say you want to write a script that uses pi in some calculation. Instead of creating a variable called pi and assigning it the value of 1.31415, you can use 1.31415 directly in your calculations. Values that aren't stored in variables are called *literals.*

Here are a few examples of using literals in JavaScript:

```
alert("Sorry, you entered your
    e-mail address incor-
    rectly.") // string literal

x = 1.31415 * someVariable //
    floating-point literal

if (theAnswer == true) //
    boolean literal

document.write("The total
    number of users is " +
    1234) // integer literal
```

Why, I declare! (Functions, that is)

A function declaration requires the `function` keyword. You'll probably write a great many functions; they're a good way to organize your script statements into discrete little chunks that each do something specific (instead of having one huge script with dozens of lines, one right after another). Think of a function as a named bundle of JavaScript statements that can be used over and over again just by calling the name of the function.

Organizing your script into functions, like organizing your closet, can seem like loads of up-front work for nothing — after all, you don't *have* to do it. Your script (and your closet) will work as designed, even if they're a mess. The payoff comes when you have a problem (or the perfect brown leather belt) hiding somewhere in all that confusion and you want to find it in a hurry!

Here's the syntax for a function declaration:

```
function name([parameter] [, parameter] [..., parameter]) {
    statements
    return value
}
```

And here's an example:

```
function calculateTotal(numberOrdered, itemPrice) {
    var result = numberOrdered * itemPrice
    return result
}
```

Your function can take as many arguments as you want it to (including none at all), separated by commas. You generally refer to these argument values in the body of the function (otherwise, why bother to use them at all?), so be sure to name them something meaningful. In other words, I could have substituted x and y for `numberOrdered` and `itemPrice` in the code snippet above, and the code would work just as well. It just wouldn't be very easy to read or maintain!

Because the optional *return* statement is so important, I devote a whole section to its use (*Return to Sender,* which you can find right after this section.)

Okay, you know how to declare a function. Now I bet you'd like to know how to call one — and I'd like to oblige you! You call a function by specifying the name of the function, followed by an open parenthesis, comma-delimited parameters, and a closing parenthesis.

For example:

```
. . .
function calculateTotal(numberOrdered, itemPrice) {
    var result = numberOrdered * itemPrice
    return result
} // Now the function is defined, so it can be called
...
// The statement below calls calculateTotal()
alert("Total purchases come to " +
      calculateTotal(10, 19.95))
```

A *function call* is the technical term for — what else — calling a function. See the line of code that reads `calculateTotal(inputNumber, inputPrice)`? That line is a function call.

Notice also that you can embed a function call within another expression. That is, `calculateTotal(inputNumber, inputPrice)` is actually part of the expression being sent to the `alert()` method. (You find out all about methods in "Methods Defined" later in this chapter; for now, you can think of them as special kinds of functions.)

Return to sender

You use the `return` keyword to return a value from a function. To understand why you might want to return a value from a function, imagine yourself asking a friend to go look up some information for you. If your friend went ahead and did the research you asked, but neglected to pass it along to you, you'd be pretty disappointed, wouldn't you? Well, imagine that you are a bit of JavaScript code calling a function, and your friend is the function you're calling. It's the same principle: no matter how many useful things it does, if a function doesn't return some sort of result to the piece of code that needs it, it hasn't finished its job.

The syntax for `return` is simple:

```
return expression
```

Here's how it looks in action:

```
function calculateTotal(numberOrdered, itemPrice) {

    var result = numberOrdered * itemPrice
    return result
} // Now the function is defined, so it can be called

...
document.write("The total amount to remit to us is " +
        calculateTotal(3, 4.99))
```

Operators are standing by

Operators are like conjunctions. Remember fifth grade English? (Or if you were a cartoon connoisseur, maybe you remember *Conjunction Junction, What's Your Function?* "And, but, and or, they'll take you pretty far. . . .") Ahem.

Operators, like conjunctions, enable you to join multiple phrases together to form expressions.

Two categories of operators exist: *binary,* meaning two items (or *operands*) must be sandwiched on either side of the operator, and *unary,* meaning only one operand is required.

Table 3-1 gives you a rundown of the basic operators. The JavaScript interpreter always evaluates the expression to the right of the equal sign first, and only then does it assign the evaluated value to the variable — with two exceptions: the unary decrement operator (--), and the unary increment operator (++).

Table 3-1		JavaScript Operators		
In all these examples, x is initially set to 11.				
Operator	**Meaning**	**Example**	**Result**	**How Come?**
%	modulus	x = x % 5	x = 1	11 / 5 = 2 with 1 remainder, so modulus returns 1 in this case
++	increment	x = x++	x = 11	++ is applied *after* assignment when you put it *after* the var
		x = ++x	x = 12	++ is applied *before* assignment when you put it *before* the var
--	decrement	x = x--	x = 11	-- is applied *after* assignment when you put it *after* the var
		x = --x	x = 10	--is applied *before* assignment when you put it *before* the var

(continued)

Table 3-1 *(continued)*

In all these examples, x is initially set to 11.

Operator	Meaning	Example	Result	How Come?
-	negation	x = -x	x = -11	Turns positive numbers negative and vice versa
+	addition	x = x + x	x = 22	11 + 11 is 22

Some of the operators are pretty normal; most of us are familiar with addition and negation, for example. The increment operators are a little weird, though, because not only are they a new thing (you never see ++ or - - outside of a computer program listing), but depending on whether you put them before or after the variable, they behave differently!

Just as in math, an order of evaluation is applied to a statement that contains multiple operators. Unless you set phrases off with parentheses, the JavaScript interpreter observes the precedence order shown in Table 3-2 (from the comma, which has the lowest order of precedence, to the parentheses, which has the highest).

Table 3-2	JavaScript Operator Precedence (From Lowest to Highest)
Operator	Syntax
semicolon	; (separates JavaScript statements that appear on the same line)
comma	,
assignment	=, +=, -=, *=, /=, %=
conditional	? :
logical "or"	||
logical "and"	&&
equality	==, !=
relational	<, <=, >, <=
mathematical	+, -, *, /, %
unary	!, -, ++, -- (negation, increment, and decrement operators)
call	( )

So, how exactly does this work? Like this: Suppose the JavaScript interpreter runs into the following statement in your script:

```
alert("Grand total: " + getTotal() + (3 * 4 / 10) + tax++)
```

The interpreter knows its job is to evaluate the statement, so the first thing it does is scan everything between the alert() parentheses. When it finds the next set of parentheses, it knows that's where it needs to start. It thinks to itself, "Okay, first I'll get the return value from getTotal(). Then I'll evaluate (3 * 4 / 10). Within (3 * 4 / 10), I'll do the division first, and *then* the multiplication. Now I'll add one to the *tax* variable. Okay, the last thing I have to do is add the whole thing to come up with a string to display."

Frankly, it's okay if you can't remember the precedence order. Just group expressions in parentheses like you did back in high school algebra class. Because parentheses outrank all the other operators, you can force JavaScript to override its default precedence order and do evaluate expressions the way that makes the most sense to *you!*

Your assignment for tomorrow

Assignment operators enable you to assign values to variables. Besides being able to make a straight one-to-one assignment, though, you can also use some assignment operators as a kind of shorthand to bump up a value based on another value. Table 3-3 describes how this process works.

Table 3-3	JavaScript Assignment Operators (From Lowest to Highest Precedence)	
Assignment	*Alternate approach*	*Description*
x = y	(none)	(assignment)
x += y	x = x + y	(addition)
x -= y	x = x - y	(subtraction)
x *= y	x = x * y	(multiplication)
x /= y	x = x / y	(division)
x %= y	x = x % y	(modulus)

The order of precedence in Table 3-3 is from lowest to highest, so the JavaScript interpreter will evaluate any modulus operations first, and then division, and then multiplication, and so on.

Compared to what?

When comparing two values or expressions, you can compare for equality as shown in Table 3-4.

Table 3-4	JavaScript Comparison Operators	
Operator	*Example*	*Meaning*
== (two equal signs)	x == y	x is equal to y
!=	x != y	x is not equal to y
<	x < y	x is less than y
>	x > y	x is greater than y
<=	x <= y	x is less than or equal to y
>=	x >= y	x us greater than or equal to y
?:	x = (y < 0) ? -y : y	if y is less than zero, assign -y to x; otherwise, assign y to x

It's only logical

Logical operators take logical (also called *Boolean*) operands, and they also return Boolean values. A *Boolean value* can be just one of two possibilities: *true* or *false*. (No fuzzy logic here!) When you see two expressions separated by a logical operator, the JavaScript interpreter first resolves the expressions to see whether each is *true* or *false,* and then resolves the entire statement. If an expression equates to a nonzero value, that expression is considered to be *true*; if an expression equates to zero, that expression is considered to be *false.* Table 3-5 describes the logical operators available in JavaScript.

Table 3-5	JavaScript Logical Operators	
Operator	*Meaning*	*Example*
&&	and	if (x == y && a != b)
||	or	if (x < y || a < b)
!	not	if (!x)

Watch out!

A common mistake, even (especially?) among seasoned programmers, is to use a single equal sign (=, an *assignment* operator) in place of a double equal sign (==, a *comparison* operator) or vice versa. The statement x = 6 *assigns* the value of 6 to x; x == 6, on the other hand, *compares* 6 to x but doesn't assign any value at all! Mistakenly typing == when you mean = (or vice versa) is a very common programming bug.

```
if (x = 6) { // At first
  glance, this looks like it
  compares 6 to x, but it
  doesn't -- it assigns 6 to
  x!

    document.writeln("x is 6,
    all right.")

}
```

Creationism: new, this

The new operator allows you to create your very own objects in JavaScript. (For a list of built-in objects, check out "Object Models Always Pose Nude," later in this chapter.)

When you use the new operator with a function that defines a type of object, you can create an instance (or a dozen instances) of that type of object.

The best way to explain this is by an example:

```
function person(inputName, inputAge, inputSex,
         inputOccupation) {
    this.name = inputName
    this.age = inputAge
    this.sex = inputSex
    this.occupation = inputOccupation
}
```

First off, you need to define a generic type of object. You're already familiar with functions, so this example — defining a generic type of object called person — should look familiar too. The person() function takes four parameters, one each for name, age, sex, and occupation. Then the person() function immediately assigns these input values to its own attributes. (name is set to inputName, age to inputAge, and so on).

(In this example, the this keyword is shorthand for person. The JavaScript interpreter knows that you're inside a function called person(), so it automatically substitutes the function name for the this keyword so that you don't have to spell out the whole function name.)

Now, whenever you want to create a specific, concrete instance of person, here's what you do:

```
jennifer = new person("Jennifer McLaughlan", 33, "F", "lion
            tamer")
```

The code snippet above uses the new operator, in conjunction with the predefined, generic person() function, to create a specific instance of person whose name is Jennifer McLaughlan, age is 33, sex is F, and occupation is lion tamer.

After the preceding statement is performed, you can use the object jennifer as you would any built-in object in JavaScript.

If you think that objects with properties but no methods are kind of boring, you're right. Here's how you add your own methods to the objects you create:

```
function ftalk(kindOfPet){
    if (kindOfPet == "dog") {
        document.writeln("bow-wow!")
    }
  else {
        if (kindOfPet == "cat") {
            document.writeln("meow-meow-meow")
        }
    }
}
function pet(inputName, inputKind, inputColor) {
    this.name = inputName
    this.kind = inputKind
    this.color = inputColor
        this.talk = ftalk(inputKind)
}
```

Conceptually, all you do to add a method to an object is to create two JavaScript functions and reference one from the other.

For example: see the definition of the pet() function? It contains three properties: name, kind, and color. It also has one method, called talk. You know that talk is a method and not a property because it's being assigned a function, not a variable.

Bear with me here; it'll all make sense when you see it in action!

The following code first creates an instance of pet and names that instance Boots; then it calls the talk() method associated with boots.

```
Boots = new pet("Boots", "cat", "orange striped")
Boots.talk
```

Here's how the JavaScript interpreter executes these two JavaScript statements:

1. **The first statement passes three variables to the** `pet()` **constructor function and assigns the resulting object to a variable called** `Boots`.

   When this first statement has finished processing, the `Boots` variable contains an object associated with the following three properties:

   - Boots.name = "Boots"
   - Boots.kind = "cat"
   - Boots.color = "orange striped"

2. **The second statement (**`Boots.talk`**) passes the value of** `Boots.kind`, **which is "cat", to the** `ftalk()` **function.**

3. **The** `ftalk()` **function contains an** `if` **statement that says, "if the input variable is** `cat` **, then print** `meow-meow-meow` **to the screen."**

   So, because the string "cat" *was* passed to the `ftalk()` function, you see "meow-meow-meow" on the screen.

If creating your own objects and methods isn't clear to you right now, it will be after you've had a chance to load and play with ch2_objects.htm, located on the companion CD.

Leftovers again?

A couple of JavaScript operators, `typeof` and `void`, just don't seem to fit in any other operator category. You'll understand what I mean when you see how each is used.

typeof

The `typeof` operator can be applied to any JavaScript object to find out what type of object it is. For example, if you apply the `typeof` operator to a string, it will return `"string"`; if you apply it to a number, it will return `"number"`; if you apply it to *true,* it will return `"boolean"` — and so on, for every kind of object that exists. Here's how `typeof` looks in action:

```
typeof "My friend Flicka"      // returns "string"
typeof false                   // returns "boolean"
typeof 69                      // returns "number"
typeof document.lastModified   // returns "string"
typeof Math                    // returns "function"
typeof someVariable            // returns variable type
```

Take a look at the HTML file ch3_typeof.htm to see what typeof returns for all kinds of JavaScript objects.

Into the void

The void operator is a strange beast; you use it to tell JavaScript to do *nothing*. (Only programmers would make up an operator whose sole purpose in life is to do nothing, don't you think?) Perhaps you think there's not much call for an operator that does nothing. Well, you'd be right — *except* in one pretty important instance: when you want to use a programming construct that demands the value of a function, but (for whatever reason) you don't want to give it one.

I won't spend much time on this operator, because chances are you won't need to use it often, if at all. For now, just be aware that void( ) exists, and that it can be used to "fake out" an attribute that requires a value.

Suppose, for example, that you want to use the HTML <AREA> and <MAP> tags to create an image that responds when users drag their mouse across that image, but does nothing when users click on that image. The <AREA> tag requires you to provide a value for the HREF attribute, as shown below. But if you provide a value for HREF, the image will respond when users click on it — and you don't want that!

In such a case, you can "fake out" the HREF attribute by using void( ), like this:

```
<AREA HREF="javascript:void(0)" ...>
```

Object Models Always Pose Nude

Because JavaScript is *object-based*, when you program in JavaScript you get to take advantage of a pre-defined *object model*.

Human beings tend to think in terms of object models naturally, so object-based languages like JavaScript are typically much easier to handle than their procedural counterparts. (Examples of procedural languages include BASIC, C, and COBOL.)

Here's a real-world example of an object model.

If I tell you my friend Ralph works in an office, you might reasonably assume that Ralph has a boss, a few co-workers, sits at a desk, and does some kind of work. How do you know all this without my having to come right out and tell you? Because you've seen or heard of other offices; perhaps you've even worked in one yourself. In other words, you're familiar with the office *model* — so even though you don't know anything about Ralph's particular office just yet, you can correctly guess a great deal.

In fact, all I have to do is fill in a few specific details (the names of Ralph's co-workers, what kind of work he does, what his office looks like, and so on) for you to have a complete picture of how my friend spends his day.

That's the beauty of an object model: it helps people communicate clearly and efficiently.

JavaScript's object model (called the *document object model*, or *DOM* for short) is no exception. Specifically, it helps you communicate what you want your script to do — clearly and efficiently — to the JavaScript interpreter. (The JavaScript interpreter is the part of a Web browser that executes a script. You can see the JavaScript interpreter in action in Chapter 2.)

The DOM performs this oh-so-useful task by describing

- ✔ All of the *objects* that go into making up a Web page, such as forms, links, images, buttons, and text.

- ✔ The descriptive *properties* associated with each of the DOM objects. For example, an image object can be associated with specific properties describing its height and width.

- ✔ The behaviors, or *methods,* associated with each of the DOM objects. For example, a JavaScript method called `blink()` allows you to display blinking text on a Web page.

- ✔ The special built-in methods, called *event handlers*, associated with automatic and user-initiated events. For instance, loading a Web page into a browser is considered an event; so is clicking a button. The event handlers you use to trigger some JavaScript code when these events occur are called `onLoad` and `onClick`, respectively.

Read on for an in-depth look at each of these four categories and how you can use them to create your own powerful JavaScript scripts!

Conceptually, the DOM is the same whether you're viewing a Web page in Internet Explorer, Netscape Navigator, or another browser entirely. In practice, however, the versions of the DOM implemented for Internet Explorer and Netscape Navigator are slightly different. See the last two sections of this chapter for details.

For example, in an object-oriented language such as C++ or Smalltalk, if you have a class of objects called *push button,* you can inherit from it to define two new classes called *red round pushbutton* and *skinny green pushbutton.* Because JavaScript is object-based and not object-oriented, you can use its built-in objects (all of which are detailed in Appendix C) and create brand-new ones, but you can't create new *classes* of objects based on the ones you're given. Using JavaScript you can't, for instance, create a new, reusable class of button derived from the HTML push button.

Object-ivity

In computer parlance, an *object* is a software representation of a real-world thing. Theoretically, any person, place, thing, or concept (hey, sounds like a noun, doesn't it?!) can be represented as an object.

In practice, however, most of the objects you work with in JavaScript fall into the first three of the following four categories:

- ✔ **Objects defined using HTML tags, such as documents, links, applets, text fields, windows, and so on.** (For the purposes of this book, JavaScript scripts are always attached to HTML documents. Using JavaScript, you can access any object defined in the HTML document to which a script is attached. To see an example of a script accessing HTML objects, check out Listing 2-2 in Chapter 2.)

- ✔ **Objects defined automatically by Web browsers.** One example is the `navigator` object which, despite its name, holds configuration and version information about whichever browser is currently in use, even if that browser happens to be Internet Explorer. (To see an example of a script accessing a browser object, flip to Chapter 4.)

- ✔ **Objects that are built into JavaScript, such as Date and Number.** To see an example of a script accessing built-in JavaScript objects, take a look at Chapter 5.

- ✔ **Objects you yourself have created using the JavaScript new operator.** (To see an example of how you can create and access your own objects using JavaScript, check out Chapter 5.)

Just like their real-world counterparts, software objects are typically associated with specific characteristics and behaviors. Because this is a computer topic, though, we can't call these bits of information *characteristics* and *behaviors*. No, that would take all the fun out of it. Programmers call characteristics *properties* (or *attributes*) and call behaviors *methods* — except for certain event-related behaviors whose names begin with "on," such as onLoad, onResize, and onSubmit. Programmers call these special "on" methods *event handlers*.

Properties and attributes are really the same thing, but some JavaScript programmers tend to differentiate between properties (which belong to JavaScript objects) and attributes (which are associated with HTML objects).

Because most of the JavaScript code you write involves objects, properties, methods, and event handlers, understanding what with these object-oriented terms means is essential for folks planning to write their own scripts. One way to keep these terms straight is to think back to sixth-grade English class. Objects are always nouns; properties are adjectives; methods are verbs; event handlers are verbs with "on" tacked to their fronts. Got it? Take a look at Table 3-6 to see examples of some common object definitions.

Table 3-6		Sample Object Definitions		
Kind of Object (Noun)	*Object (Adjective)*	*Property (Verb)*	*Method*	*Event handler ("on" + Verb)*
HTML	button	name	click()	onClick
		type		
		value		
HTML	link	href	-----	onClick
		port		onMouseOver
		protocol		onKeyPress
		...		...
HTML	form	action	reset()	onReset
		elements	submit()	onSubmit
		length		
		...		
Browser	Navigator	appVersion	javaEnabled()	-----
		appName		
		language		
		platform		
JavaScript	Number	MAX_VALUE	toString()	-----
		MIN_VALUE		
Custom	customer	name	changeAddress()	
		address	changeName()	
		creditHistory	placeOrder()	

For sale by owner: Object properties

Properties are attributes that describe an object. Most of the objects available in JavaScript have their own set of properties. (Appendix C contains a listing of JavaScript properties arranged alphabetically.)

An `image` object, for example, is usually associated with the following properties:

Property	Description
src	The file name of the image to embed in an HTML document
name	The internal name of the image (the one you reference using JavaScript code)
height	The height of the image, in pixels
width	The width of the image, in pixels
border	The thickness of the border to display around the image, in pixels
complete	Whether or not the image loaded successfully (true or false)
hspace	The number of pixels to pad the sides of the image with
vspace	The number of pixels to pad the top and bottom of the image with
lowsrc	The file name of a small image to load first

At runtime, all object properties have a corresponding value, whether it's explicitly defined or filled in by the Web browser. For example, consider an image object created with the following HTML code:

```
<BODY>
...
<IMG SRC="myPicture.jpg" NAME="companyLogo" HEIGHT="200"
        WIDTH="500" BORDER="1">
...
</BODY>
```

Assuming you have a file on your computer named myPicture.jpg, at runtime, when you load the above HTML snippet into your Web browser and query the properties, the corresponding values appear as follows:

Property name	Value
document.companyLogo.src	c:///file:/myPicture.jpg
document.companyLogo.name	companyLogo
document.companyLogo.height	200
document.companyLogo.width	500
document.companyLogo.border	1
document.companyLogo.complete	true

To see an example of this HTML and JavaScript code in action, take a look at ch3_properties.htm located on the companion CD.

In the code snippets above, the name of each property is *fully qualified*. If you've ever given a friend from another state driving directions to your house, you're familiar with fully-qualifying names — even if you've haven't heard it called that before now. It's the old narrow-it-down approach:

"Okay, as soon as you hit Texas, start looking for the signs for Austin. On the south side of Austin you'll find our suburb, called Travis Heights. Once you hit Travis Heights, start looking for Sledgehammer Street. As soon as you turn onto Sledgehammer, you can start looking for 111 Sledgehammer. That's our house."

The JavaScript interpreter is like that out-of-state friend. It can locate and provide you with access to any property — but only if you describe that property by beginning with the most basic description (in most cases, the `document` object) and narrowing it down from there.

In the image example above, the document object (which you create using the HTML `<BODY>...</BODY>` tags) contains the image called `companyLogo`. The `companyLogo` image, in turn, contains the properties `src`, `name`, `height`, `width`, `border`, and `complete`. That's why you type `document.companyLogo.src` to identify the `src` property of the image named `companyLogo`; `document.companyLogo.width` to identify the `width` property; and so on.

Note, too, that in the HTML code above, the values for `src`, `name`, `height`, `width`, and `border` are taken directly from the HTML definition for this object. The value of `true` that appears for the `complete` property, however, appears courtesy of your Web browser. If your browser had not been able to find and successfully load the myPicture.jpg file, the value of the complete property associated with this object would have been automatically set to `false`.

In JavaScript as in other programming languages, success is represented by *true* or the number 1; failure is represented by `false` or 0.

There's a method to this madness!

A *method* by any other name (some programmers call them *behaviors* or *member functions*) is a function that defines a particular behavior that an object can exhibit.

Take, for example, your soon-to-be-old friend the HTML button. Because all you can really do to an HTML button is click on it, the button object has just one method associated with it: the `click()` method. When you invoke a button's `click()` method using JavaScript, the result is the same as though a user clicked on that button.

Unlike objects, properties, and event handers, methods in JavaScript are always followed by parentheses, like this: `click()`. This convention helps remind programmers that methods often (but not always) require *parameters*. A parameter is any tidbit of information that a method needs in order to do its job.

For example, the `alert()` method associated with the `window` object allows you to create a special kind of pop-up window (an *alert* window) to display some information on the screen. Because there is no point in creating a blank pop-up window, the `alert()` method requires you to pass it a parameter containing the text you want to display:

```
function checkTheEmaillAddress () {
    ...
    window.alert("Sorry, the e-mail address you entered is
            not complete.  Please try again.")
}
```

Some objects, like the built-in window object, are associated with scads of methods. You can open a window, using the `open()` method; display some text on a window, using the `write()` and `writeln()` methods; scroll a window up or down, using the `scroll()`, `scrollBy()`, and `scrollTo()` methods; and so on.

Just as you do when referring to an object, a property, or an event handler, when you refer to a method in JavaScript you must preface that method with the specific name of the object to which it belongs. For example:

JavaScript code snippet	*What it does*
`annoyingText.blink()`	Calls the `blink()` method associated with the `string` object; specifically, causes the `string` object called `annoyingText` to blink on and off
`self.frame1.focus()`	Calls the `focus()` method associated with the `frame` object; specifically, sets the input focus to a frame called `frame1` (which itself is associated with the primary document window)

JavaScript code snippet	What it does
`document.infoForm.requestForFreeInfoButton.click()`	Calls the `click()` method associated with the `button` object; specifically, this code clicks the button named requestForFreeInfoButton, which is contained in the form called `infoForm`. (The `infoForm` form is contained in the primary HTML document.)

To see an example of a method call in JavaScript, take a look at ch3_methods.htm located on the companion CD.

You see another example of methods in action in Chapter 2, and Appendix C lists the methods available to you in JavaScript's document object model.

How do you handle a hungry event? Event Handlers!

An *event handler* is a special kind of method that a JavaScript-enabled Web browser triggers automatically when a specific event occurs. Event handlers give you, the JavaScript programmer, the ability to perform whatever instructions you like — from performing calculations to displaying messages — based on events such as:

- ✔ A user loading a Web page into a browser
- ✔ A user stopping a Web page from loading
- ✔ A user entering or changing some information in an input field
- ✔ A user clicking on an image, button, or link
- ✔ A user submitting or resetting a form

For example, when a user loads a Web page into a browser, the `onLoad` event handler associated with that page (or *document*) executes; when a user clicks on an HTML button, that HTML button's `onClick` event handler executes; and so on.

Here's an example of how you call a built-in event handler:

```
<BODY
    onLoad="window.alert('Hello!');"
    onUnload="window.alert('Goodbye!');"
>
...
</BODY>
```

Why use methods?

Many of the methods defined in JavaScript's document object model are things that users can do simply by clicking a mouse: for example, stopping a window from loading (the `stop()` method), focusing on a particular input field (the `focus()` method), printing the contents of a window (the `print()` method), and so on. Why, then, go to the all the trouble of including method calls in your script?

In a word, *automation*. Say you want to create a Web page that does several things in response to a single event. For example, when a user loads your Web page, you may want to set focus to a particular input field, open a small "What's new" window, and display today's date automatically. Using methods, you can do all of this — without the user's having to do a thing!

To see an example of calling event handlers in JavaScript, check out ch3_events.htm located on the companion CD.

Take a look at the code snippet listed above. Do you see two event handlers associated with the `document` object? (The document object is defined in HTML using the `<BODY>...</BODY>` tags.) One of the event handlers is named `onLoad`; the other, `onUnload`.

As you may be able to guess, loading this code into a Web page causes a "Hello!" message to appear. Loading another page, or closing the browser altogether, causes a "Goodbye!" message to appear. Event handling is a wonderful thing. With it you can figure out when and precisely how a user interacts with any part of your Web page, and you can respond to that action as you see fit.

Appendix C contains a list of all the event handlers that JavaScript supports. To see additional examples of JavaScript event handlers in action, check out Chapter 2.

Company functions

Like methods, *functions* are behaviors — but that's where the similarity ends. Unlike methods, functions aren't associated with a particular object. Instead, functions are stand-alone bits of JavaScript code that can be reused over and over again. The JavaScript language provides a handful of built-in functions, but you can create your own, as well — as many as you need.

Here's an example. Say you want to create an HTML form that asks users to enter their age and the number of pets they own. You could create a JavaScript function that examines a number and makes sure it's between certain reasonable parameters — say, 0 and 100. Once you create such a function, you can call it twice: once to validate the age users type in, and once to validate the number of pets they own. This ability to create reusable functions can save you quite a bit of time if you plan to create a lot of JavaScript-enhanced Web sites.

Listing 3-2 shows you how you define and use a function in JavaScript:

Listing 3-2:   Defining and Calling a Custom Function in JavaScript

```
<SCRIPT LANGUAGE="JavaScript">

function checkNumber(aNumber) {

    if (aNumber > 0 && aNumber < 100) {

        ///////////////////////////////////////////////////
        ///////
        // If the number is greater than zero and less than
            100,
        // pop up a "congratulations" message and return a
            value
        // indicating success

        ///////////////////////////////////////////////////
        ///////

        alert("The number you specified is valid (it is
            between 0 and 100).")
        return 1
    }

    ///////////////////////////////////////////////////////
    // Otherwise, the number is either negative or over 100,
        so
    // return a value indicating failure
    ///////////////////////////////////////////////////////

    else {
        alert("The number you specified is invalid (not
            between 0 and 100).  \nPlease try again.")
        return 0
    }
}

...
<FORM NAME="myForm">

...
Please type in a number: <INPUT TYPE="text" SIZE="5"
            NAME="inputNumber">
```

(continued)

Listing 3-2 *(continued)*

```
...
<INPUT TYPE="button" VALUE="Push to validate number"
       onClick="checkNumber(document.myForm.
             inputNumber.value);"

</FORM>
```

Don't worry if you see some unfamiliar symbols inside the `checkNumber()` function definition, like > and &&; you find out what these symbols mean in "JavaScript Syntax" earlier in this chapter.

To see this function example in action, check out ch3_functions.htm located on the companion CD.

For now, take a look at the penultimate line in the code snippet, the one where the `checkNumber()` function is being called:

```
<INPUT TYPE="button" VALUE="Push to validate number"
       onClick="checkNumber(document.myForm.
             inputNumber.value);"
```

Notice that `checkNumber()` is being called with a single argument (`document.myForm.inputNumber.value`)? That single argument represents the number that a user typed into the HTML form. ("For Sale By Owner: Object Properties" earlier in this chapter explains why you must fully qualify a property this way.) When a user clicks the button marked "Push to validate number," the `checkNumber()` function springs into action, takes a look at the input number passed to it, and pops up a message telling the user whether the number is valid (that is, falls inside the range of 0 to 100) or not.

Because functions are so useful in JavaScript, you see lots of examples of them in this book. For now, just remember

- ✔ You define a function inside the `<SCRIPT>...</SCRIPT>` tags, which you see explained in detail in Chapter 2.

- ✔ You let the JavaScript interpreter know a function is coming by starting it with the special JavaScript keyword `function`, followed by a pair of curly braces {}.

- ✔ In between the curly braces you put any JavaScript statements you like.

Appendix C lists a handful of built-in JavaScript functions. For additional examples of creating and calling your own functions, see Chapter 2.

Netscape Navigator's Object Model

Netscape Navigator's document object model, or DOM, describes all of the objects you can access in JavaScript to create cool scripts that execute flawlessly in Netscape Navigator.

When you want to reference any of the following objects in your script, you use that object's *fully-qualified* name, as shown in the "Syntax" column below.

The window object is the only exception to this rule. By default, every Web page contains one all-encompassing granddaddy window, no matter how many additional windows you may choose to include. Because this overall window is a given, you don't have to mention it specifically when you refer to one of the objects it contains.

For example, the following two JavaScript code snippets both set the src property of an Image object named myImage equal to "happycat.jpg":

```
window.document.myForm.myImage.src="happycat.jpg"
document.myForm.myImage.src="happycat.jpg"
```

You can find an exhaustive list of all of the objects in Navigator 6.0's DOM implementation, including associated properties, methods, and event handlers, in Appendix C. Or check out Netscape's DOM reference at

```
http://developer.netscape.com/tech/dom/
```

Object	Syntax
window	window (optional)
document	document
applet	document.applets[0]
anchor	document.*someAnchor*
area	document.*someArea*
classes	document.classes
form	document.*someForm*
button	document.*someForm.someButton*
checkbox	document.*someForm.someCheckbox*
fileUpload	document.*someForm.someFileElement*
hidden	document.*someForm.someHidden*
image	document.*someForm.someImage*
password	document.*someForm.somePassword*
radio	document.*someForm.someRadio*
reset	document.*someForm.someReset*
select	document.*someForm.someSelect*
submit	document.*someForm.someSubmit*
text	document.*someForm.someText*

(continued)

Object	Syntax
textarea	document.*someForm.someTextarea*
ids	document.ids
layers	document.layers
link	document.*someLink*
object	document.*someObject*
plugin	docment.embeds[0]
tags	document.tags
frame, parent, self, top (all of these are also synonyms for window)
history	history
location	location
locationbar	locationbar
menubar	menubar
navigator	navigator
personalbar	personalbar
scrollbar	scrollbar
statusbar	statusbar
toolbar	toolbar

JavaScript data types

Much of what you want to do with a JavaScript script involves programmer-defined objects, such as the values that a user types into your HTML form, some calculations you make based on those values, and so on.

Most programming languages require you to declare special placeholders, called *variables*, to hold each piece of data you want to work with. Not only that, but most programming languages require you to specify — up front — what *type* of data you expect those variables to contain. (This requirement makes it easy for those languages' compilers, but tough on us programmers!)

JavaScript expects you to declare variables to represent bits of data, too. (See "JavaScript Syntax" earlier in this chapter to see how you declare a variable in JavaScript.) But because JavaScript is a *loosely-typed* language, you don't necessarily have to declare the type of a variable up front; nor do you have to perform cumbersome type conversions the way you do in languages like C and C++. Here's an example:

```
var visitor // Defines a variable called "visitor" of
            // no particular type

visitor = "emily@emilyv.com"    // Sets "visitor" equal to
                      // the text string"emily@emilyv.com"
```

```
visitor = 3        // Resets "visitor" to a numeric value

visitor = null     // Resets "visitor" to null
```

You can get away without specifying string or numeric data types explicitly, as shown in the code snippet above, because the JavaScript interpreter takes care of figuring out what type of value is associated with any given variable at runtime.

Having said that, there *are* two data types that JavaScript requires you to specify explicitly: the Array and Date data types. You must declare variables of type Array and Date explicitly because the JavaScript interpreter needs to know certain extra details about these types of values in order to store them properly. Table 3-7 describes `Array`, `Date`, and all the other data types JavaScript supports.

Table 3-7	JavaScript Data Types
Data Type	*Description*
`Array`	**Ordered collection**
Examples:	
	`var animals = new Array("cat", "dog", "mouse")` `// load array`
	`var firstAnimal = animals[0] // access first` `array element`
	`var secondAnimal = animals[1] // access second` `element`
	`var thirdAnimal = animals[2] // access third` `element`
`Boolean`	**True/false data type (Values of `true` or `false` only)**
Examples:	
	`var cookieDetected = false`
	`var repeatVisitor = true`
`Date`	**Time and date data type**
Examples:	
	`var today = new Date() // current time/date via` `system clock`

(continued)

Table 3-7 *(continued)*

Data Type	Description
	`var newYearsDay = new Date(2001, 01, 01) //` `specific date`
`null`	A special data type denoting non-existence (note that null is not the same as 0)
Examples:	
	`if (emailAddress == null) { // check for null`
	`alert("Please enter an e-mail address")`
	`}`
`Number`	Numerical data type
Examples:	
	`var numberHits = 1234 // implied numeric` `data type`
	`var numberHits = new Number(1234) // explicit`
`String`	String (text) data type
Examples:	
	`alert("This is a string") // implied string with` `double quotes`
	`alert('So is this') // implied string with` `single quotes`
	`var myString = new String("Yet another string")` `// explicit`

Leftovers: The Math object

JavaScript provides a utility object for you use in your script endeavors. This object — the `Math` object — isn't part of the document object model proper (that is, it doesn't represent a conceptual component of a Web page). It isn't a data type, either. It's simply a stand-alone object provided for you to use whenever you need mathematical constants or functions. Here are a few examples:

```
var x = Math.PI // assigning "x" the value of pi
var y = Math.round(158.32) // assigning "y" the result of
           rounding 158.32
var z = Math.sqrt(49) // assigning "z" the square root of 49
```

Check out Appendix C for a full list of all the properties and methods associated with the Math object.

Microsoft Internet Explorer's Object Model

Microsoft's document object model is often referred to as the DHTML DOM, which is alphabet soup-ese for *dynamic hypertext markup language document object model.* (DHTML, or *dynamic HTML,* refers to the fact that you use scripting languages like JavaScript to make Web pages interactive — which translates to *dynamic* in action-oriented marketing-speak!)

While Microsoft's DHTML DOM is based on the same standard that Netscape Navigator's is based on — the World Wide Web consortium's DOM specification — it varies a bit from Netscape's implementation. This variation is important to keep in mind, because if your script references objects that exist in one DOM and not another, your script will run in just that one object-supporting browser. (Skip to Chapter 4 to find tips for creating cross-platform scripts that work in both browsers.)

Microsoft's DHTML DOM describes all the objects you can access with JavaScript to create cool scripts that execute flawlessly in Internet Explorer.

You can find an exhaustive list of all of the objects in Internet Explorer 5.5's DOM implementation, including associated properties, methods, and event handlers, in Appendix C. Or check out Microsoft's own DHTML DOM reference at

```
http://msdn.microsoft.com/workshop/author/dhtml/reference/
            objects.asp
```

Object	*Syntax*
window	window (optional)
document	document
applet	document.applets[0]
anchor	document.*someAnchor*
area	document.*someArea*
form	document.*someForm*
button	document.*someForm.someButton*
checkbox	document.*someForm.someCheckbox*
file	document.*someForm.someFileElement*
hidden	document.*someForm.someHidden*
image	document.*someForm.someImage*
password	document.*someForm.somePassword*
radio	document.*someForm.someRadio*
reset	document.*someForm.someReset*
select	document.*someForm.someSelect*
submit	document.*someForm.someSubmit*
text	document.*someForm.someText*

(continued)

Object	Syntax
textarea	document.*someForm.someTextarea*
link	document.*someLink*
object	document.*someObject*
plugin	docment.embeds[0] (no, this isn't a typo!)
embed	docment.embeds[0]
frame	*someFrame*
frameset	*someFrameset*
history	history
location	location
navigator	navigator
clientInformation	clientInformation

Part II
Adding Intelligence to Your Web Pages

The 5th Wave   By Rich Tennant

AT THE REAL PROGRAMMERS DATING BAR

WHOA! LOOK AT THE POCKET PROTECTORS ON THIS ONE!

In this part . . .

In this part, you find practical ways to create Web pages that appear differently to different users. Chapter 4 shows you how to modify the way your pages appear automatically based on which browser your users are running. Chapter 5 shows you how to incorporate time and date information into your pages; and Chapter 6 describes how you can create Web pages that "remember" visitors.

Best of all, you see real live working examples of all the techniques presented in Part II. (The examples are also included on the CD-ROM at the back of this book, so you don't even have to type the code.)

Chapter 4

I Spy! Detecting Your Users' Browser Environment

In This Chapter

▶ Understanding how (and why) JavaScript support differs among browsers

▶ Applying strategies for cross-platform script creation

▶ Querying browser objects

▶ Manipulating strings

▶ Taking advantage of advanced JavaScript features with a browser-detection script

The biggest challenge facing Web developers today isn't hardware- or software-based: it's *wetware*-based. (Wetware — a term that refers to the supposed squishiness of the human brain — is geek-speak for "human beings.") And that challenge is . . . trying to get the companies who create Web browsers to agree on a single, standard implementation of browser-supported technologies like JavaScript!

With the current situation, the brand of browser someone has installed — along with the browser's version and the underlying operating system — all affect that someone's ability to view your JavaScript-enabled Web pages. As a JavaScript developer, you need to be aware of the differences in JavaScript implementations among browsers, and write your scripts accordingly. If you don't, you may end up creating a whiz-bang script that runs only on *your* computer!

JavaScript: The Non-standard Standard

Back in the old days, before the Web came along, developers knew exactly what hardware and software their audience would use to run their applications before they wrote a lick of code. (In other words, these developers knew their applications' *target platforms* in advance.) Using this information, developers could implement their applications with confidence, secure in the knowledge that their application code would behave in the field just as it did in their testing labs.

Not so on the Web. Users can choose to view Web pages — or, more accurately, Web-based applications — with whatever target platform they choose. They might, for instance, use a Macintosh, PC, UNIX box, or hand-held device running some version of Navigator, Internet Explorer, or any of the other dozens of Web browsers available on the market. Unfortunately, your users' choices affect their ability to run your JavaScript-enabled Web pages, as you see in this chapter.

The two latest versions of the most popular Web browsers — Internet Explorer and Netscape Navigator — do support JavaScript. But despite their creators' claims of support for something called the *ECMA standard,* created by the European Computer Manufacturers Association, which I discuss in detail in the next section, both browsers support slightly different versions of both these elements:

- The JavaScript language
- The document object model that the JavaScript language was designed to access

Can't we all just get along? The ECMA Standard

Netscape (with some help from Sun Microsystems) invented JavaScript clear back in the early 1990s, so it's no surprise that JavaScript support first appeared in Netscape's browser (Netscape Navigator 2.0, if you're a history buff).

Soon after, Microsoft released version 3.0 of Internet Explorer, which featured support for their own JavaScript-compatible scripting language — called JScript. Minor differences existed between these two browsers' scripting implementations, however, and as each successive version appeared, those differences continued to grow.

In 1998, Netscape decided to hand over the task of creating a formal JavaScript standard to the ECMA, an international standards body comprising companies from all over the world. (Both Netscape and Microsoft are ECMA members.) In theory, this was a great thing! It allowed a relatively impartial group of folks to decide the best, most efficient way to implement a cross-browser Web scripting language. Unfortunately — in software as in life — the reality of real-world implementation hasn't quite yet achieved the perfection promised by the standard.

The ECMAScript language specification, called ECMA-262, describes how a scripting language *should* be implemented in an ECMA-compliant browser; not how it *is* implemented. So even though ECMAScript has the potential to unify JavaScript implementations and guarantee developers a consistent, cross-browser JavaScript execution platform, differences in JavaScript support still exist between the latest Navigator and Internet Explorer browsers. One reason for these differences is the inevitable lag time between creating a standard and then scurrying to implement and release it; another reason is the inherent tendency of software companies to embellish standards with additional, proprietary features. (The same tendency that led to the need for a standard in the first place!)

The bottom line is this: Although ECMAScript offers the potential for increased consistency across browsers, the final word on JavaScript implementation comes from the browsers themselves — *not* the specification.

Whacking your way through the browser maze

From the latest reports, both Microsoft and Netscape have promised to support the ECMAScript standard in future versions of their respective browsers. Check to make sure that the version of Internet Explorer or Netscape Navigator that you use fully supports the ECMAScript standard. Even if the version doesn't support it, you still have the language features that you need.

Features you can live without

Some proprietary features that were supported in Internet Explorer and Netscape Navigator before the ECMAScript and World Wide Web Consortium DOM standard came along may not be long for this world. (In other words, the two browsers may drop support for these features as Microsoft and Netscape race for the "most standard-compliant" prize.)

Even if the following features continue to be supported, however, I caution you strongly against including them in your JavaScript code if at all possible. Steering clear of these features helps ensure that your scripts can be seen by the widest possible audience.

Netscape proprietary features

```
document.layers[]
document.tags
document.ids
document.classes
```

Microsoft proprietary features

```
document.all
document.styleSheets[]
<MARQUEE> and <BGSOUND>
```

Even if Internet Explorer and Netscape Navigator *were* fully ECMAScript-compliant (and offered no additional features), the same JavaScript script still might not execute identically in both browsers. Why? For JavaScript to be a truly cross-browser language, both the syntax and the document object model. would have to be consistent. The DOM is crucial because these are the objects created by HTML tags and with which JavaScript interacts.

ECMA-262 takes JavaScript halfway to cross-browser nirvana by defining a standard language specification, but it doesn't define the document object model. As you see in Chapter 3, the document object models for the two browsers are far from identical, despite the efforts of the World Wide Web Consortium to define a unified standard.

Fortunately, as you see in the next section, you don't have to depend on differences between JavaScript implementation and object models in order to write great cross-browser scripts!

The Browser Detective Script

The most reliable way to figure out which browsers are loading your script is to ask! You "ask" programmatically, using JavaScript, by adding a bit of code to the front of your script that queries the document object model for browser-specific details. When you determine which make, model, and version of browser is attempting to load your JavaScript-enabled Web page, you can display your page accordingly.

The easiest way to implement this functionality is to use the <MARQUEE> tag, which is an HTML tag (and corresponding scripting object) supported by Internet Explorer (beginning with version 3.x). Trouble is, Navigator and many other browsers don't support the <MARQUEE> tag at all! When a non-marquee-supporting browser loads a Web page containing the <MARQUEE> tag, it may display the scrolling text statically or not at all; ignore your marquee-related JavaScript code, or generate a JavaScript error.

One way to ensure that your viewers see what you want them to see is to use JavaScript to see whether the browser loading your script is Internet Explorer, version 3.x or higher. If it is, you can use the <MARQUEE> tag with confidence. If the browser *isn't* Internet Explorer version 3.x or higher, you can display the scrolled information in an alternate eye-catching fashion — for example, as a bolded, centered heading.

Listing 4-1 shows the code for a script that examines browser settings and displays a string of text either 1) as a scrolling marquee, or 2) as a bolded, centered heading, depending on whether the browser loading the script is Internet Explorer 3.x and up or not. This browser "sniffer" script is patterned after the one Netscape provides at

```
http://developer.netscape.com/docs/examples/javascript/browse
r_type_oo.html.
```

A custom fit, every time

Creating different versions of each of your Web pages for each and every different browser version in existence ensures an optimum experience for all of your users. It also represents a maintenance nightmare!

A good design approach to follow is this:

1. Provide absolutely essential information (such as contact information) in the form of plain, old, every-browser-supports-it text — rather than, say, a scrolling JavaScript marquee.

2. Provide additional information and effects using cross-browser techniques wherever possible. For example, layers aren't implemented in all browsers, but depending on the effect you want to achieve, you may be able to get by using an image-swapping technique (like the one you see in Chapter 9) or

an animated GIF file instead. GIF stands for graphics interchange format. You can find more information on animated GIFs, including links to free animation software, at

```
http://animation.about.com/
arts/animation/msubgif.htm
```

3. If you want to take advantage of the latest and greatest Web effects (and who doesn't, from time to time?), implement them in conjunction with a browser "sniffer" script like the one shown in this chapter. For example, suppose you want to create a JavaScript-enabled Web page that does these things:

✔ Draws viewers' attention by scrolling a line of text

✔ Allows the user to stop (and restart) the scrolling action

Take a quick peek at Listing 4-1; then check out Figures 4-1 and 4-2, which show how this script appears in Netscape Navigator 6.0 and Microsoft Internet Explorer 5.5, respectively. I spend the remainder of this chapter describing exactly how the script in Listing 4-1 works, step by step, so you can apply the principles you see here to your own browser-sniffing scripts!

The file shown in Listing 4-1, which is named list0401.htm, is located on the companion CD. Check it out in your own browser!

Listing 4-1:   Sniffing out Browser Versions

```
<HTML>

<HEAD><TITLE>JavaScript browser "sniffer" (from JavaScript
          For Dummies, 3rd edition)</TITLE>

<SCRIPT LANGUAGE="JavaScript">
function Is () {

    // convert all characters to lowercase to simplify
          testing
```

(continued)

Listing 4-1 *(continued)*

```
var agt=navigator.userAgent.toLowerCase();

// *** BROWSER VERSION ***
// Note: On IE5, these return 4, so use is.ie5up to
        detect IE5.

this.major = parseInt(navigator.appVersion);
this.minor = parseFloat(navigator.appVersion);

this.nav = ((agt.indexOf('mozilla')!=-1) &&
        (agt.indexOf('spoofer')==-1) &&
            (agt.indexOf('compatible') == -1) &&
            (agt.indexOf('opera')==-1) &&
            (agt.indexOf('webtv')==-1));

this.nav2 = (this.nav && (this.major == 2));
this.nav3 = (this.nav && (this.major == 3));
this.nav4 = (this.nav && (this.major == 4));
this.nav4up = (this.nav && (this.major >= 4));
this.navonly = (this.nav && ((agt.indexOf(";nav") != -1)
        ||
                (agt.indexOf("; nav") != -1)) );
this.nav5 = (this.nav && (this.major == 5));

this.nav6 = ((this.nav) && (this.major == 5) &&
        (this.minor == 5));

this.ie = (agt.indexOf("msie") != -1);
this.ie3 = (this.ie && (this.major < 4));
this.ie4 = (this.ie && (this.major == 4) &&
            (agt.indexOf("msie 5.")==-1) );
this.ie4up = (this.ie && (this.major >= 4));
this.ie5 = (this.ie && (this.major == 4) &&
            (agt.indexOf("msie 5.")!=-1) );
this.ie5up = (this.ie && !this.ie3 && !this.ie4);

// KNOWN BUG: On AOL4, returns false if IE3 is embedded
        browser
// or if this is the first browser window opened. Thus
        the
// properties is.aol, is.aol3, and is.aol4 aren't 100%
        reliable.

this.aol = (agt.indexOf("aol") != -1);
this.aol3 = (this.aol && this.ie3);
this.aol4 = (this.aol && this.ie4);
this.opera = (agt.indexOf("opera") != -1);
this.webtv = (agt.indexOf("webtv") != -1);

// *** JAVASCRIPT VERSION CHECK ***

if (this.nav2 || this.ie3)
    this.js = 1.0
```

```
else if (this.nav3 || this.opera)
    this.js = 1.1
else if ((this.nav4 && (this.minor <= 4.05)) || this.ie4)
    this.js = 1.2
else if ((this.nav4 && (this.minor > 4.05)) || this.ie5)
    this.js = 1.3
else if (this.nav5)
    this.js = 1.4
else if (this.nav6)
    this.js = 1.5

// NOTE: In the future, update this code when newer v's
        of JS
// are released. For now, we try to provide some upward
// compatibility
// so that future versions of Nav and IE will show they
        are at
// *least* JS 1.x capable. Always check for JS v
        compatibility
// with > or >=.

else if (this.nav && (this.major > 6))
    this.js = 1.6

// HACK: no idea for other browsers; always check
// for JS version with > or >=

else this.js = 0.0;


// *** PLATFORM ***
this.win = ( (agt.indexOf("win")!=-1) ||
             (agt.indexOf("16bit")!=-1) );

// NOTE: On Opera 3.0, the userAgent string includes
// "Windows 95/NT4" on all
// Win32, so you can't distinguish between Win95 and
        WinNT.

this.win95 = ((agt.indexOf("win95")!=-1) ||
              (agt.indexOf("windows 95")!=-1));

// is this a 16 bit compiled version?

this.win16 = ((agt.indexOf("win16")!=-1) ||
              (agt.indexOf("16bit")!=-1) ||
              (agt.indexOf("windows 3.1")!=-1) ||
              (agt.indexOf("windows 16-bit")!=-1) );

this.win31 = ((agt.indexOf("windows 3.1")!=-1) ||
              (agt.indexOf("win16")!=-1) ||
              (agt.indexOf("windows 16-bit")!=-1));
```

(continued)

Listing 4-1 *(continued)*

```
// NOTE: Reliable detection of Win98 may not be
// possible. It appears that:
// - On Nav 4.x and before you'll get plain "Windows" in
// userAgent.
// - On Mercury client, the 32-bit version will return
// "Win98", but
// the 16-bit version running on Win98 will still return
// "Win95".

this.win98 = ((agt.indexOf("win98")!=-1) ||
            (agt.indexOf("windows 98")!=-1));

this.winnt = ((agt.indexOf("winnt")!=-1) ||
            (agt.indexOf("windows nt")!=-1));

this.win32 = ( this.win95 || this.winnt || this.win98 ||
            ((this.major >= 4) && (navigator.platform
    ==
                "Win32")) || (agt.indexOf("win32")!=-1)
    ||
                (agt.indexOf("32bit")!=-1) );

this.os2 = ((agt.indexOf("os/2")!=-1) ||
            (navigator.appVersion.indexOf("OS/2")!=-1) ||
            (agt.indexOf("ibm-webexplorer")!=-1));

this.mac = (agt.indexOf("mac")!=-1);

this.mac68k = (this.mac && ((agt.indexOf("68k")!=-1) ||
            (agt.indexOf("68000")!=-1)));

this.macppc = (this.mac && ((agt.indexOf("ppc")!=-1) ||
            (agt.indexOf("powerpc")!=-1)));

this.sun = (agt.indexOf("sunos")!=-1);
this.sun4 = (agt.indexOf("sunos 4")!=-1);
this.sun5 = (agt.indexOf("sunos 5")!=-1);
this.suni86= (this.sun && (agt.indexOf("i86")!=-1));
this.irix = (agt.indexOf("irix") !=-1); // SGI
this.irix5 = (agt.indexOf("irix 5") !=-1);
this.irix6 = ((agt.indexOf("irix 6") !=-1) ||
            (agt.indexOf("irix6") !=-1));
this.hpux = (agt.indexOf("hp-ux")!=-1);
this.hpux9 = (this.hpux && (agt.indexOf("09.")!=-1));
this.hpux10= (this.hpux && (agt.indexOf("10.")!=-1));
this.aix = (agt.indexOf("aix") !=-1); // IBM
this.aix1 = (agt.indexOf("aix 1") !=-1);
this.aix2 = (agt.indexOf("aix 2") !=-1);
this.aix3 = (agt.indexOf("aix 3") !=-1);
this.aix4 = (agt.indexOf("aix 4") !=-1);
this.linux = (agt.indexOf("inux")!=-1);
this.sco = (agt.indexOf("sco")!=-1) ||
            (agt.indexOf("unix_sv")!=-1);
```

```
    this.unixware = (agt.indexOf("unix_system_v")!=-1);
    this.mpras = (agt.indexOf("ncr")!=-1);
    this.reliant = (agt.indexOf("reliantunix")!=-1);
    this.dec = ((agt.indexOf("dec")!=-1) ||
                (agt.indexOf("osf1")!=-1) ||
                (agt.indexOf("dec_alpha")!=-1) ||
                (agt.indexOf("alphaserver")!=-1) ||
                (agt.indexOf("ultrix")!=-1) ||
                (agt.indexOf("alphastation")!=-1));
    this.sinix = (agt.indexOf("sinix")!=-1);
    this.freebsd = (agt.indexOf("freebsd")!=-1);
    this.bsd = (agt.indexOf("bsd")!=-1);
    this.unix = ((agt.indexOf("x11")!=-1) || this.sun ||
                this.irix || this.hpux ||
                this.sco ||this.unixware || this.mpras ||
                this.reliant || this.dec || this.sinix ||
                this.aix || this.linux || this.bsd ||
                this.freebsd);
    this.vms = ((agt.indexOf("vax")!=-1) ||
                (agt.indexOf("openvms")!=-1));

} // end Is() function declaration

var is;
var isIE3Mac = false;

// this section is designed specifically for IE3 for the Mac

if ((navigator.appVersion.indexOf("Mac")!=-1) &&
    (navigator.userAgent.indexOf("MSIE")!=-1) &&
    (parseInt(navigator.appVersion)==3)) {
        isIE3Mac = true;
}
else {
    is = new Is();
    var builtInScroll;
    if (is.ie3up || is.ie4up || is.ie5up) {

        // the MARQUEE element is supported, so use it

        builtInScroll = '<FORM NAME="myForm"><MARQUEE ID=abc
            DIRECTION=LEFT BEHAVIOR=SCROLL
            SCROLLAMOUNT=2>JavaScript For
            Dummies...</MARQUEE><INPUT TYPE="button"
            VALUF="Start scrolling" NAME="startscroll"
            onClick="document.all.abc.start()"><INPUT
            TYPE="button" VALUE="Stop scrolling"
            NAME="stopScroll"
            onClick="document.all.abc.stop()"></FORM>';

    }
```

(continued)

Listing 4-1 *(continued)*

```
    else {

        // display an attractive, non-scrolling alternative

        builtInScroll = '<CENTER><H1>JavaScript For
            Dummies...</H1></CENTER>'
    }

    document.write(builtInScroll)

}


</SCRIPT>

</HEAD>
<BODY>

</BODY>
</HTML>
```

Order in the court!

The code in Listing 4-1 might look a little intimidating at first, but it's pretty straightforward when you understand what's going on. (And you do, after you finish this chapter!)

The first thing you want to notice is the order of the JavaScript statements. The JavaScript interpreter processes JavaScript statements in top-down order, so here's the order in which the interpreter interprets the code in Listing 4-1:

1. **The** `Is()` **function declaration is the first statement that appears after the opening** `<SCRIPT>` **tag, so this function declaration is processed first.**

   The JavaScript interpreter processes the `Is()` function and holds it in memory, ready to spring into action as soon as a line of code calls the `Is()` function.

2. **After the closing curly brace that marks the end of the** `Is()` **function declaration, you see the** `if . . . else` **statement that determines whether or not the browser is Internet Explorer version 3 running on a Macintosh.**

   The JavaScript interpreter processes this `if . . . else` statement second.

3. **Within the else portion of that** if . . . else **statement, you see one last** if . . . else **statement.**

   This last if . . . else statement calls the Is() function to determine whether the loading browser is Internet Explorer version 3 or later.

Take a look at listing 4-2 to see these three statements, and how they appear in relation to one another. This radically excerpted version of the "sniffer" script demonstrates the top-down order in which JavaScript statements are processed.

Listing 4-2:   Code Showing the Sniffer Process

```
<HTML>
<HEAD><TITLE>JavaScript browser "sniffer" (from JavaScript
         For Dummies, 3rd edition)</TITLE>

<SCRIPT LANGUAGE="JavaScript">

function Is () {


    . . .
}

var is;
var isIE3Mac - false;

// this section is designed specifically for IE3 for the Mac

if ((navigator.appVersion.indexOf("Mac")!=-1) &&
    (navigator.userAgent.indexOf("MSIE")!=-1) &&
    (parseInt(navigator.appVersion)==3)) {
        isIE3Mac = true;
}
else {
    is = new Is();
    var builtInScroll;


    if (is.ie3up || is.ie4up || is.ie5up) {

        // the MARQUEE element is supported, so use it

        builtInScroll = '<FORM NAME="myForm"><MARQUEE ID=abc
            DIRECTION=LEFT BEHAVIOR=SCROLL
            SCROLLAMOUNT=2>JavaScript For
            Dummies...</MARQUEE><INPUT TYPE="button"
            VALUE="Start scrolling" NAME="startscroll"
            onClick="document.all.abc.start()"><INPUT
```

(continued)

Listing 4-2 *(continued)*

```
            TYPE="button" VALUE="Stop scrolling"
            NAME="stopScroll" onClick="document.
            all.abc.stop()"></FORM>';

    }

    else {
        // display an attractive, non-scrolling alternative

        builtInScroll = '<CENTER><H1>JavaScript For
            Dummies...</H1></CENTER>'

    }

    document.write(builtInScroll)

}
```

You can place JavaScript scripts in either the head of a Web document, as shown in Listing 4-2 (between the opening HTML <HEAD> tag and the closing HTML </HEAD> tag) or the body (between the opening HTML <BODY> tag and the closing HTML </BODY> tag). You can even place scripts in both the head <u>and</u> the body of a Web document, if you're so inclined!

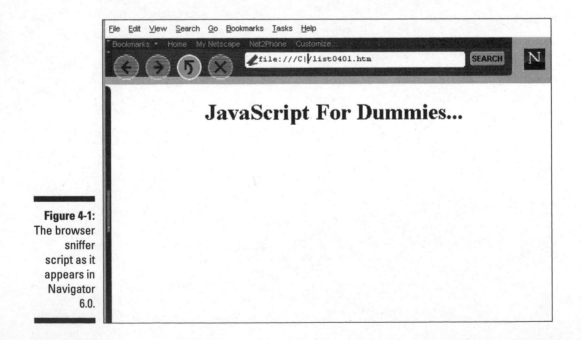

Figure 4-1:
The browser sniffer script as it appears in Navigator 6.0.

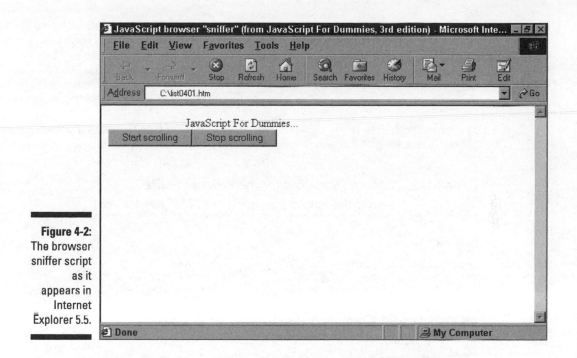

Figure 4-2:
The browser
sniffer script
as it
appears in
Internet
Explorer 5.5.

Variables: Think global, act local

Variables are named placeholders you define in JavaScript, and then stuff with whatever values you like. If you haven't worked with variables before, they might strike you as a strange concept at first — but trust me, they soon become your best programming friend!

Places, everybody!

Two things to keep in mind when you're considering script placement:

✔ Scripts placed in the head of a Web document are processed before scripts placed in the body of a Web document.

A good design practice is to place a script containing all the custom functions you create in the head of your Web document. That way, the JavaScript interpreter encounters them right up front, ensuring that your functions are accessible from any

JavaScript statements that appear later, in the body of the document.

✔ You are not limited to one script per document head or body; you may include as many scripts as you like in either section. (One reason why you might want to attach multiple scripts to a single Web document is if you plan to take advantage of external scripts. You can find out more about external scripts, including how and why to create, find, and attach them, in Chapter 14.)

Variables help you keep track of all the bits of information you work with in a script. You use variables in everyday life all the time, although you might not think of it that way. For example, your checkbook balance is a variable. The value of your checkbook balance might be $100 one month and $100,000 the next, but the name you use to describe it — *checkbook balance* — remains the same.

The browser sniffer script described in this chapter makes use of many variables. Take a look at the script excerpt in Listing 4-3 to see what I mean!

Listing 4-3:   Defining Variables for the Browser Sniffer
Script: the `agt`, `major`, and `minor` Variables

```
function Is () {
    . . .

    // Making the browser string lowercase
    // and storing it separately helps us pick it apart and
    // hunt for certain values in it later on
    // in the script.  The "navigator" object refers to
    // the executing browser, whatever it is (Navigator
    // or Internet Explorer).

    var agt=navigator.userAgent.toLowerCase();

    this.major = parseInt(navigator.appVersion);
    this.minor = parseFloat(navigator.appVersion);

    . . .
}
```

The first variable declaration you see in Listing 4-3 is the declaration and assignment of a variable called `agt`. (`agt` is short for *user agent*, which is programmer-ese for "the specific instance of the browser loading this script right here and now.")

The JavaScript statement that declares the `agt` variable also loads it with a value: the value returned by the `toLowerCase()` method call associated with the `userAgent` object, which itself is associated with the `navigator` object. Whew!

Let me break that statement down for you, so you can see exactly what's going on here.

This part of the code . . .	*Does this*
`var agt`	Declares a variable called `agt`
`=`	The assignment operator; assigns the value on its right to the variable on its left

This part of the code . . .	Does this
`navigator.userAgent.` `toLowerCase()`	Calls the `toLowerCase()` method of the `userAgent` object. (The `userAgent` object is contained inside the `navigator` object.) The `toLowerCase()` method returns the value of the `userAgent` string in all lower-case letters.
	Denotes the end of this JavaScript statement.

The `navigator` object refers to the executing browser, which may (or may not) be Netscape Navigator. Both Navigator and Internet Explorer support the `navigator` object.

Say what you mean, mean what you say

Technically, you can declare a variable in JavaScript with or without using the `var` keyword. For example, the following two variable declarations are both valid:

```
function someFunction() {

    . . .

   var x = 123 // This function is the scope of x (even if
   another x
   // was declared earlier in the script as a global
   // variable
   y = 123  // Could retain value of a previously declared global
   variable

    . . .

}
```

The difference between the two different declarations? The first declaration — the one using the `var` keyword — is more formal; it ensures that only one variable named x is visible within any given scope. The second function may cause confusion because any other y variable declared earlier as a global variable is also visible within this function.

In effect, the `var` keyword tells the JavaScript interpreter to ignore all other variables bearing the same name — global or local — that it encounters in any given scope.

I suggest you get in the habit of using the `var` keyword to declare all of your variables. Doing so helps prevent hard-to-find errors in your JavaScript code due to accidentally giving a global variable and a local variable the same name. (To see an example of how leaving off the var keyword can cause surprising results in a script, check out var.htm on the companion CD-ROM.)

The semi-colon end-of-statement operator is optional — *unless* you try to cram several statements onto the same line. If you place more than one JavaScript statement on the same line, you must separate them with semi-colons.

As an example, when you load the code snippet in Listing 4-3 into the Internet Explorer 5.5 browser, you see these values:

✔ The value for `navigator.userAgent` is Mozilla/4.0 (compatible; MSIE 5.5; Windows 95)

✔ The value assigned to the `agt` variable is mozilla/4.0 (compatible; msie 5.5; windows 95)

In JavaScript, as in other programming languages, variables can either be *local* or *global*. *Local* variables are variables that you define inside a function — like the variables you see in Listing 4-3. Local variables are accessible (or *visible*) only inside the function containing the local variable declaration.

Global variables, on the other hand, are variables that you define at the top of a script, before any function declarations. Because you declare them outside the *scope* of any single function, global variables are accessible from all the functions in a script. The *scope* of a variable refers to the JavaScript statements from which that variable is accessible. If you define a variable in a function, that function is the variable's scope; if you define a variable at the beginning of a script, all the functions in the script comprise that variable's scope.

I cover string manipulation methods like `toLowerCase()`in more detail in the next section. For now, continuing with the variable declaration theme, take a peek at the second variable declaration and assignment statement in Listing 4-3:

```
this.major = parseInt(navigator.appVersion);
```

The preceding statement introduces a built-in JavaScript keyword: the `this` keyword. `this` is shorthand for "this here object that I'm in right now." (At least, that's the way we say it in Texas!)

Using `this` turns an ordinary function into an object generator. When you call a function containing `this` statements using the `new` operator, as shown here, you create a brand-new instance of an object.

```
var is = new Is();   // creates a new instance of the Is
            object
```

The above statement creates a new variable, called `is`, and assigns it a brand-new object generated by calling the `Is()` function. And because statements in the `Is()` function (as you see in Listing 4-3) assign values to `this.major` and `this.minon`, those values are available from the newly created `is` variable, as well! Take a look:

```
var abc = new Is()
// Now you can access abc.major and abc.minor

var is = new Is()
// Now you can access is.major and is.minor

var browser = new Is()
// Now you can access browser.major and browser.minor
```

String manipulation (Don't worry, it's ethical!)

The bulk of the browser "sniffer" script demonstrated in this chapter, as you may recall from Listing 4-1, is made up of JavaScript statements that examine *strings* to determine the make, model, and version of the loading browser. For example, the following line asks: Is "this" loading browser Internet Explorer, or not?

```
this.ie = (agt.indexOf("msie") != -1);
```

A JavaScript *string* is much like an English word or sentence: it can contain letters, numbers, and even special characters, like spaces or punctuation marks. In the preceding JavaScript statement, `"msie"` is a string.

Because we humans tend to think in words and sentences, examining and manipulating strings is a pretty common thing to do in JavaScript. (By manipulating, I mean changing the case of the characters, extracting characters, combining two or more strings — that kind of thing.) Fortunately, the document object model and JavaScript's built-in string support offer lots of functions and methods you can use to do just that!

In this section, you get a step-by-step look at the string manipulation statements used in the browser "sniffer" script.

String fling

Every time you create a `string` object, — which you can do using any of the following JavaScript statements — you automatically get a bunch of built-in properties and methods, courtesy of JavaScript. I introduce you to some of the most common methods in this chapter. To get a full rundown on all of the properties and methods available for your own string manipulation endeavors, visit

```
http://developer.netscape.com/docs/manuals/js/client/jsref/st
     ring.htm#1193137
```

You can create straightforward strings like this:

Creating a string

```
var string1 = "My dog has fleas."
```

```
var string2 = 'So does my cat.'
```

```
var string3 = new String("What just bit me?")
```

To add strings for more complex results or displaying combinations of field values, use these examples:

Example	Result
`var string4 = string1 + string2 + string3`	Concatenates `string1`, `string2`, and `string3` and assigns the result to `string4`
`var string5 += string1`	Adds `string1` to the end of `string5`

Using the `length` property like this, and the result represents the length of `string1`.

```
string1.length
```

The following examples are some useful string methods:

Method	Return Value
`string1.toLowerCase()`	Returns string1 in all lowercase
`string1.toUpperCase()`	Returns string1 in all uppercase
`string1.indexOf("abc")`	Returns the position number if "abc" is found in string1; otherwise, returns -1
`string1.concat(string2, string3)`	Concatenates (combines) `string1`, `string2`, and `string3`
`string1.substring(11, 16)`	Returns a substring of `string1` that's exactly five characters long, beginning with character 11 (`fleas`)

The examples in Listing 4-4 show you how to examine and manipulate strings. The code for this listing comes from the sniffer script.

**Listing 4-4:   Working with Strings in
                the Sniffer Script**

```
function Is () {
    . . .
    // Change the value of navigator.userAgent to lower case
    // and assign the result to the variable called "agt"
    var agt=navigator.userAgent.toLowerCase();

    // Use the built-in JavaScript function parseInt()
    // to turn the first couple of characters of
           navigator.appVersion
    // into an integer assign this value to the variable
           called "major"

    this.major = parseInt(navigator.appVersion);

    // Check to see whether the strings 'moozilla',
           'spoofer',
    // 'compatible', 'opera', or 'webtv' are in this
           browser's
    // configuration details; if so, set the "this is a
    // Navigator-compatible browser" flag (the variable
           called
    // nav) to true.
    this.nav = ((agt.indexOf('mozilla')!=-1) &&
                (agt.indexOf('spoofer')==-1) &&
                (agt.indexOf('compatible') == -1) &&
                (agt.indexOf('opera')==-1) &&
                (agt.indexOf('webtv')==-1));
```

toLowerCase ( )

Take a look at the first variable assignment statement in Listing 4-4: the one
that assigns a value to the agt var. As you can see, this statement is calling the
toLowerCase() method of the userAgent object (which is a string object).

If you display the value for navigator.userAgent all by itself (inside the
Netscape Navigator 6.0 browser), this is what you see:

```
Mozilla/5.0 (Windows; N; Win95; en-US; m14) Netscape6/6.0b1
```

Calling the toLowerCase() method on the preceding string returns the following result, which is immediately assigned to the agt variable:

```
mozilla/5.0 (windows; n; win95; en-us; m14) netscape6/6.0b1
```

Why change a string to all lowercase letters? Because doing so makes testing
that string for specific patterns much easier. You don't have to worry about
capitalization!

The object of your desire

How on earth are you supposed to know that the `navigator` object contains an object called `userAgent` that contains specific browser configuration details? And how on earth are you supposed to figure out what those configuration details look like — exactly — so you can examine them and make sense out of them?

I'm glad you asked!

The document object model describes all of the document- and browser-related details you work with in JavaScript. As you see in Chapter 3, many of the objects defined in the DOM have descriptive names. For example, you can probably guess what the objects `image`, `form`, and `button` refer to — and what properties and methods they contain — if you are familiar with HTML images, forms, and buttons.

The contents of a few objects, however, such as `navigator`, aren't quite as obvious at first blush. The best way to get familiar with the objects available to you is to skim through this book, which contains examples of common

tasks you want to perform using JavaScript. If you want to use an object not demonstrated in this book, take a look at

> http://developer.netscape.com/d ocs/manuals/js/client/jsref /objintro.htm

(Be sure to click on the link marked `Next`) and

> http://msdn.microsoft.com/work- shop/author/dhtml/refer- ence/objects.asp

The latter of these two links provides detailed object model descriptions for Navigator and Internet Explorer, respectively.

To find out the contents of the `navigator` object (essential if you want to extend the browser "sniffer" example shown in this chapter), take a peek at http://www.it97.de/ JavaScript/JS_tutorial/bstat/navobj.html. This comprehensive Web site contains representative `navigator` contents for virtually every browser on planet Earth!

As you might expect, JavaScript supports the `toUpperCase()` method on strings, as well. See the section, "String fling" for details.

parseInt()

The second variable assignment you see in Listing 4-4 is this one:

```
this.major = parseInt(navigator.appVersion);
```

This statement uses the built-in JavaScript function `parseInt()` to transform the first numbers it encounters in the `navigator.appVersion` string to an integer (technically speaking, a JavaScript Number object that can be used in mathematical calculations). Say, for example, that `navigator.appVersion` contains the following value (which it does if you're running Internet Explorer 5.5):

```
4.0 (compatible; MSIE 5.5; Windows 95)
```

The value returned by `parseInt(navigator.appVersion)`is: 4

The parseInt() function assumes a base 10 conversion unless you tell it otherwise. You request a non-base-10 conversion by passing an optional radix parameter to the parseInt() function, like this:

```
parseInt(aString, "16") // base 16 calculation
```

indexOf()

The third and final variable assignment you see in Listing 4-4 is this one:

```
this.nav = ((agt.indexOf('mozilla')!=-1) &&
            (agt.indexOf('spoofer')==-1) &&
            (agt.indexOf('compatible') == -1) &&
            (agt.indexOf('opera')==-1) &&
            (agt.indexOf('webtv')==-1));
```

The statement above uses the indexOf() method associated with string objects to determine which, if any, of five strings the agt variable contains.

Here's how the index() method works. You pass it the string you're looking for, and if it finds a match, it returns the number of characters it had to count in before it found the match. If no match exists, index() returns the value -1.

Suppose the agt variable contains the following string at runtime (which it does, if you're running Netscape Navigator 6.0):

```
mozilla/5.0 (windows; n; win95; en-us; m14) netscape6/6.0b1
```

When the JavaScript interpreter runs the third and final variable assignment you see in Listing 4-4, it assigns the value true to the this.nav variable. Why? Because the JavaScript interpreter steps through these tests:

- **Locates a match.** It finds mozilla in mozilla/5.0 (windows; n; win95; en-us; m14) netscape6/6.0b1.

- **Compares the match result.** agt.indexOf() returns a value of 0, because the interpreter has to count in 0 characters before it finds a match. Because 0 is not equal to (!=) -1, the first condition is true.

- **Doesn't find any more matches.** None of spoofer, compatible, opera, nor webtv are contained in the "mozilla/5.0 (windows; n; win95; en-us; m14) netscape6/6.0b1" string, so each of these other conditions tests true, as well.

- **Assigns the result to** this.nav. Because all of the conditions test true, the interpreter places a value of true in the this.nav variable.

Talkin' about my JavaScript generation

The purpose of all the code I discuss in the previous sections of this chapter is to determine, at runtime, precisely what kind of browser is loading a particular script. After you know what browser you're dealing with comes the fun part: you get to display a Web page appropriate for that type of browser! And that's exactly what you see how to do in this section.

Take a look at Listing 4-5 to see the portion of the browser "sniffer" example that generates two different Web pages, based on whether the loading browser is Internet Explorer or some other browser.

Listing 4-5:   Generating Two Different Web Pages
Based on the Type of Loading Browser

```
. . .
var builtInScroll;
if (is.ie3up || is.ie4up || is.ie5up) {
      // the MARQUEE element is supported, so use it
    builtInScroll = '<FORM NAME="myForm"><MARQUEE ID=abc
          DIRECTION=LEFT BEHAVIOR=SCROLL
          SCROLLAMOUNT=2>JavaScript For
          Dummies...</MARQUEE><INPUT TYPE="button"
          VALUE="Start scrolling" NAME="startscroll"
          onClick="document.all.abc.start()"><INPUT
          TYPE="button" VALUE="Stop scrolling"
          NAME="stopScroll"
          onClick="document.all.abc.stop()"></FORM>';
          }
    else {
       // display an attractive, non-scrolling alternative
       builtInScroll = '<CENTER><H1>JavaScript For
          Dummies...</H1></CENTER>'
    }
    document.write(builtInScroll)
}
</SCRIPT>
```

Here's what the code in Listing 4-5 does. First off, it declares a variable called `builtInScroll`.

Then, it determines whether the loading browser is Internet Explorer. The line of JavaScript that makes this determination is

```
if (is.ie3up || is.ie4up || is.ie5up)
```

In English, the preceding statement checks to see if the loading browser is Internet Explorer version 3 or up (ie3up), Internet Explorer version 4 or up (ie4up), or Internet Explorer version 5 or up (ie5up).

When this `if` condition resolves to `true` — in other words, if the loading browser *is* Internet Explorer version 3, 4, 5, or greater, the code in Listing 4-5 sets the variable `builtInScroll` equal to a bunch of HTML statements. These statements, when executed, display an Internet Explorer-proprietary scrolling marquee on the page.

When, on the other hand, this `if` condition resolves to `false` — in other words, if the loading browser is *not* Internet Explorer version 3, 4, 5, or greater, then the code in Listing 4-5 sets the variable `builtInScroll` to a bunch of HTML statements that quietly display the message as a heading (rather than as scrolling text).

Finally, the `document.write(builtInScroll)` statement writes the contents of the `builtInScroll` variable to the Web page, causing one of two distinctly different displays to appear.

Another common use for the browser detection script demonstrated in this chapter is to determine in advance whether a browser has a specific plug-in loaded before you attempt to call or manipulate that plug-in from your JavaScript code. For more information on plug-ins, check out Chapter 14.

Chapter 5

Making Every Date Count

In This Chapter

▶ Capturing current time and date information

▶ Getting familiar with the built-in Date object

▶ Performing date calculations

▶ Displaying time and date information on your Web pages

▶ Creating and attaching an external script

*J*avaScript provides a special, built-in object, called Date. You can use this object to capture and manipulate date and time information. Using this object allows you to display the current date on your Web pages, customize what your users see based on what time of day or night it is, and even keep track of how long users linger on your site!

How About a Date?

You use the built-in Date object to store and manipulate date and time information in JavaScript. Because it's an object, Date comes complete with lots of handy methods you use to access date and time information. This chapter show you some of these, including as getTime(), getMinutes(), getMonth(), and getSeconds(). (Most of the methods Date supports are listed in the table titled, "Marking Time".)

Before you can use Date methods, however, you first must create a variable of type Date. You create a variable of type Date using the new operator, like this:

```
new Date()
new Date(milliseconds)
new Date(dateString)
new Date(yr_num, mo_num, day_num [, hr_num, min_num, sec_num,
        ms_num])
```

Replace these elements of the syntax like this:

milliseconds is the number of milliseconds that have elapsed since January 1, 1970, 00:00:00

dateString is a string representing a date in this format: February 3, 1915

yr_num is a four-digit integer representing the year; for example: 2000

mo_num is an integer between 0 and 11 that represents month

day_num is an integer between 0 and 30 that represents day

hr_num is an integer between 0 and 11 that represents hours (optional)

min_num is an integer between 0 and 59 that represents minutes (optional)

sec_num is an integer between 0 and 50 that represents seconds (optional)

ms_num is an integer representing milliseconds: for example, 7878 (optional)

The Date syntax boils down to this: You have these two basic ways you can create a Date in JavaScript:

✔ **You can provide specific date information.** If you pass the Date constructor information such as month, year, day, or time, the Date constructor creates a Date object using those values. (If you skip a few optional values, the Date constructor fills them in with zeros for you.) You see an example of this approach in Listing 5-1.

✔ **You can provide no date information.** If you don't pass the Date constructor any values, it creates a Date object containing the current date and time. You see an example of this in Listing 5-2.

To experiment with the full version of the code in Listing 5-1, load the file list0501.htm from the companion CD.

Listing 5-1: **Constructing a Date Object Using Specific Date/Time Information**

```
...
// Creates a date from a string
var birthDay = new Date("October 21, 1963")

// Creates a date from year, month, date, hours,
// minutes, and seconds
var graduation = new Date(1990, 7, 12, 10, 30, 01)
```

```
// Creates a date from the number of milliseconds
// elapsed since 1970. (Hey, ya gotta start
// somewhere!)
var wedding = new Date(710485200000)

// Display the newly created dates.
// "\n" inserts a new line in the display, so that
// the three pieces of information display on three
// separate lines in the alert box.
alert("Date #1 = " + birthDay
       + "\nDate #2 = " + graduation
       + "\nDate #3 " + wedding)
...
```

Figure 5-1 shows you what the code in Listing 5-1 looks like when you load it into Netscape Navigator 6.0. Notice how the `Date` constructor adds the day of the week for you automatically.

JavaScript, like many other programming languages, counts a bit differently than we humans do. Specifically, it begins counting months with 0, not with 1. So, to create a date of January, the first month of the year, you must specify a value of 0 for mo_num.

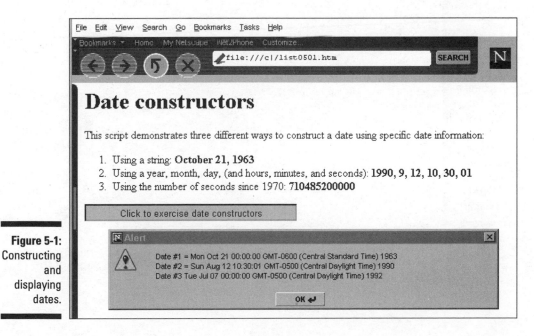

Figure 5-1:
Constructing
and
displaying
dates.

The code snippet in Listing 5-2 shows how the `Date` constructor, when called with no arguments at all, pulls the current date and time.

If you like, you can load the code in Listing 5-2 (list0502.htm on the companion CD) into your own browser. The file on the CD contains the full HTML for this simple page.

Listing 5-2:   Load this Web Page to See What Time It Is!

```
<SCRIPT LANGUAGE="JavaScript">
    document.write("This page last updated: " + new Date())
</SCRIPT>
```

The result, as you see in Figure 5-2, is the current date and time (the date and time at which this script was loaded into *my* Web browser).

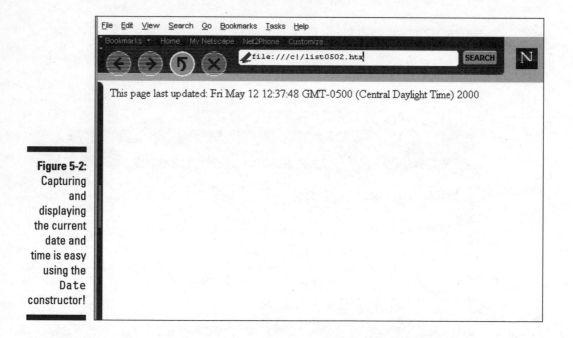

Figure 5-2:
Capturing and displaying the current date and time is easy using the Date constructor!

This page last updated: Fri May 12 12:37:48 GMT-0500 (Central Daylight Time) 2000

The `Date` object supports dozens of methods. Table 5-1 lists some of the most common.

Table 5-1	Marking Time with Date Methods
Method	*Value returned*
getDate()	Returns the day of the month for the specified date, according to local time
getDay()	Returns the day of the week for the specified date according to local time
getFullYear()	Returns the year of the specified date according to local time
getHours()	Returns the hour in the specified date according to local time
getMilliseconds()	Returns the milliseconds in the specified date according to local time
getMinutes()	Returns the minutes in the specified date according to local time
getMonth()	Returns the month in the specified date according to local time
getSeconds()	Returns the seconds in the specified date according to local time
getTime()	Returns the numeric value corresponding to the time for the specified date according to local time
getUTCDate()	Returns the day (date) of the month in the specified date according to universal (Greenwich Mean) time
getUTCDay()	Returns the day of the week in the specified date according to universal time
getUTCFullYear()	Returns the year in the specified date according to universal time
getUTCHours()	Returns the hours in the specified date according to universal time
getUTCMilliseconds()	Returns the milliseconds in the specified date according to universal time
getUTCMinutes()	Returns the minutes in the specified date according to universal time
getUTCMonth()	Returns the month according in the specified date according to universal time

(continued)

Table 5-1 *(continued)*

Method	Value returned
getUTCSeconds()	Returns the seconds in the specified date according to universal time
getYear()	Returns the year in the specified date according to local time
parse()	Returns the number of milliseconds in a date string since January 1, 1970, 00:00:00, local time
setDate()	Sets the day of the month for a specified date according to local time
setFullYear()	Sets the full year for a specified date according to local time
setHours()	Sets the hours for a specified date according to local time
setMilliseconds()	Sets the milliseconds for a specified date according to local time
setMinutes()	Sets the minutes for a specified date according to local time
setMonth()	Sets the month for a specified date according to local time
setSeconds()	Sets the seconds for a specified date according to local time
setTime()	Sets the value of a Date object according to local time
setUTCDate()	Sets the day of the month for a specified date according to universal time
setUTCFullYear()	Sets the full year for a specified date according to universal time.
setUTCHours()	Sets the hour for a specified date according to universal time
setUTCMilliseconds()	Sets the milliseconds for a specified date according to universal time
setUTCMinutes()	Sets the minutes for a specified date according to universal time
setUTCMonth()	Sets the month for a specified date according to universal time

Method	Value returned
setUTCSeconds()	Sets the seconds for a specified date according to universal time
setYear()	Sets the year for a specified date according to local time
toGMTString()	Converts a date to a string, using the Internet GMT conventions
toLocaleString()	Converts a date to a string, using the current locale's conventions
toString()	Returns a string representing the specified Date object
toUTCString()	Converts a date to a string, using the universal time convention
UTC()	Returns the number of milliseconds in a Date object since January 1, 1970, 00:00:00, universal time

For details on what parameters each of these methods expect — along with examples of how you use them and additional, more esoteric Date methods — take a peek at Netscape's site:

```
http://developer.netscape.com/docs/manuals/js/client/jsref/
        date.htm
```

Not Your Ordinary Date

Because JavaScript stores date information as a collection of properties, you don't have to settle for a single representation of a given date. Figure 5-2 earlier in this chapter shows you the default format for date display:

```
Fri May 12 12:37:48 GMT-0500 (Central Daylight Time) 2000
```

But what if you want to display something a little different than the computer-ese looking message shown here? For example, what if you want to display the date in a more friendly fashion, such as

```
Good afternoon! It's 12:37 p.m.
```

or perhaps

```
May 12, 2000
```

Using the built-in property-accessing methods JavaScript provides, you can do just that! I've broken out these two examples into the following two sections, "Finding time" and "Spelling it out."

Finding time: The time formatting script

Take a look at Listing 5-3 to see how you can examine the time component of a JavaScript date.

You can play around with the code you see in Listing 5-3, including the HTML tags, by loading list0503.htm from the companion CD into your own Web browser.

Listing 5-3: Accessing the Time Portion of a JavaScript Date

```
<SCRIPT LANGUAGE="JavaScript">

    var today = new Date()
    var hours = today.getHours()
    var minutes = today.getMinutes()
    var greeting
    var ampm

    // We consider one in the morning until just before noon
          "morning"

    if (hours <= 11) {
        greeting = "Good morning!"
        ampm="a.m."

        // JavaScript reports midnight as 0, so change
        // it to 12 for display purposes.

        if (hours == 0) {
            hours = 12
        }
    }
    // We consider noon until five o'clock "afternoon"
    else if (hours > 11 && hours < 18) {

        greeting = "Good afternoon!"
        ampm="p.m."
// We don't want to see military time, so
        // subtract 12
```

```
        if (hours > 12) {
            hours-=12
        }
    }

    // We consider six until eight "evening"
    else if (hours > 17 && hours < 21) {
        greeting = "Good evening!"
        ampm="p.m."
        hours-=12
    }

    // We consider nine o'clock until midnight "night"
    else if (hours > 20) {
        greeting = "Good night!"
        ampm="p.m."
        hours-=12
    }

    // We want the minutes to display with "0" in
    // front of them if they're single-digit.  (For
    // example, rather than 1:4 p.m.,
    // we want to see 1:04 p.m.

    if (minutes < 10) {
        minutes = "0" + minutes
    }

    // Display the formatted time on the screen.
    // ("\n" inserts a new line on the page to help
    // format the message nicely.)
    document.write(greeting + "\nIt's " + hours + ":" +
        minutes + " " + ampm);

</SCRIPT>
```

To see how the code in Listing 5-3 looks when it loads into Netscape Navigator 6.0, take a look at Figure 5-3. You can access date properties via built-in methods to display dates and times in whatever custom format you choose.

Here's how the code in Listing 5-3 works. First, a new Date object is created (called today). Next, the hours and minutes are plucked from the Date object, using the getHours() and getMinutes() methods, respectively. After you have the hours (an integer between 0 and 24, depending on what time of day it is), you can determine whether it's morning, afternoon, evening, or night. To do this you compare the contents of the hours variable to a range appropriate for morning (1:00 a.m. to 11:00 a.m., in this script example), for afternoon (12:00 p.m. to 5:00 p.m., in this script example) and so on.

File Edit View Search Go Bookmarks Tasks Help

Bookmarks ▾   Home   My Netscape   Net2Phone   Customize...

file:///c|/emily/write/jsfd3e/scripts/list   SEARCH   N

Good afternoon! It's 1:10 p.m.

Figure 5-3:
Now you're
showing
your guest
a nice time.

As it classifies the current hour as a.m. or p.m., the code in Listing 5-3 sets the display variables `ampm` and `greeting`. At the end of the script, those display variables are used, along with the `hours` and `minutes` variables, to construct the text shown in the body of the Web page.

Spelling it out: The date formatting script

In this section I show you how to examine a JavaScript date, format it attractively, and display it on a Web page. Because this is the kind of script you may want to use on more than one Web page, I also show you how to implement this script as an *external script*, so that you can create it once and then reuse it over and over again from inside many different HTML documents.

An external script is a bunch of JavaScript statements saved separately from any HTML document. External JavaScript script filenames, by convention, always contain a .JS extension.

Some old browsers — notably Internet Explorer 3.x and older — do not support external JavaScript scripts.

Take a look at Listing 5-4 to see an external JavaScript script that displays the current date in a nice custom format.

The script you see in Listing 5-4 can be found on the companion CD. Look for the filename list0504.js.

Listing 5-4: This External JavaScript Script Formats a Date

```
<!--Hide from browsers that do not support JavaScript

// Get the current date
today = new Date();

// Get the current month
month = today.getMonth();

// Attach a display name to the month number

switch (month) {
    case 0 :
        displayMonth = "January"
        break
    case 1 :
        displayMonth = "February"
        break
    case 2 :
        displayMonth = "March"
        break
    case 3 :
        displayMonth = "April"
        break
    case 4 :
        displayMonth = "May"
        break
    case 5 :
        displayMonth = "June"
        break
    case 6 :
        displayMonth = "July"
        break
    case 7 :
        displayMonth = "August"
        break
    case 8 :
        displayMonth = "September"
        break
    case 9 :
        displayMonth = "October"
        break
    case 10 :
        displayMonth = "November"
        break
    case 11 :
```

(continued)

Listing 5-4 *(continued)*

```
        displayMonth = "December"
        break

    default: displayMonth = "INVALID"
}

document.writeln(displayMonth + " " + today.getDate() + ", "
        + today.getYear());

// stop hiding -->
```

The code in Listing 5-4 first gets the current date and time, and pokes it into a variable called `today`. It then gets the month portion of the current date and pokes *that* into a variable called, appropriately enough, `month`.

With the value for `month` in hand, the code in Listing 5-4 uses the JavaScript `switch` statement to determine the corresponding month name — January, February, March, and so on. (For more information on the `switch` statement, including why it's so much easier to use than a long bunch of `if . . . then` statements, check out Chapter 3's discussion on conditionals.)

Finally, the code in Listing 5-4 displays the month name, day, and year as shown in Figure 5-4. Before you peek at Figure 5-4, though, take a quick look at Listing 5-5. Listing 5-5 shows you the `<SCRIPT>` tags you to attach the external JavaScript script shown in Listing 5-4 to an HTML file.

Listing 5-5:   Attaching the External Script Called
**   list0504.js to an HTML File**

```
<SCRIPT LANGUAGE="JavaScript" SRC="list0504.js">
</SCRIPT>
```

Browsers look for .js files in the same directory in which the referencing HTML file is located. If you want to store your .js files in a separate directory, make sure you reflect that directory in the value for the SRC attribute. For example, `SRC="../script/list05045.js"` tells browsers to search for the .js file in the /script directory located directly below the directory containing the HTML file.

Load list0505.htm from the companion CD into your Web browser to experiment with the code shown in Listing 5-5.

When you use external scripts, such as the one defined in Listing 5-4 and referenced in Listing 5-5, keep the following points in mind:

✔ While the latest versions of both Netscape Navigator and Internet Explorer support external scripts, not all browsers do.

✔ Implementing your scripts as separate files (rather than including them directly in your HTML files) allows you to reuse or share scripts easily. That saves time and effort!

✔ External scripts can't be viewed by others the way internal scripts can. For example, clicking View⇨Source in Internet Explorer or View⇨Page Source in Netscape Navigator lets users see internal JavaScript statements. But JavaScript statements implemented as external scripts can't be viewed this way! Users can see the name of your external script file, but the actual JavaScript statements contained in that file are hidden safely away from view.

The way JavaScript handles dates changed between JavaScript version 1.2 (supported in Navigator 4.05 and earlier versions) and JavaScript version 1.3 (supported in Navigator 4.06 and later versions). Browsers that support JavaScript version 1.3 or earlier contain two significant date-related bugs: they cannot properly process dates earlier than 1970, and their date calculating abilities are platform-dependent. Fortunately, these bugs no longer exist in JavaScript version 1.3. If manipulating dates in JavaScript is crucial to your project, take a look at Chapter 4, to see how to verify that your users are running JavaScript version 1.3 or later.

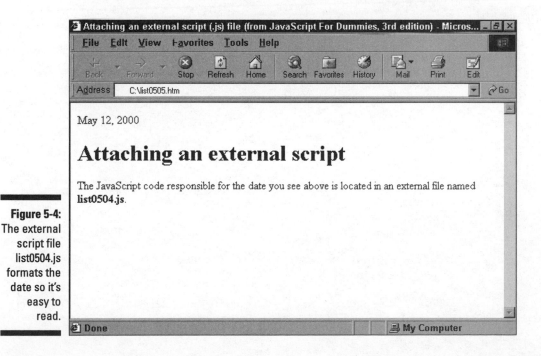

Figure 5-4:
The external script file list0504.js formats the date so it's easy to read.

Chapter 6

That's How the Cookie Crumbles

In This Chapter

▶ Taking a close look at cookies

▶ Understanding the benefits and limitations of cookies

▶ Setting and retrieving cookie values

▶ Creating a script to recognize previous visitors to your site

*U*nlike a traditional client/server configuration, in which both the client and the server have to agree to begin and end every conversation, the Web is *stateless*. Stateless means that, by default, neither Web browsers nor Web servers keep track of their conversations for later use. Like two ships that pass in the night, browsers and servers interact only when a user downloads a Web page, and then they immediately forget the other ever existed!

Cookies — tiny text files that a Web server can store on a client's computer via a Web browser — were designed to change all that. Using cookies to keep track of browser-to-server interactions, Web developers can create intelligent Web sites that "remember" details about each and every user who visits them. You can even create cookies with built-in expiration dates, so that information stored as cookies is maintained for only a limited period of time — say, a week or a month.

The Cookie Sampler

You can use JavaScript, Perl, VBScript, or any other Web-savvy language to store small text files called *cookies* on your site visitor's computer. Because the whole point of using cookies is for server-side applications to keep track of client information, however, cookies are typically created and set by CGI programs rather than by JavaScript scripts. (CGI stands for Common Gateway Interface. CGI programs, which are usually written in either Perl or C/C++, live on Web servers; their job in life is to transmit data back and forth between a Web server and a Web client.) So while typically you interact with existing cookies using JavaScript rather than create them, in "The Repeat Visitor Script" later in this chapter, I show you how to create a script that uses a cookie to identify repeat visitors and greet them by name.

Before I dive into the code, however, I'd like to explain exactly what cookies are and how they work.

Why use cookies?

Cookies allow you to store information about a user's visit on that user's computer and retrieve it later, on subsequent visits. This ability is a boon for Web developers, because it allows them to create Web sites that offer repeat visitors personalized displays.

Two of the most common reasons Web developers use cookies:

✔ **To identify visitors.** You can detect when a user has previously visited your site and customize what that user sees on subsequent visits. For example, you can greet visitors by name, tell them what's changed on your site since their last visit, display customized pages based on their previous purchasing or site navigation habits, and so on.

✔ **To save transaction state.** You can store the status of any lengthy transactions between your site and your visitors' browsers to safeguard against interruptions. For example, imagine that I'm filling out a lengthy form on your Web site when — all of a sudden — my dog chases the cat under my desk. They scuffle, and before I know what's happening, my computer plug comes sailing out of the wall socket! If your site uses cookies, I can throw my beasts out in the backyard, plug my machine back in, reload your Web page — and pick right up where I left off. If your site *doesn't* use cookies, I have to start filling out the form from the beginning.

Cookie security issues

Cookies have been used safely for a few years now, and because their use is strictly governed by Web browsers, they rank mighty low on the list of potential security threats. Still, they are highly controversial in some programmer circles for two reasons:

✔ **Cookies jump the traditional bounds of a Web browser by storing information directly on users' hard drives.** Some folks fear that cookies can damage their computers, either by storing such huge amounts of data on their hard drives that their computers no longer work properly, or by infecting their computers with viruses.

Fortunately, cookies come with built-in safeguards against both these threats! No matter whether you use JavaScript or some other language, you can't get past the following common-sense limits that Web browsers impose:

- **Where cookies are placed.** Internet Explorer 5.5, for example, stores cookies as individual text files and places them in the following directory:

```
C:\Windows\Profiles\[yourUserName]\Cookies
```

Netscape Navigator 6.0 bunches cookies together in a single file, called cookies.txt, and places that file in the following directory:

```
C:\Program Files\Netscape\Users50\default\cookies.txt
```

- **How large cookie files can be**. Both Internet Explorer and Netscape Navigator limit cookie files to 4K.

- **How many cookies any given Web site can place on a user's hard drive.** Both Internet Explorer and Netscape Navigator set the limit at 20 cookies per site, and an overall total of 300 cookies per browser.

- **Which sites have access to cookies.** Cookie visibility is configurable. (You see how to configure cookie access in the "Tasting cookies" section in this chapter.) But no matter how you configure a cookie, the most visible it can ever be is to sites in a single domain. For example, a cookie created by a page at www.someDomain.com can *never* be viewed by a page at www.someOtherDomain.com.

✔ **Cookies enable Web developers to gather detailed marketing information about users without those users' knowledge or consent.** Using cookies in conjunction with client-side applications like CGI programs and Java applets, Web developers can save, examine, and interpret virtually every interaction between a user and a Web site. Every click, every keystroke, every credit card purchase can be used to customize what a user sees the *next* time he visits a cookie-enabled Web site.

Fortunately, users who feel uncomfortable with the Big Brother-like aspect of cookies have a choice: they can configure their browsers to limit cookie support or turn it off altogether. (You see an example of this in the very next section.)

Tasting cookies

One of the best ways to understand how cookies work is to take a look at them from a user's perspective. In this section I show you how to configure cookie support in your browser, visit a cookie-enabled site, and examine an actual cookie file. When you finish, you have all the background you need to be able to jump right into cookie-making JavaScript code!

Configuring cookie support

Netscape Navigator and Internet Explorer both allow users to specify a level of cookie support.

In Netscape Navigator 6.0, you configure cookie support by following these steps:

1. **Click Edit⇨Preferences⇨Advanced⇨Cookies.**

2. **Select one of the following options from the cookie menu that appears, as shown in Figure 6-1:**

   - Accept all cookies

   - Accept only cookies earmarked for return to their originating server (as opposed to any server in the originating domain),

   - Disable cookie support altogether

As you might guess, users who disable cookie support can't benefit from the cookie-accessing scripts you create with JavaScript. One way to alert users that they need to turn on cookie support to get the most out of your site is to tell them! Just include the following sentence to the top of your cookie-enabled Web pages: `This Web site requires you to turn on cookie support.`

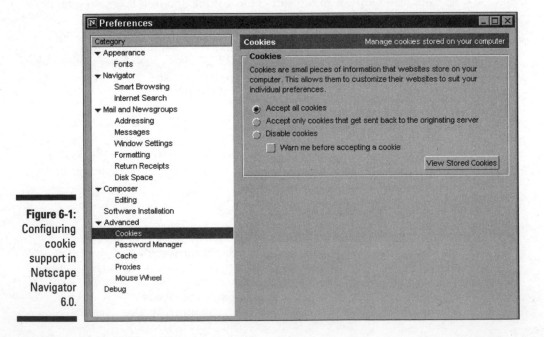

Figure 6-1: Configuring cookie support in Netscape Navigator 6.0.

To configure cookie support in Internet Explorer:

1. **Tools⇨Internet Options.**

2. **Click the Security tab.**

3. **Click on a Web content zone.**

4. **Click Custom Level.**

5. **Scroll down the Security Settings dialog box until you see the cookie options, as shown in Figure 6-2.**

   • **Allow Cookies That Are Stored on Your Computer**

     Disable: Does not allow any cookies to be stored on your computer

     Enable: Allows cookies from any site to be stored on your computer

     Prompt: Tells Internet Explorer to let you know every time a site attempts to store a cookie on your computer so you can allow or disallow each cookie

   • **Allow Per-session Cookies (not stored)**

     Disable: Prohibits any transient cookies to be set up in memory on your computer

     Enable: Allows transient cookies from any and all sites

     Prompt: Specifies that Internet Explorer should alert you every time a site attempts to create a transient cookie so you can allow or disallow each one

Visiting a cookie-enabled site

Once your browser is configured to accept cookies, you can surf to cookie-enabled sites with impunity! Cookies are often used to recognize visitors and present them with a custom greeting and options, as shown in Figure 6-3. (You see how to create a similar custom greeting later in this chapter in "The Repeat Visitor Script.")

Exploring a cookie file

The previous section shows you the results of a site that uses cookies; this section shows you what goes on underneath the covers when you visit a cookie-enabled site.

In Netscape Navigator 6.0, you can examine the cookie file by clicking Edit⇨Preferences⇨Advanced⇨Cookies and clicking the View Stored Cookies button. The resulting Cookie Manager dialog box appears, as shown in figure 6-4.

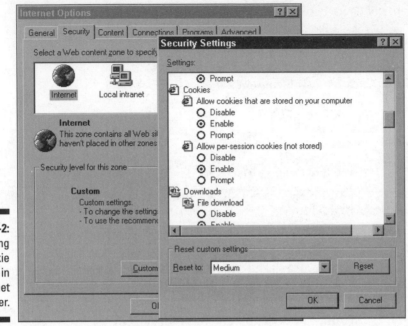

Figure 6-2:
Configuring cookie support in Internet Explorer.

Figure 6-3:
The results of a cookie: a customized greeting from the folks at Amazon. com.

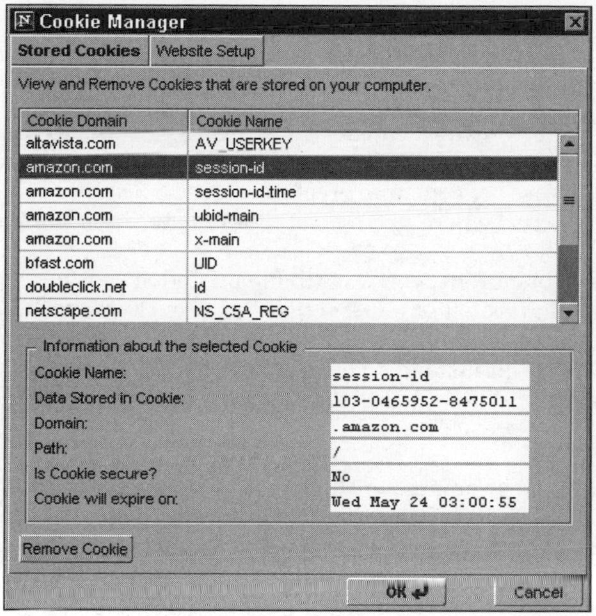

Figure 6-4:
Taking a
look inside
one of the
cookies set
by the
amazon.com
domain.

You can use either of these two additional ways to examine cookies generated by Netscape Navigator:

- ✔ Type JavaScript:alert(document.cookie); in the Netscape search window of a loaded Web page and click Search to see a pop-up window containing all the cookies associated with that page.

- ✔ You can get your hands on the raw cookie file by loading the C:\Program Files\Netscape\Users50\default\cookies.txt (which is the text file in which Netscape Navigator 6.0 stores cookies) into your favorite editor.

Internet Explorer stores individually generated cookie files in the following directory: C:\Windows\Profiles\[*userName*]\Cookies. Cookie filenames take the form of userName@*domain*[*timesAccessed*].txt. For example, on my machine, the following file exists after a visit to Amazon.com:

```
C:\Windows\Profiles\emily\Cookies\emily@amazon[3].txt
```

You can also type JavaScript:alert(document.cookie); In the Address window of Internet Explorer after you have loaded a Web page. When you click Go, you see a pop-up window containing all of the cookies associated with that page.

The Repeat Visitor Script

In this section, you see how to create a script that registers a user by saving the user's name to disk using a cookie. On subsequent visits to the site, the script accesses the cookie from disk, recognizes the user's name, and uses the information to display a custom greeting. Figure 6-5 shows stage one of the repeat visitor script where users must first register their names.

In many real-life applications, you want to create and access cookies using a server-side technology such as a CGI script. Because CGI scripting is beyond the scope of this book, in this chapter I show you how to create and access cookies using JavaScript instead. (The syntax between CGI scripting languages and JavaScript differs, but the basic ways you interact with cookies are the same.)

After users register their names, as shown in Figure 6-5, they never see the registration form again. Users can close their browsers, turn off their machines, and go away on vacation for a week. When they return and attempt to access the registration page again, the script recognizes that they've already registered and loads the For Registered Users Only Page using a customized greeting (see Figure 6-6).

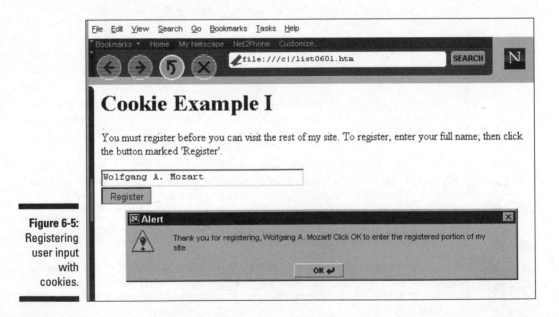

Figure 6-5:
Registering
user input
with
cookies.

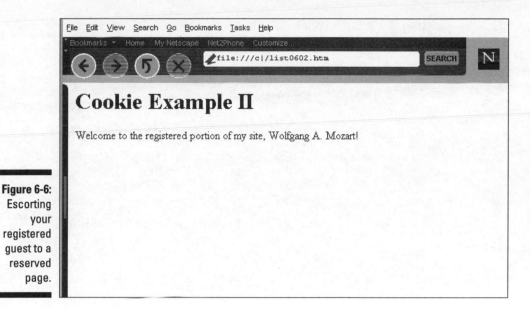

Cookie Example II

Welcome to the registered portion of my site, Wolfgang A. Mozart!

Figure 6-6:
Escorting
your
registered
guest to a
reserved
page.

I implemented the repeat visitor script in two parts based on the two actions in the Figures 6-5 and 6-6:

- ✔ **Cookie Example I ("unregistered users" page).** This script registers a user's name, stores a cookie on that user's machine, and loads the "registered users only" page.

- ✔ **Cookie Example II ("registered users only" page).** This script accesses the cookie and displays a custom greeting.

When you create a cookie, you specify an expiration date. After the specified expiration date, the cookie can no longer be accessed. An expiration of `null` marks a cookie as `transient`. (Transient cookies stay around in memory only as long as the user's browser session lasts; they are not saved to disk.) In the example in Listing 6-1, you see an expiration date of one year from the time the cookie is created.

Those two scripts are shown in Listing 6-1 and 6-2, respectively. You can find the repeat visitor scripts, in their entirety, in list0601.htm and list0602.htm on the companion CD-ROM.

Listing 6-1:   Cookie Example I: The Registration Form

```
<HTML>
<HEAD><TITLE>Cookie Example I: The Registration Page (from
          JavaScript For Dummies, 3rd edition)</TITLE>

<SCRIPT LANGUAGE="JavaScript">
```

(continued)

Listing 6-1 *(continued)*

```
<-- Begin hiding

function getCookieVal (offset) {

    // This function returns the portion of the
    // "myCookie=userName'" string
    // between the = and the ;
    var endstr = document.cookie.indexOf (";", offset);

    if (endstr == -1) {
        endstr = document.cookie.length;
    }

    return unescape(document.cookie.substring(offset,
        endstr));
}

function getCookie (cookieName)  {

    // We have to pick apart the cookie text.  To do this, we
            start
    // by figuring out how many characters are in the string
    // "myCookie="

    var arg = cookieName + "=";
    var argLength = arg.length;

    // Now find out how long the entire cookie string is
    var cookieLength = document.cookie.length;

    // If cookies were stored as objects, life would be much
            easier!
    // As it is, we must step through the contents of a
            cookie
    // character by character to retrieve what is stored
            there.

    var i = 0;

    // While the "i" counter is less than the number of
            characters in
    // the cookie . . .
    while (i < cookieLength) {

        // Offset the "j" counter by the number of characters
            in
        // "myCookie=".
        var j = i + argLength;

        // If you find "myCookie=" in the cookie contents
        if (document.cookie.substring(i, j) == arg) {
            // return the value associated with "myCookie="
```

```
            return getCookieVal(j)
        }
        // i = document.cookie.indexOf(" ", i) + 1;
        //}
        if (i == 0) {
            break
        }
    }
    return null;
}

function setCookie(name, value) {

    // Capture all the arguments passed to the setCookie()
          function.

    var argv = setCookie.arguments;

    // Determine the number of arguments passed into this
          function
    var argc = setCookie.arguments.length;

    // We expect the third argument passed in to be the
    // expiration date.
    // If there isn't a third argument, set the expires
    // variable to null.
    // (An expiration date of null marks a cookie as
    // transient.  Transient cookies are not saved to disk.)
    var expires = (argc > 2) ? argv[2] : null;

    // We expect the fourth argument passed in to be the
          path.
    // If there isn't a fourth argument, set the path
          variable
    // to null.
    var path = (argc > 3) ? argv[3] : null;

    // We expect the fifth argument passed in to be the
          domain.
    // If there isn't a fifth argument, set the domain
          variable
    // to null.
    var domain = (argc > 4) ? argv[4] : null;

    // We expect the sixth argument passed in to be true or
          false,
    // depending on whether this cookie is secure (can be
          transmitted
    // only to a secure server via https) or not.
    // If there isn't a sixth argument, set the secure
          variable
    // to false.
```

(continued)

Listing 6-1 *(continued)*

```javascript
    var secure = (argc > 5) ? argv[5] : false;

    // Set the cookie.
    document.cookie = name + "=" + escape(value) +
        ((expires == null) ? "" : ("; expires=" +
            expires.toGMTString())) +
        ((path == null) ? "" : ("; path=" + path)) +
        ((domain == null) ? "" : ("; domain=" + domain)) +
        ((secure == true) ? "; secure" : ""));
}


function register(userName, value) {

    if (userName == "" || userName == null) {
        // The name is missing, so register this user as
            "Unknown User."
        userName = "Unknown User"
    }

    // If no cookie called 'MyCookie' exists . . .
    if(getCookie('myCookie') == null) {

        // Set the expiration date to today.
        var expdate = new Date()

        // Set the expiration date (which JavaScript stores
            as milliseconds
        // to a date exactly one year in the future.
        expdate.setTime(expdate.getTime() + (1000 * 60 * 60 *
            24 * 365));

        setCookie('myCookie', userName, expdate);
        alert ("Thank you for registering, " + userName + "!
            Click OK to enter the registered portion of my
            site.");

        // Whisk the user to the page reserved for
            registered users.
        location.href = "list0602.htm"

    }
}


///////////////////////////////////////////////////////
// This code checks to see if a cookie named 'myCookie'
// exists on the user's machine.
//
// If it has, the user has already registered, so whisk
// the user to registered-users-only portion of the site.
//
```

```
// If no cookie called 'myCookie' exists on the user's
// machine, ask the user to register.
///////////////////////////////////////////////////////

// If the "myCookie" cookie exists . . .

if(getCookie('myCookie') != null) {

    // Then redirect the user's browser to the
    // password-protected page called "list0602.htm"

    location.href="list0602.htm"
}


// End hiding -->
</SCRIPT>
</HEAD>

<BODY>
//#2 (from here to the closing </BODY> tag)
<H1>Cookie Example I</H1>

<FORM NAME="loginForm">
You must register before you can visit the rest of my site.
        To register, enter your full name; then click the
        button marked 'Register'.
<P>
<INPUT TYPE="text" NAME="fullName" SIZE=35>
<BR>
<INPUT TYPE="button" VALUE="Register"
        onClick="register(loginForm.fullName.value)">
</FORM>
</BODY>
</HTML>
```

Here's a quick run-down on how the JavaScript interpreter handles the code
in Listing 6-1:

1. **The interpreter first checks to see if a cookie named** myCookie **exists.**

   If such a cookie does exist, the interpreter — understanding that this
   user has previously registered — loads list0602.htm.

2. **If no such cookie exists, the interpreter loads the registration page,
   complete with an input field and a button marked Register.**

3. **When a user clicks the Register button, the interpreter begins executing the** register() **function, which in turn invokes the** setCookie()
   method to store a cookie on the user's machine.

   The cookie contains the user's name and an expiration date.

4. **After the** register() **function stores the cookie, the** register()
   function loads the For Registered Users Only page.

Mixing a master cookie recipe

The `cookie` property of the `document` object holds all of the cookies associated with a document.

To create a cookie, you must define a variable/value pair that represents the name of the cookie and the cookie's content (`name=value`). Because cookie values can't contain semicolons, commas, or white space, it's a good idea to use the built-in JavaScript `escape()` function when storing a cookie's value, and the built-in JavaScript unescape() function when retrieving a cookie's value. (`escape()` encodes any semicolons, commas, and white space that exist in a string; `unescape()` reconstitutes them.) Other than this restriction, a cookie value can contain just about anything you like! (Some programmers come up with fancy encryption schemes; others stick with simple text-based strings.)

In addition to the mandatory name and value, you may define the following optional, semicolon-delimited attributes for a cookie (see Table 6-1).

Table 6-1	JavaScript Cookie Attributes
Attribute	*Description*
`expires=`*expirationDate*`;`	The date, in milliseconds, after which the cookie expires (and is deleted by the Web browser). Expiration dates are normally stored in the standard Greenwich Mean Time format. (You format a date in GMT using the `toGMTString()` method of the Date object.)
`path=`*path*`;`	The path of the CGI program to which the cookie contents can be transmitted. The default is the root path of the originating server.
`domain=`*domain*`;`	The domain (for example, `www.acme.com`) to which a cookie can be transmitted. Restricted by default, (see the "Cookie security issues" section for details).
`secure`	Specifies that this cookie can be transmitted only via a secure protocol such as `https`.

To create a cookie and store it on disk, all you need to do is set the `document.cookie` property equal to a string containing the required name/value pair and any optional, semicolon-delimited cookie attributes, as shown in the following code snippet taken from Listing 6-1:

```
document.cookie = name + "=" + escape(value) +
    ((expires == null) ? "" : ("; expires=" +
        expires.toGMTString())) +
    ((path == null) ? "" : ("; path=" + path)) +
    ((domain == null) ? "" : ("; domain=" + domain)) +
    ((secure == true) ? "; secure" : "");
```

The cryptic, odd-looking syntax — `(condition) ? something : somethingElse` — is JavaScript shorthand for "if this condition is true, then add *something*; otherwise, add *somethingElse*."

For example, here's how the JavaScript interpreter interprets the following JavaScript phrase: "If the value for `expires` is null, then add `""` to `document.cookie`; otherwise, add the string `expires=someGMTFormattedDate` to document.cookie:

```
((expires == null) ? "" : ("; expires=" +
            expires.toGMTString()))
```

You can find out more about the conditional `?:` operator in Chapter 3.

You can set attributes for a cookie using JavaScript (specifically, the `expires`, `path`, `domain`, and `secure` attributes, as described in the section "Mixing a master cookie recipe"), but you can't access those attributes using JavaScript. (In contrast, you *can* access a cookie's value, as shown in Listings 6-1 and 6-2.)

After you give out your cookies, only the Web browser is privy to cookie attributes. This seemingly odd state of affairs — being able to set attributes you can't retrieve — actually makes sense, when you think about it. All of these attributes are security-related; preventing them from being altered helps maintain cookies' integrity and safety.

Listing 6-2: Cookie Example II: Displaying the Custom Greeting

```
<HTML>
<HEAD><TITLE>Cookie example II (from JavaScript For Dummies,
        3rd edition)</TITLE>

<SCRIPT LANGUAGE="JavaScript">

<-- Begin hiding

function getCookieVal (offset) {
    var endstr = document.cookie.indexOf (";", offset);
    if (endstr == -1) {
        endstr = document.cookie.length;
    }
```

(continued)

Listing 6-2 *(continued)*

```
        return unescape(document.cookie.substring(offset,
            endstr));
}

function getCookie (name) {


    var arg = name + "=";

    var argLength = arg.length;
    var cookieLength = document.cookie.length;

    var i = 0;
    while (i < cookieLength) {
        var j = i + argLength;
        if (document.cookie.substring(i, j) == arg) {
            return getCookieVal(j)
            i = document.cookie.indexOf(" ", i) + 1;
        }
        if (i == 0) {
            break
        }
    }
    return null;
}



////////////////////////////////////////////////////////////
// This code checks to see if a cookie named 'myCookie'
// exists on the user's machine.
//
// If it has, the user has already "logged in" with a valid
// userid and password, so display the site; otherwise,
// display an error.
////////////////////////////////////////////////////////////

// If the "myCookie" cookie exists . . .

// #1 (down to document.write(documentText)

var nameOfVisitor = getCookie('myCookie')

insert // #2 (down to closing brace associated with if
            statement)
if(nameOfVisitor != null) {

    var documentText = "<BODY><H1>Cookie Example
            II</H1>Welcome to the registered portion of my
            site, "
    documentText += nameOfVisitor
    documentText += "!</BODY>"
}
```

```
insert // #3 (down to closing brace associated with else
        statement)
else {
   var documentText = "<BODY><H1>Cookie Example II</H1>Sorry!
        Only registered users can access this
        page.</BODY>"
}

document.write(documentText)

// End hiding -->
</SCRIPT>
</HEAD>
</HTML>
```

In Listing 6-2, here's what's going on:

1. The JavaScript interpreter looks for a cookie named myCookie on the user's machine.

2. If a cookie named myCookie exists, the JavaScript interpreter constructs and displays a custom greeting using the registered user's name.

3. If no such cookie exists, the JavaScript interpreter constructs an error message.

You can't expire me . . . I quit!

You can't delete a cookie directly using JavaScript, for the simple reason that only browsers can actually write to disk. (It's this security measure that prevents cookies from being able to wreak havoc on users' hard drives.)

What you *can* do in JavaScript is to alter a cookie's expiration date to a date far in the past. Doing so will cause the Web browser to delete the newly expired cookie automatically.

```
function deleteCookie () {
    var expired = new Date();
    // You can't delete a cookie file directly from the user's
    // machine using JavaScript, so mark it as expired by
    // setting the expiration date to a date in the past.

    // First, set the exp variable to a date in the past . . .
    expired.setTime (expired.getTime() - 1000000000);

    // Then, get the cookie
    var cookieValue = getCookie ('myCookie');

    // Finally, set the cookie's expiration date to the long-past
    date.
    document.cookie ='myCookie' + "=" + cookieValue + ";
                    expires=" + expired.toGMTString();

}
```

Part III

Making Your Web Pages Interactive

The 5th Wave   By Rich Tennant

"OH, I'LL GET US IN — I USED TO RUN TECH SUPPORT AT AN INTERNET ACCESS COMPANY."

In this part . . .

In this part, you find practical ways to create Web pages that respond appropriately to user interaction. Chapter 7 shows you how to create push buttons that kick off scripts each time users click on them. In Chapters 8 and 9 you see how to use JavaScript to make graphic images respond when users click on, or drag their mouse over, those images. Chapter 10 rounds out this part by showing you how to gather and verify input from the folks who visit your Web site — including time-tested tips to help you design user-friendly Web pages and communicate effectively with your users.

Chapter 7

Button Up!

In This Chapter

▶ Getting acquainted with HTML button elements

▶ Understanding JavaScript event handlers

▶ Attaching event handlers to HTML `button`, `submit`, `reset`, and `radio` elements

As you probably know if you've had a chance to dip into any of the other chapters in this book, JavaScript helps you transform static Web pages into interactive Web-based applications. And, what's the feature that makes this client-side interactivity possible? The humble and lovable *event handler*. You can think of event handlers as little software bungee cords that bind custom JavaScript code to *events* such as clicking a button or a link, loading a page, typing data into an input field, and so on.

You see examples of event handlers throughout this book; for now, in this chapter, I focus on the event handlers most developers want to explore first — the event handlers associated with HTML buttons. Here you find out how to create and attach essential scripts not just to `button` and `radio` elements, but the all-important form-controlling `submit` and `reset` elements, as well.

Pick A Button — Any Button!

HTML defines a handful of `button` elements: push buttons, radio buttons, and two special built-in buttons, `submit` and `reset`. Each of these buttons — when accompanied by a JavaScript event handler definition — allows visitors to your Web site to interact with your page.

Here's how it works. In the life of a button, several *events* can occur. That button can be clicked, double-clicked, receive input focus, and lose input focus, for example. JavaScript event handlers can detect and handle each of these separate events — click, double click, focus, and blur. Take a look at the following code to see what I mean.

```
<INPUT TYPE="button" NAME="pushButton" VALUE="Push me!"
onClick="doSomething()"
```

The preceding statement, which is a mixture of HTML syntax and inline JavaScript code, defines an HTML button element. Along with the TYPE, NAME, and VALUE attributes, this statement defines an onClick event handler for the button. At runtime, when a user clicks the button marked Push Me, the JavaScript interpreter automatically calls the function doSomething().

JavaScript statements assigned to an event handler, like the one shown above, are the only JavaScript statements that can appear outside the bounds of the beginning and ending <SCRIPT> . . . </SCRIPT> tags.

Table 7-1 lists all of the button-related events you can handle using JavaScript. (A full description of those events appears in the sidebar, "Handling the big events on page and screen!")

In the section, "Custom tailored buttons: the button and radio elements," I show you in detail how to define event handlers for the button and radio elements. Because the reset and submit buttons work differently, they merit their own discussion; I cover them in the section, "Off-the-rack buttons: the reset and submit elements."

Table 7-1	HTML Button-related Event Handlers	
Element	**HTML Definition**	**Supported event handlers**
button	<INPUT TYPE="button" . . . >	onClick
		onDblClick
		onMouseDown
		onMouseUp
		onFocus
		onBlur
radio	<INPUT TYPE="radio" . . . >	(same as button)
reset	<INPUT TYPE="reset" . . . >	(same as button)
submit	<INPUT TYPE="submit" . . . >	(same as button)
form	<FORM . . . >	onReset
		onSubmit

Netscape Navigator and Internet Explorer provide different levels of support for event handlers, as they do so many other features of JavaScript (and HTML and HTML extensions and . . . Well, you get the picture). Additionally, because event handling is inherently platform-dependent, browsers implemented on Macintosh and Unix systems offer differing levels of support for events. The bad news: at the time of this writing, neither Microsoft nor Netscape currently offers an up-to-date reference that thoroughly documents implemented JavaScript event handling support for the latest versions of Navigator or Internet Explorer. The good news? Most of the events you want to handle using JavaScript are documented in the following sidebar. For additional event handling information, visit the respective browsers' site:

```
http://developer.netscape.com/docs/manuals/js/client/jsref/
           handlers.htm
```

```
http://msdn.microsoft.com/workshop/author/dhtml/reference/
           events.asp
```

Handling the big events on page and screen!

Buttons aren't the only client-side objects that support event handlers; forms, images, and many other objects do, as well, as shown in Table 7-2.

Table 7-2	Client-side Objects that Support Event Handlers	
Event handler	*Supporting objects*	*Event (event handler triggered when . . .)*
onAbort	Image	The image loading is interrupted.
onBlur	Button, Checkbox, FileUpload, Password, Radio, Reset Select, Submit, Text, Textarea, window (frame)	The element loses input focus (clicking out of, or tabbing away from, an element takes away that element's input focus).
onChange	Checkbox, FileUpload, Password, Radio, Select, Text, Textarea	The element changes (for example, the user types text into a Text element or clicks on a Radio button) *and* loses input focus.

(continued)

Table 7-2 *(continued)*

Event handler	Supporting objects	Event (event handler triggered when . . .)
onClick	Button, Checkbox, document, FileUpload, Image, Link, Password, Radio, Reset, Select, Submit, Text, Textarea	The element is clicked a single time (combination of onMouseDown and onMouseUp).
onDblClick	Button, Checkbox, document, FileUpload, Image, Link, Password, Radio, Reset, Select, Submit, Text, Textarea	The element is clicked twice in quick succession (double-clicked).
onError	Image	The image doesn't finish loading, for some reason (perhaps the image file doesn't exist or is corrupted).
onFocus	Button, Checkbox, FileUpload, Frame, Password, Radio, Reset, Select, Submit, Text, Textarea, window (frame)	The element gains input focus.
onKeyDown	Button, Checkbox, document, FileUpload, Image, Link, Password, Radio, Reset, Select, Submit, Text, Textarea	The user presses a key.
onKeyPress	Button, Checkbox, document, FileUpload, Image, Link, Password, Radio, Reset, Select, Textarea	The user presses and releases a key (combination of the onKeyDown and onKeyUp event handlers).
onKeyUp	Button, Checkbox, document, FileUpload, Image, Link, Password, Radio, Reset, Select, Submit, Text, Textarea	The user releases a previously-pressed key.
onLoad	Image, window (frame)	The element loads successfully.

Event handler	Supporting objects	Event (event handler triggered when . . .)
onMouseDown	Button, Checkbox, document, FileUpload, Image (and Area), Link, Password, Radio, Reset, Select,Submit, Text, Textarea	The user presses a mouse button (but doesn't release it).
onMouseOut	Image (and Area), Link	The mouse moves off the element.
onMouseOver	Image (and Area), Link	The mouse moves over the element.
onMouseUp	Button, Checkbox, document, FileUpload, Image (and Area, Link, Password, Radio, Reset, Select, Submit, Text, Textarea	The user releases a previously-clicked mouse button.
onMove	window (frame)	The user moves or resizes the window or frame.
onReset	form	The form is reset; either the user clicks a reset button, or the programmer invoked the form.reset() method.
onResize	window (frame)	The user resizes the window or frame.
onSubmit	form	The form is submitted; either the user clicks a submit button, or the programmer invoked the form.submit() method.
onUnload	window	The user unloads a document (either by closing the browser or by loading another document).

Custom tailored buttons: The button and radio elements

Attaching event handlers to the button and radio elements is the easiest and best way to experiment with event handling in JavaScript.

The code in Listing 7-1 shows a script that defines a set of radio buttons and a regular push button, all of which are associated with event handlers. Take a look at Figures 7-1 and 7-2 to see this code in action! Figure 7-1 shows this JavaScript-enabled page contains a button element and three radio elements.

Figures 7-2 and 7-3 show the use of alert boxes that react to the users actions on the page.

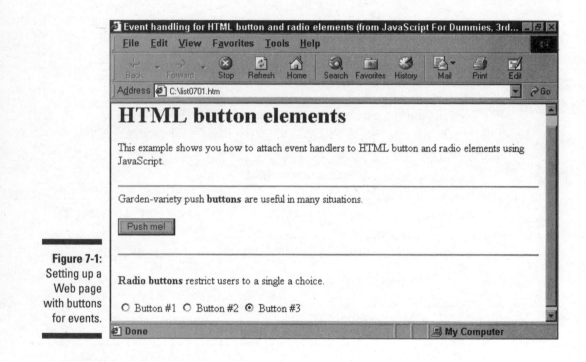

Figure 7-1:
Setting up a
Web page
with buttons
for events.

Figure 7-2:
Clicking the
button
marked
Push Me
invokes the
button
element's
onClick
event
handler.

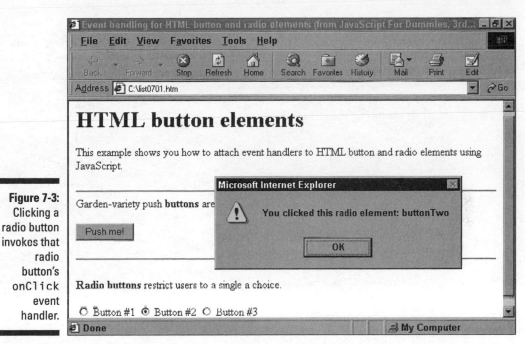

Figure 7-3: Clicking a radio button invokes that radio button's `onClick` event handler.

Load the file list0701.htm from the companion CD to see how the example in Listing 7-1 appears in *your* browser.

Listing 7-1: **Creating** `onClick` **Event Handlers for Button and Radio Elements**

```
<HTML>
<HEAD><TITLE>Event handling for HTML button and radio
            elements (from JavaScript For Dummies, 3rd
            edition)</TITLE>
<SCRIPT LANGUAGE="JavaScript">

///////////////////////////////////////////////////////
// You can alter this script to exercise any event
// handler associated with a button element.  (A list
// of all the event handlers associated with buttons
// is provided in Chapter 7 of JavaScript For Dummies,
// 3rd edition.)
//
// To see the onDblClick event handler in action, for
// instance, all you need to do is replace (inside
// the HTML button declaration)
//
// onClick="showEvent(this, 'click')"
//
```

(continued)

Listing 7-1 *(continued)*

```
// with
//
// onDblClick="showEvent(this, 'double click')"
//////////////////////////////////////////////////

function showEvent(incomingButton, event) {

    alert("You " + event + "ed this " + incomingButton.type +
          " element: " + incomingButton.value)
}

</SCRIPT>

</HEAD>
<BODY>
<FORM NAME="myForm">
<H1>HTML button elements</H1>
<P>
This example shows you how to attach event handlers to HTML
            button and radio elements using JavaScript.
<P>
<HR>
Garden-variety push <B>buttons</B> are useful in many
            situations.
<P>
<INPUT TYPE="button" NAME="pushButton" VALUE="Push me!"
// the onClick event handler for the button
onClick="showEvent(this, 'click')"
>
<P>
<HR>
<P>
<B>Radio buttons</B> restrict users to a single a choice.
<P>
<INPUT TYPE="radio" NAME="radioGroup" VALUE="buttonOne"
// the onClick event handler for the first radio button
onClick="showEvent(this, 'click')"
> Button #1

<INPUT TYPE="radio" NAME="radioGroup" VALUE="buttonTwo"
// the onClick event handler for the second radio button

onClick="showEvent(this, 'click')"
> Button #2

<INPUT TYPE="radio" NAME="radioGroup" VALUE="buttonThree"
// the onClick event handler for the third radio button

onClick="showEvent(this, 'click')"
> Button #3
```

```
</FORM>
</BODY>
</HTML>
```

Looking at Listing 7-1, you see four different button definitions: one `button` element, and three `radio` button elements. Inserted in each one of these HTML definitions is the following line of event handler-defining JavaScript code:

```
onClick="showEvent(this, 'click')"
```

This line of code causes the JavaScript interpreter to call the `showEvent()` function as soon as the user clicks the associated button. The built-in JavaScript value `this` is sent to `showEvent()` along with the string `'click'`, which enables the `showEvent()` function to create and display the customized messages you see in Figures 7-2 and 7-3.

Note that the value for the `onClick` event handler must be surrounded by quotes. (Single quotes work, but double quotes, as shown, are standard programming practice.)

You can set the value for an `onClick` event handler to any valid JavaScript statement. You can even set the value to a string of statements, as long as you separate them with semicolons, like this:

```
onClick="showEvent(this, 'click'); somethingElse();
         doThisNow()"
```

(Check out Chapter 2 for more information on the `this` keyword.)

Off-the-rack buttons: The reset and submit elements

The `reset` and `submit` elements are special buttons which, when clicked, reset and submit HTML forms, respectively. (It's nice to know some things still do what they say.)

Keep in mind that because no CGI script is specified in the <BODY> of the HTML document shown in this example (Listing 7-2), form data is not actually submitted to a Web server; the only result from clicking the Submit button is a change in the Address field shown in Figure 7-5 and the document reloading. "The Order Form Script" section describes the HTML necessary to transmit form data to a Web server via a CGI script when a user clicks the Submit button.

As you can see from Table 7-1, the reset and submit elements support the same event handlers that all the buttons support: `onClick`, `onDblClick`, `onMouseDown`, `onMouseUp`, `onFocus`, and `onBlur`. But the event handlers associated with resetting and submitting a form (`onReset` and `onSubmit`) are associated not with the reset and submit buttons, as you might expect; instead, they are associated with the HTML form being reset or submitted.

The code in Listing 7-2 shows a script that defines a few radio buttons, a submit button, and a reset button. The code you see in Listing 7-2 is located on the companion CD (in a file named list0702.htm).

If you choose to load the code in Listing 7-2 in your own browser, you notice that the built-in Reset and Submit functions occur *after* the event handling instructions finish processing. For example, clicking the reset button displays a message *and* resets the form; clicking the submit button displays a message *and* submits the form.

Listing 7-2:   Attaching onReset **and** onSubmit
                 Event Handlers to the form **Object**

```
<HTML>
<HEAD><TITLE>HTML reset and submit elements (from JavaScript
          For Dummies, 3rd edition)</TITLE>
</HEAD>
<BODY>
<FORM NAME="myForm" onReset="alert('You pushed reset')"
          onSubmit="alert('You pushed submit')" >
<H1>HTML button elements</H1>
<P>
<HR>
<P>
<B>Radio buttons</B> restrict users to a single a choice.
<P>
<INPUT TYPE="radio" NAME="radioGroup" VALUE="buttonOne"
> Button #1

<INPUT TYPE="radio" NAME="radioGroup" VALUE="buttonTwo"
> Button #2

<INPUT TYPE="radio" NAME="radioGroup" VALUE="buttonThree"
> Button #3

<P>
<HR>
<P>
<B>Submit buttons</B> automatically submit form contents to
          the CGI program defined in the HTML <BODY> tag, if
          any.
<P>
<INPUT TYPE="submit" NAME="submitButton">
<P>
<HR>
<P>
<B>Reset buttons</B> allow users to clear a form and start
          fresh.
<P>
<INPUT TYPE="reset" NAME="resetButton">
</FORM>
</BODY>
</HTML>
```

The code in Listing 7-2 associates the onReset and onSubmit event handlers with the form named myForm.

The JavaScript interpreter automatically executes the code associated with the onReset event handler when the user clicks the reset button, and the code associated with the onSubmit event handler when the user clicks the submit button. Take a look at Figures 7-4 and 7-5 to see an example of what happens when you click the Submit button; it executes the onSubmit event handler associated with the form. Clicking the Reset button resets the form by clearing any radio buttons or other form elements the user has set by executing the onReset event handler associated with the form.

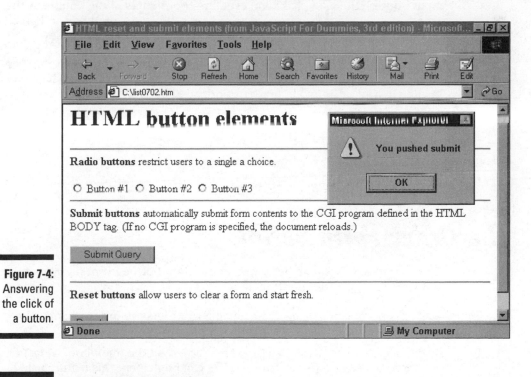

Figure 7-4:
Answering
the click of
a button.

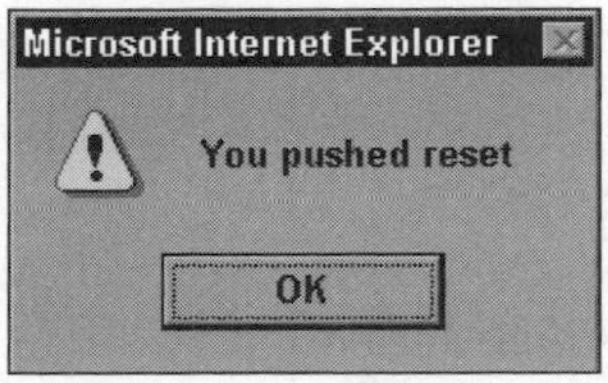

Figure 7-5:
Responding
to events
lets your
users know
the action is
successful.

In most cases, you want to perform more sophisticated processing than a simple pop-up message when a form is reset or submit; for example, you might want to check the contents of the form and stop the submission process if certain conditions aren't met. The order form script described in the next section shows you how to just that!

Both Navigator and Internet Explorer support the concept of an Event object designed for advanced event-handling scenarios. In theory, you can use the Event object to capture and examine nitty-gritty details about an event that has occurred. For example, if a user clicks a mouse button, you can use the methods and properties associated with the Event object to determine which mouse button the user clicks and even the coordinates of the pointer at the time of the click. If a user presses a key, you can use the methods and properties associated with the Event object to determine which key (or key combination) your visitor presses; and so on. JavaScript support for the Event object isn't well defined, stable, or consistent between browsers at the time of this writing. For more information on the Event object and how it's implemented in Navigator and Internet Explorer, respectively, visit

```
http://developer.netscape.com/docs/manuals/js/client/jsref/ev
          ent.htm
```

```
http://msdn.microsoft.com/workshop/author/dhtml/reference/obj
          ects/obj_event.asp.
```

The Order Form Script

This example brings together the most common button event handlers to simulate a real-world order form that:

- ✔ Accepts a user's name and a number of widgets to order, as shown in Figure 7-6.

- ✔ Calculates and displays a total price based on the number of widgets ordered, as shown in Figure 7-7. You can implement this feature using the onClick event handler associated with the button element.

- ✔ Pops up helpful descriptions when the user tabs to or clicks the mailing options, as shown in Figure 7-8. This feature uses the onFocus event handler associated with the radio element.

- ✔ Resets global variables used in the price calculation when the user clicks the Reset button. This feature is implemented using the onReset event handler associated with the form element.

- ✔ Checks to make sure the user enters a valid number of widgets before submitting the form, as shown in Figures 7-9 (before) and 7-10 (after). This feature uses the onSubmit event handler associated with the form element.

The examples in Chapter 10 extend this example even further by providing a handful of common input validation scripts.

The sample code in Listing 7-3 is located on the companion CD (list0703.htm). Check it out! The order form example demonstrates the `onClick`, `onFocus`, `onReset`, and `onSubmit` event handlers.

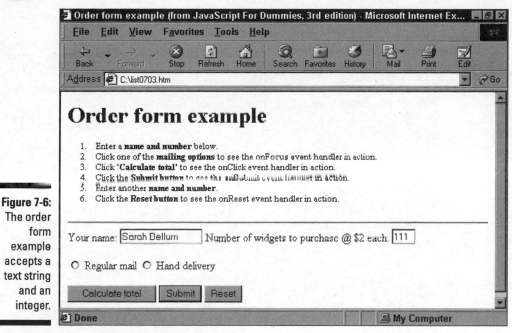

Figure 7-6:
The order form example accepts a text string and an integer.

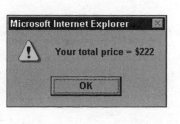

Figure 7-7:
The onClick event handler of the Calculate Price button calculates widget price.

Listing 7-3: Creating the Interactive Order Form with Event Handlers

```
<HTML>
<HEAD><TITLE>Order form example (from JavaScript For Dummies,
          3rd edition)</TITLE>
<SCRIPT LANGUAGE="JavaScript">

// Declare a global value
var numWidgets

function clearGlobalValues() {

    ////////////////////////////////////////////////////////

    // Set the global variable to an empty string

    ////////////////////////////////////////////////////////

    numWidgets=""
}

function checkOrder() {

    ////////////////////////////////////////////////////////
    // If the user ordered something, go ahead and submit the
    // form data to the server; otherwise, don't bother.
    ////////////////////////////////////////////////////////

    if (numWidgets == "" || numWidgets == null || numWidgets
          == 0) {
      alert("Please specify a number of widgets to order and
          click Submit again.")
      return false
    }
    else {
      ////////////////////////////////////////////////////
      // If this script defines values for the METHOD and
          ACTION
      // attributes associated with the HTML <FORM> element,
      // the form contents are automatically sent to the CGI
          script
      // specified by the value for the ACTION attribute.
      //
      // For example, if this script defined the following
      // <FORM> definition, the form contents would
          automatically
      // be transmitted to the tmail.cgi CGI script located
          on
      // the /cgi-bin/tmail directory (of the Web server on
```

```
        // which this HTML file is located).
        //
        // <FORM NAME="myForm"
        // onSubmit="return checkOrder()"
        // METHOD="POST"
        // ACTION="/cgi-bin/tmail/tmail.cgi">
        //////////////////////////////////////////////////

        alert("Thank you for your order!")
        return true
    }

}

function calcTotalPrice() {

    //////////////////////////////////////////////////

    // Set the global variable "numWidgets" equal to the
         value
    // the user typed in (unless the user typed in a value
    // earlier; then don't set it).

    //////////////////////////////////////////////////

    if (!numWidgets) {
        numWidgets = document.myForm.numberWidgets.value
    }

    alert("Your total price = $" + (numWidgets * 2))
}

</SCRIPT>

</HEAD>
<BODY>

<FORM NAME="myForm" onSubmit="return checkOrder()"
                    onReset="clearGlobalValues()">

<H1>Order form example</H1>
<FONT SIZE="2">
<OL>
<LI>Enter a <B>name and number</B> below.
<LI>Click one of the <B>mailing options</B> to see the
         onFocus event handler in action.
<LI>Click <B>'Calculate total'</B> to see the onClick event
         handler in action.
```

(continued)

Listing 7-3 *(continued)*

```
<LI>Click the <B>Submit button</B> to see the onSubmit event
          handler in action.
<LI>Enter another <B>name and number</B>.
<LI>Click the <B>Reset button</B> to see the onReset event
          handler in action.
</OL>
</FONT>
<HR>
Your name:
<INPUT TYPE="text" SIZE="15" NAME="userName">
Number of widgets to purchase @ $2 each:
<INPUT TYPE="text" SIZE="3" NAME="numberWidgets">
<P>
<INPUT TYPE="radio" NAME="mailOptions" VALUE="regular"

onFocus="alert('There is no extra charge for this option.')">
          Regular mail
<INPUT TYPE="radio" NAME="mailOptions" VALUE="regular"

onFocus="alert('Please note that hand delivery is not
          available for non-U.S. orders')"> Hand delivery
<P>
<INPUT TYPE="button"  NAME="calcTotal" VALUE="Calculate
          total"
onClick="calcTotalPrice()">
<INPUT TYPE="submit" VALUE="Submit">
<INPUT TYPE="reset">
</FORM>
</BODY>
</HTML>
```

One important thing to keep in mind when implementing the onSubmit event handler: the only way you can prevent the submission process is to return a value of false (0) from the event handling code.

Take a look at the statement from Listing 7-3 that defines the onSubmit event handler:

```
onSubmit="return checkOrder()"
```

See the return right before the call to the checkOrder() function? That return keyword accepts the return value from checkOrder() and passes it back to the Web browser to let the Web browser know whether it can submit the form data or not. A return value of 0 (or false) prevents the data from being submitted; a non-zero value like true (1) gives the Web browser the go-ahead to submit the form data. If you forget to add in the return keyword as shown in the statement above, checkOrder() checks the user's input data and then submits the form anyway, regardless of its findings!

You can prevent the Web browser from automatically resetting a form or following a link as easily as you can prevent it from automatically submitting a form. To do so, just include the return keyword and return a value of false to the onReset event handler associated with the form element or the onClick event handler associated with a link element.

The Submit button is hardwired in Web browsers to submit all of the elements in a form to the server-side program defined for the ACTION attribute of the HTML <FORM> tag. For example, the following <FORM> definition causes all of the myForm data to be sent automatically to the tmail.cgi CGI script on submission. (The value for METHOD affects how form data is sent to that CGI script.)

```
<FORM NAME="myForm"
onSubmit="return checkOrder()"
METHOD="POST"
ACTION="/cgi-bin/tmail/tmail.cgi">
```

Figure 7-8:
The
onFocus
event
handler
displays a
helpful
message as
soon as the
user tabs to
the first
radio button.

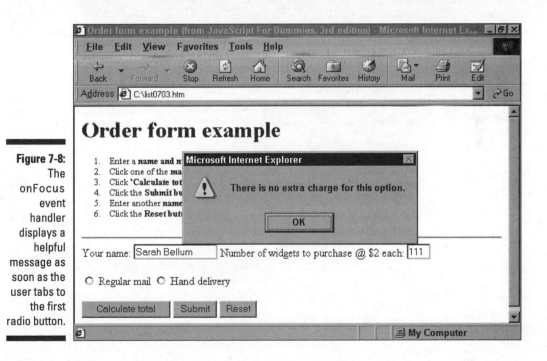

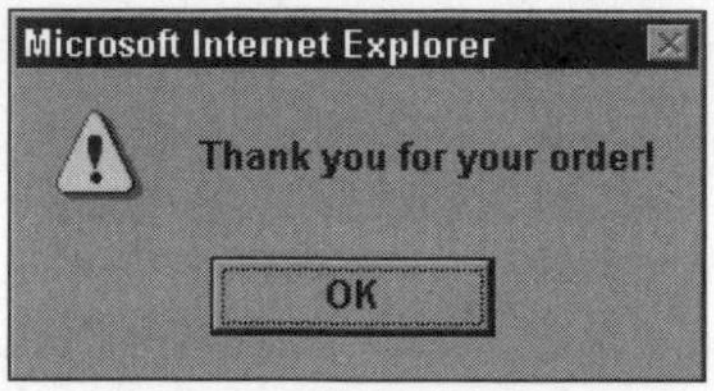

Figure 7-9:
The
onSubmit
event
handler
verifies form
data before
submitting it.

Figure 7-10:
The result of
the form
submission
process
(note the
change in
the contents
of the
Address
field).

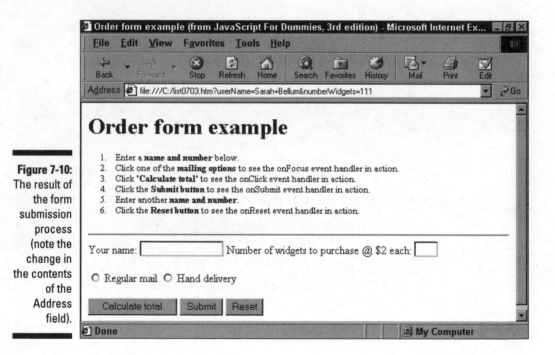

Chapter 8

Picture Perfect

· ·

In This Chapter

▶ Making images clickable using JavaScript

▶ Creating interactive navigation bars

▶ Exploring JavaScript mouse event handlers

· ·

As anyone who's surfed the Web can tell you, a good picture *is* worth a thousand words. Images add visual punch to your site. They also let you incorporate information that would be downright impossible to present as well using any other way. (Can you imagine trying to describe a collection of antique lamps without using photo images?)

Because images are represented as programmable objects in JavaScript, you can go the static image one better and create *interactive* images: images that respond appropriately when a user clicks or drags a mouse over them. Read on for all the juicy details!

A Picture by Any Other Name

You add a picture to a Web page by including the `<IMG>` tag into your HTML source code, like this:

```
<IMG SRC="somePicture.jpg" . . . >
```

For example, take a look at HTML snippet shown in Listing 8-1, which appears in full on the CD as list0801.htm:

Listing 8-1: Creating an Image Object with the HTML `<IMG>` Tag

```
. . .
<IMG SRC="splash.jpg" WIDTH=241 HEIGHT=208
    TITLE="Essential resources for the professional and
            aspiring writer"
    ALT="Writing for the Web splash image"
>
```

The code you see in Listing 8-1 accomplishes these:

- ✔ Inserts an image file named splash.jpg into a space 241 pixels wide by 208 pixels high using the SRC, HEIGHT, and WIDTH attributes of the <IMG> tag, respectively.

- ✔ Defines a tooltip message using the TITLE attribute of the <IMG> tag. The contents of the TITLE attribute appear automatically when a user running Microsoft Internet Explorer mouses over this image.

- ✔ Defines an alternate text description for the image using the ALT attribute of the <IMG> tag. The contents of the ALT attribute appear in browsers that can't display images, as well as in browsers that have been configured not to display images and in situations where an image just plain doesn't exist. Figure 8-2 shows you how the code in Listing 8-1 appears in Internet Explorer 5.5 with image loading turned off.

Check out Figure 8-1 to see how the line of HTML code in Listing 8-1 appears in Internet Explorer 5.5. Placing your mouse cursor over an image in Internet Explorer displays the contents of the image's TITLE attribute.

Picture this

One thing to keep in mind when you create interactive images with JavaScript is that users have the ability to turn off image loading in their browsers. If you rely on an image to convey the bulk of your page's information and interactivity, and your users have configured their browsers so that images don't appear, your page will be ineffective, to say the least!

If you're wondering why a Web surfer would choose not to see images, it's because image files are relatively large and take a long time to download at modest connection speeds. Not every user has a cable modem; plenty of us are making do with 56K dial-up connections that are subject to occasional cut-offs! Because images are often gratuitous (yours won't be, I'm sure!), users without a lot of time to spend may choose to turn off image loading in order to get their online tasks accomplished in the shortest amount of time.

These are the steps your users take to turn off image loading:

Navigator users

1. Click Edit⇨Preferences

2. Click the Advanced option

3. Uncheck the checkbox next to Automatically load images.

Internet Explorer users

1. Click Tools⇨Internet Options

2. Click the Advanced tab.

3. Scroll down to Multimedia and uncheck the checkbox next to Show Pictures.

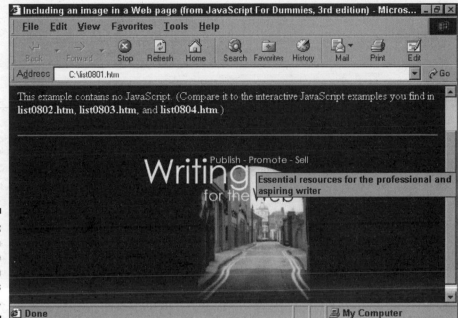

Including an image in a Web page (from JavaScript For Dummies, 3rd edition) - Micros...

File   Edit   View   Favorites   Tools   Help

Back   Forward   Stop   Refresh   Home   Search   Favorites   History   Mail   Print   Edit

Address   C:\list0801.htm   Go

This example contains no JavaScript. (Compare it to the interactive JavaScript examples you find in list0802.htm, list0803.htm, and list0804.htm.)

Writing for the Web

Publish - Promote - Sell

Essential resources for the professional and aspiring writer

Done   My Computer

Figure 8-1:
Displaying a
message
based on
the mouse's
location.

For up-to-the-minute details on support for the Image object in Navigator and Internet Explorer, check out these sites:

```
http://developer.netscape.com/docs/manuals/js/client/jsref/im
           age.htm
```

```
http://msdn.microsoft.com/workshop/author/dhtml/reference/obj
           ects/img.asp
```

As you can see from Figures 8-1 and 8-2, the TITLE attribute you define as part of the HTML <IMG> tag provides a bit of interactivity. It displays a helpful message automatically when a user running Internet Explorer mouses over the defined image.

But what if you want more interactivity? What if you want to display your helpful message more discreetly — say, at the bottom of the window? (Some professional Web designers consider this approach less confusing to Web novices than creating a message that temporarily obscures everything around the mouse pointer.) What if you want different parts of an image to pop up *different* messages or respond to different mouse clicks?

Well, you're in luck: those scenarios are tailor-made for JavaScript! As you see in the following sections, making plain old HTML images interactive is a simple matter of adding a few JavaScript event handlers.

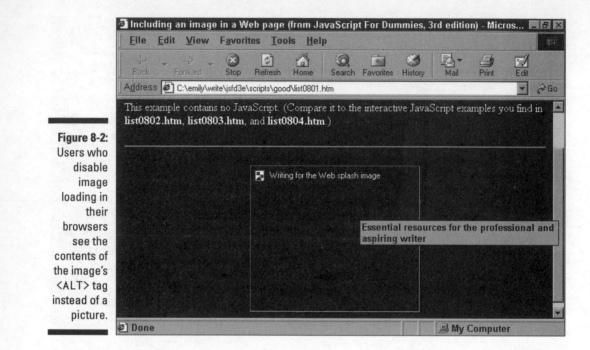

Figure 8-2:
Users who disable image loading in their browsers see the contents of the image's <ALT> tag instead of a picture.

The Splash Page Script

In this section, you see how to create an image that meets these demands:

✔ Displays a message in the status bar of the document window when a user rolls the mouse pointer over the image.

✔ Responds to a mouse click.

Figures 8-3 and 8-4 show how the interactive image you create in this section appears in Netscape Navigator.

The code in Listing 8-2 creates the pages in these figures by attaching JavaScript code to an image's event handlers, which makes that image respond to mouse events.

Listing 8-2:   Responding to Mouse Events

```
<HTML>
<HEAD>

<TITLE>Using mouse event handlers to create clickable images
        (from JavaScript For Dummies, 3rd edition)</TITLE>

</HEAD>
<BODY BGCOLOR="black" TEXT="white">
```

```
<H1>Creating clickable images</H1>
Rolling your mouse pointer over the image causes a message to
        display at the bottom of the window (in a property
        of the window called the <B>status</B> bar).
        Clicking anywhere on the image causes a pop-up
        message to display.
<P>
<HR>
<P>
<CENTER>

<IMG SRC="splash.jpg" HEIGHT=208 WIDTH=241
//onClick event handler definition
    onClick="alert('Writing for the Web is an online resource
        that helps professional writers publish, promote,
        and sell their work online.')"
    TITLE="Essential resources for the professional and
        aspiring writer"
    ALT="Writing for the Web splash image"
//onMouseOver event handler definition
    onMouseOver="window.status='Click to find out more about
        us!'; return true"
//onMouseOver event handler definition
    onMouseOut="window.status=''; return true"

>
</CENTER>
</BODY>
</HTML>
```

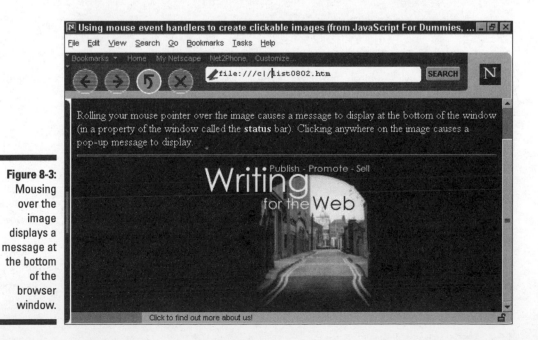

Figure 8-3:
Mousing
over the
image
displays a
message at
the bottom
of the
browser
window.

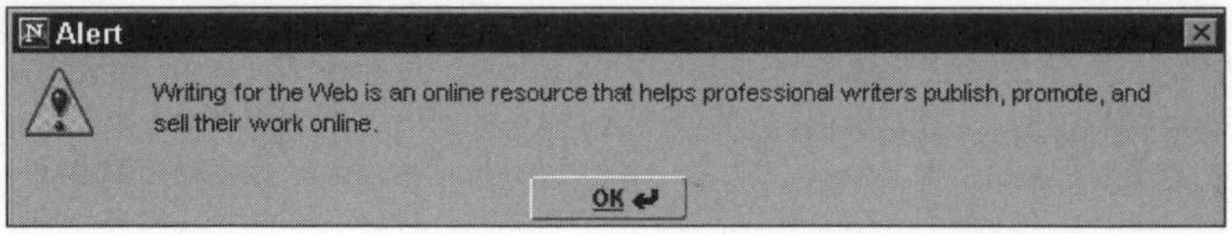

Figure 8-4:
Clicking
anywhere
on the
image
displays a
pop-up alert
message.

N Alert

⚠ Writing for the Web is an online resource that helps professional writers publish, promote, and sell their work online.

OK ↵

Three different event handlers are responsible for the image behavior you see in Figures 8-3 and 8-4: onClick, onMouseOver, and onMouseOut.

onDonner, onDasher, onPrancer, onClick

The onClick event handler responds to the click event. In other words, when a user clicks a mouse while the mouse pointer is positioned anywhere on the associated element (in this case, the splash page image), the JavaScript code associated with the onClick event handler executes automatically.

Listing 8-2 defines the message that appears in the alert box shown in Figure 8-4 by the following JavaScript statement:

```
<IMG SRC="splash.jpg" HEIGHT=208 WIDTH=241
   . . .
onClick="alert('Writing for the Web is an online resource
        that helps professional writers publish, promote,
        and sell their work online.')"
```

Other actions you might want the click event to trigger including sending an e-mail message to someone or loading another Web page. "The Best Navigation Bar None," coming up in this chapter, shows you how to do both!

The mouse detective I: onMouseOver

The onMouseOver event handler responds to the mouseover event. In other words, when users move the mouse pointer anywhere over the associated element (in this case, the splash page image), the JavaScript code associated with the onMouseOver event handler executes automatically.

Here is the line of code from Listing 8-2 responsible for the message you see displayed at the bottom of the browser window in Figure 8-3:

```
<IMG SRC="splash.jpg" HEIGHT=208 WIDTH=241
  . . .
onMouseOver="window.status='Click to find out more about
        us!'; return true"
```

The semicolon-delimited JavaScript code associated with the onMouseOver event handler shown here does these two things:

- ✔ Sets the status property of the window object equal to the message string "Click to find out more about us!" and displays the message at the bottom of the browser window, as shown in Figure 8-3.

- ✔ Returns a value of true to the onMouseOver event handler. This statement (return true) is required by pre-5.5 Internet Explorer and pre-6.0x Navigator browsers; leaving it off causes these older browsers to ignore the onMouseOver instructions.

The mouse detective II: onMouseOut

The onMouseOut event handler is the flip side of onMouseOver. In the example in the preceding section, you use onMouseOver to display a message. To get rid of that message when the user moves the mouse off the image, you must define a value for onMouseOut. (If you don't, the message continues to display, no matter where users place the mouse pointer!)

All the JavaScript statements assigned to the onMouseOut event handler in the following code snippet execute automatically when a user moves the mouse pointer out of (or off) the associated element — in this example, the splash page image.

```
onMouseOut="window.status=''; return true"
```

The semicolon-delimited JavaScript code associated with the onMouseOver event handler shown here gets the job done for these two things:

- ✔ Sets the status property of the window object equal to an empty string.

- ✔ Returns a value of true to the onMouseOut event handler. This statement (return true) is required by pre-5.5 Internet Explorer and pre-6.0x Navigator browsers; leaving it off causes these older browsers to ignore the onMouseOut instructions.

The Image object is associated with more than just the onClick, onMouseOver, and onMouseOut event handlers; it also supports the onAbort, onDblClick, onError, onKeyDown, onKeyPress, onKeyUp, onLoad, onMouseDown, and onMouseUp event handlers. You can find out more about these event handlers and how to use them in Chapter 7, where I describe each of them, along with the events they handle.

Splash Page Redux

This section takes the first splash page example (which you see in "The Splash Page Script" earlier in this chapter) to new heights.

Here you see how to carve up an image into little pieces and then associate each of those pieces with a separate event handler. The result? An intelligent image that responds differently depending on where on that image a user clicks.

HTML areas (and their associated event handlers) let you carve up images into multiple image *hot spots,* areas of an image that correspond with a message or action (see Listing 8-3). Mousing over the section of the image marked `Publish`, as shown in Figure 8-5, causes a publishing-related message to appear in the status bar. Figure 8-6 shows a similar trick for a different section of the image. And, you can designate a larger area for a more general message in the status bar (see Figure 8-7).

Figure 8-5:
Creating
correspon-
ding status
bar mess-
ages to
mouse
locations on
a page.

Figure 8-6:
Mousing
over the
section of
the image
marked
"Promote"
causes a
promotion-
related
message to
appear
in the
status bar.

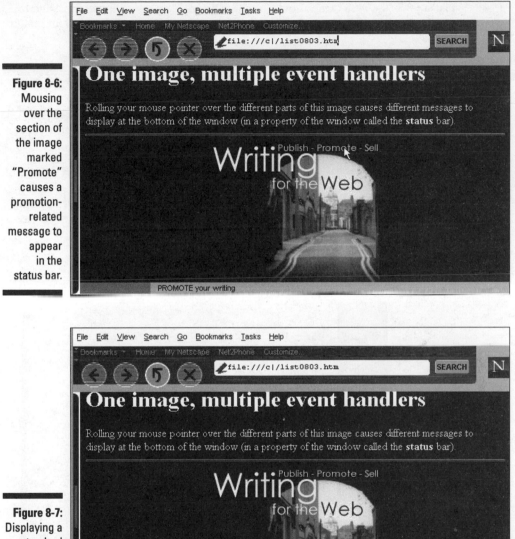

Figure 8-6:
Mousing
over the
section of
the image
marked
"Promote"
causes a
promotion-
related
message to
appear
in the
status bar.

Figure 8-7:
Displaying a
standard
message to
appear
in the
status bar.

Listing 8-3 (list0803.htm) shows you how to create a customized message to
display in the status bar when a user mouses over a specific area of an image.

Listing 8-3:   Designating Image Hot Spots

```
<HTML>
<HEAD>

<TITLE>Attaching multiple event handlers to a single image
          (from JavaScript For Dummies, 3rd edition)</TITLE>

</HEAD>
<BODY BGCOLOR="black" TEXT="white">
<H1>One image, multiple event handlers</H1>
Rolling your mouse pointer over the different parts of this
          image causes different messages to display at the
          bottom of the window (in a property of the window
          called the <B>status</B> bar).
<P>
<HR>
<P>
<CENTER>
<!--
The HTML areas "carve" up a single image. Defining separate
          event handlers for each area lets you display a
          different message in the window's status bar
          depending on where a user's mouse moves or clicks.
-->


<IMG height=208 src="splash.jpg" width=241
    useMap=#newsplash border=0>
<MAP name=newsplash>

      <AREA
      onMouseOver="window.status='Writing for the Web';
        return true"
      onMouseOut="window.status=''; return true"
      shape=POLY target=_top

        coords=1,2,1,46,78,48,80,197,240,201,239,18,93,12,
        94,2
      >

      <AREA
      onMouseOver="window.status='SELL your writing';
        return true"
      onMouseOut="window.status=''; return true" shape=RECT
        target=_top
      coords=216,0,241,16
    >

      <AREA
```

```
        onMouseover="window.status='PROMOTE your writing';
            return true"
        onMouseout="window.status=''; return true" shape=RECT
            target=_top
        coords=149,0,209,15
        >

        <AREA
        onMouseOver="window.status='PUBLISH your writing';
            return true"
        onMouseOut="window.status=''; return true" shape=RECT
            target=_top
        coords=94,0,140,14
        >
</MAP>


</CENTER>
</BODY>
</HTML>
```

HTML areas are the constructs that let you carve an image into separate pieces. The image itself stays where it is; the areas you define just let you define arbitrary ways of interacting with that image.

You can define as many areas for an image as you want, sized and shaped however you like (courtesy of the coords attribute). You define an area using the HTML <AREA> and <MAP> tags, as shown in Listing 8-3. Each area gets to define its own event handlers.

Four separate areas are defined in Listing 8-3:

- ✔ One encompasses the portion of the image that says Publish. The onMouseOver event handler associated with this area displays the message PUBLISH your writing.

- ✔ One encompasses the portion of the image that says Promote. The onMouseOver event handler associated with this area displays the message PROMOTE your writing.

- ✔ One encompasses the portion of the image that says Sell. The onMouseOver event handler associated with this area displays the message SELL your writing.

- ✔ One encompasses all of the rest of the image not described by areas 1 through 3. The onMouseOver event handler associated with this leftover area displays the generic message Writing for the Web.

In order to create distinct areas within an image, you need to know the xy coordinates that describe that area. Most graphic manipulation tools on the market today, including Macromedia Fireworks and Adobe ImageReady, allow you to import a picture, outline which areas you want to create, and then — boom! They generate the necessary coordinates for you.

The Best Navigation Bar None

One of the first things you need to do when you set about creating a Web site is to design a navigation bar. A navigation bar is like a table of contents for your Web site; it allows users to view labels describing the pages of your site (or, for large sites, the categories of pages) so that they can click immediately to whatever portion of your site interests them the most.

In this section, I show you how to create a typical navigation bar: a row of independently clickable images. In this example, each navigation "button" (not to be confused with an HTML button) acts as a link, so you get to take advantage of the properties and event handlers associated with links in designing your navigation bar. Unlike normal text links, however, each of these links is implemented as a small image.

Creating image links

As shown in Figures 8-8 and 8-9, clicking on any of the navigation buttons loads a different, related Web page. The code responsible for creating these pages appears in Listing 8-4.

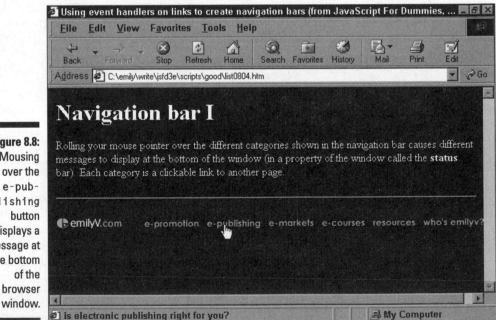

Figure 8.8: Mousing over the e-pub-lishing button displays a message at the bottom of the browser window.

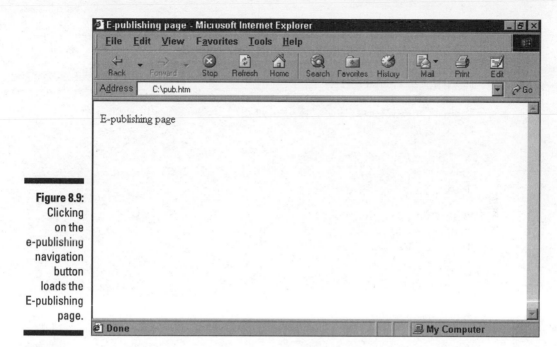

Figure 8.9:
Clicking
on the
e-publishing
navigation
button
loads the
E-publishing
page.

Listing 8-4: Creating an Image Link

```
<HTML>
<HEAD>

<TITLE>Using event handlers on links to create navigation
        bars (from JavaScript For Dummies, 3rd
        edition)</TITLE>
</HEAD>

<SCRIPT LANGUAGE="JavaScript">
//This custom function displays a message in the status bar
function displayMsg(message) {
    window.status=message
}

</SCRIPT>

<BODY BGCOLOR="black" TEXT="white">
<H1>Navigation bar I</H1>
Rolling your mouse pointer over the different categories
        shown in the navigation bar causes different
        messages to display at the bottom of the window
        (in a property of the window called the
        <B>status</B> bar).  Each category is a clickable
        link to another page.
```

(continued)

Listing 8-4 *(continued)*

```
<P>
<HR>
</P>
</HEAD>

<BODY BGCOLOR="black" TEXT="white" >

. . .

//an image implemented as an HTML link

    <A onMouseOver="displayMsg('emilyv.com home'); return
        true"
        onMouseOut="displayMsg(''); return true"
        href="mailto:emily@emilyv.com" ><IMG height=18
        src="logo.jpg" width=92 border=0></A>

    . . .

//another image implemented as an HTML link

    <A onMouseOver="displayMsg('promote your writing
        online'); return true"
        onMouseOut="displayMsg(''); return true"
        href="pro.htm"><IMG height=12
        src="pro_p.gif" width=81 border=0></A>

. . .
//another image implemented as an HTML link
    <A onMouseOver="displayMsg('is electronic publishing
        right for you?'); return true"
        onMouseOut="displayMsg(''); return true"
        href="pub.htm"><IMG height=12
        src="pub_p.gif" width=81 border=0></A>
    . . .

//another image implemented as an HTML link
    <A onMouseOver="displayMsg('find paying online markets
        for your work'); return true"
        onMouseOut="displayMsg(''); return true"
        href="mkt.htm"><IMG height=12
            src="mkt_p.gif" width=72 border=0></A>
        . . .

//another image implemented as an HTML link
    <A onMouseOver="displayMsg('take an online writing
        course'); return true"
        onMouseOut="displayMsg(''); return true"
        href="crs.htm"><IMG height=12
        src="crs_p.gif" width=67 border=0></A>
        . . .
//another image implemented as an HTML link
```

```
      <A onMouseOver="displayMsg('writing-related resources');
          return true"
        onMouseOut="displayMsg(''); return true"
        href="res.htm"><IMG height=12
        src="res_p.gif" width=65 border=0></A>
        . . .
//another image implemented as an HTML link
      <A onMouseOver="displayMsg('who is emilyv?'); return
          true"
        onMouseOut="displayMsg(''); return true"
        href="who.htm"><IMG height=12
          src="who_p.gif" width=89 border=0></A>
        . . .
</BODY>
```

The code you see in Listing 8-4 defines seven links using the HTML <A> . . .
</A> tags. Each link represents a single navigation button in the navigation
button bar. I've broken out the code below so you can see what each line does:

```
<!-- Opening HTML link (anchor) tag -->
<A

<!--onMouseOver event handler displays status bar message -->
onMouseOver="displayMsg('who is emilyv?');  return true"

<!--onMouseOut event handler turns off msg on mouse exit -->
onMouseOut="displayMsg(''); return true"

<!--Specifies page to load when this image/link is clicked -->
href="who.htm">

<!--Opening HTML image tab -->
<IMG

<!--Specifies height of image (in pixels) -->
    height=12

<!--Specifies width of image (in pixels) -->
    width=89

<!--Specifies name of image source file -->
    src="who_p.gif"

<!--Turns off the default border surround the image/link -->
    border=0>

<!--Closing HTML link (anchor) tag -->
</A>
```

Under the covers

You may choose to use an HTML/JavaScript generating tool to help you design and implement your Web pages. Such tools (some of which you can find on the companion CD) can be a great help in developing cool features such as the interactive images and hot spots shown in this chapter.

Because not all tools generate flawless code under all conditions, however — and because sometimes you want to customize generated code so that it performs *precisely* the way you want it to — even dyed-in-the-wool development tool users find the descriptions and examples in this chapter useful.

Linking to e-mail

One navigation button — the logo you see in Figure 8-8 — behaves differently than the others in response to a mouse click. Here's the code, fresh from Listing 8-4:

```
<A onMouseOver="displayMsg('emilyv.com home'); return true"
   onMouseOut="displayMsg(''); return true"
   HREF="mailto:emily@emilyv.com" ><IMG height=18
   SRC="logo.jpg" WIDTH=92 BORDER=0></A>
```

Take a look at the definition of the HREF attribute above. See the value being assigned (mailto:emily@emilyv.com)? In Figure 8-10, you see the result of clicking on the logo navigation button.

The value of an HREF attribute can be one of many different Internet protocols: file:, http:, mailto: news:, and telnet: are the most common. (When you don't specify a protocol, the interpreter assumes that the value refers to a file residing in the same directory as the HTML source file.) Instead of loading a Web page, which is what the http: protocol tells the Web browser to do when the corresponding link is clicked, the mailto: protocol instructs the Web browser to send an e-mail message to the userid that follows the colon.

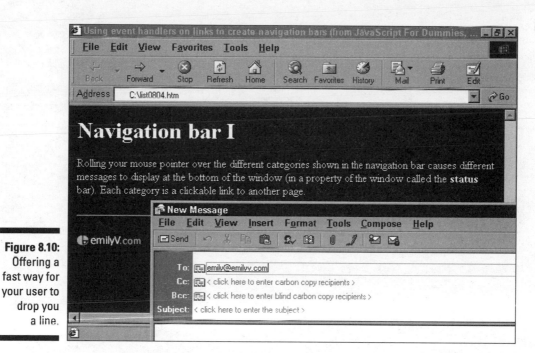

Figure 8.10:
Offering a
fast way for
your user to
drop you
a line.

Chapter 9

Roll Over, Boy! Good Mouse!

In This Chapter

▶ Creating image rollovers with JavaScript

▶ Optimizing page performance with preloaded images

▶ Getting familiar with arrays

*I*n the dark ages of Web development, folks created navigation bars using the only tool at hand at the time: simple hypertext links. There's nothing wrong with that approach; it works, and it's easy to do. (In fact, some sites still make use of links in this way.) But with a little help from JavaScript, you can replace simple links with cool *rollover* effects — dynamic navigation bars that respond visually when a user mouses, or *rolls*, over them.

Besides adding a sophisticated look to your Web pages, rollovers actually make navigating your site easier for users! Read on for details.

What's a Rollover?

The term *rollover* describes an image (typically, an image used as a navigation button) that changes color, font, size, or some other aspect when a user rolls over it with the mouse pointer. Figure 9-1 shows the e-publishing button as it appears (white) when first loaded into Internet Explorer.

As you can see from Figure 9-2, rolling the mouse over a navigation button that you implement as a rollover provides a visual cue that helps users recognize what they can expect when they click the mouse button. (The change in text color from white to purple lets users know in no uncertain terms the button the mouse is about to click!)

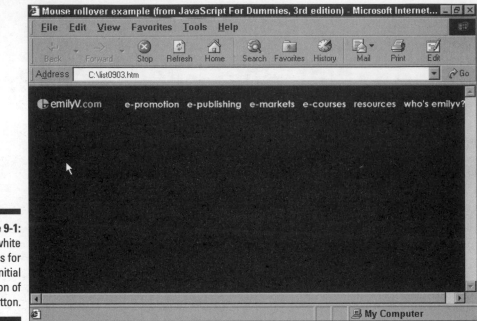

Figure 9-1:
Using white
images for
the initial
version of
the button.

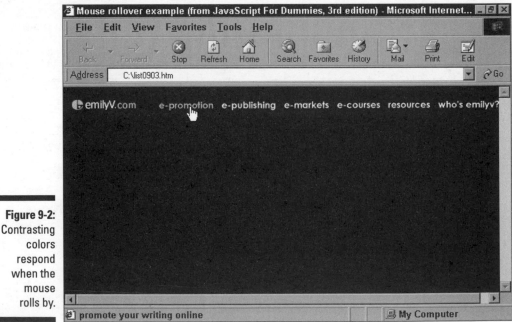

Figure 9-2:
Contrasting
colors
respond
when the
mouse
rolls by.

No law exists that says you must use rollover techniques exclusively for navigation bars. You can use rollovers to make any graphic portion of your Web site respond to mouse events. (Another common use for rollovers is to create interactive splash pages.)

Creating a mouse rollover is fairly simple (maybe easier than you can teach your dog). Just follow this plan:

1. **Choose two images of precisely the same size: one to display by default, and one to display in response to a** mouseover **event.**

   One way to keep the two versions straight is to use on/off terminology. From now on I refer to these images as the *off* image and the *on* image, respectively, since one appears when your mouse is resting somewhere *off* the image and one when your mouse is *on* it.

   You can get images one of two ways:

   • You can use pre-designed images. Many graphics tools come complete with a library of pre-designed images; you can also find images online — some free, some for purchase

   • You can create your own images using an image creation tool such as Paint Shop Pro 6, a trial copy of which you can find on the companion CD-ROM.

   One popular approach is to create a navigation button you like and save it as the *off* image — then change the color of the button and immediately save another copy as the *on* image.

   Not graphically inclined? GoGraph offers freely downloadable icons and graphics at this site:

   `(http://www.gograph.com/)`

2. **Create two JavaScript functions, one attached to the** onMouseOver **event handler and one attached to the** onMouseOut **event handlers.**

   These functions handle the swapping of one image for the other.

3. **Add an optional (but recommended) JavaScript function that pre-loads all of the images.**

   Pre-loading images helps ensure that users mousing over images for the first time don't have to wait while additional images are downloaded from the Web server one at a time.

I show you how these three elements work together in the following section, where you see how to construct a typical navigation bar with rollover effects step by step.

Adding Living Color to Perk Up a Navigation Bar

In Chapter 8, you see an example of a Web site navigation bar containing a handful of navigation image buttons — each of which responds to mouse clicks by loading a different Web page. The example in this chapter is similar, except that each button in this example actually changes appearance when the user mouses over it. I show you how this example appears in Internet Explorer (refer to Figures 9-1 and 9-2).

Pre-loading images

You aren't *required* to pre-load your rollover images, but doing so is a good idea. Using pre-loaded images make your rollovers work much more smoothly, which in turn gives your visitors a much better impression of your site (and your JavaScript skills)!

So, why pre-loading images is a good idea? By default, browsers fetch images only when they're needed for display the first time. So, by default, browsers don't bother to fetch *on* images until a user mouses onto a rollover for the very first time. Unfortunately, if the user's connection is slow or the Web server is overloaded, that fetched image can take quite a while to arrive. In the meantime, the browser display doesn't change, and the user doesn't get to see the rollover effect.

Pre-loading all images helps ensure that users see your rollover effects right away. To pre-load images, you simply create instances of the `Image` object using JavaScript; then you fill those instances with the names of the image files you want to pre-load. You do all of this as soon as the page loads; that way, while the user is busy reading the text on your Web page, the images are quietly loading in the background. By the time the user is ready to click on an image, all the *on* images are loaded in memory and ready to go!

I break down this next example in three chunks to help make clearer what's happening. Listing 9-1 shows you how to pre-load images using a custom function called, appropriately enough, `preloadImages()`. Watch the comments for the stages of the process, which I outline following the listing.

Listing 9-1:   Pre-loading Images as Soon as the Web Page Loads

```
<HEAD>
...
// This first script defines the code necessary to pre-load
        images
```

```
<SCRIPT LANGUAGE="JavaScript">

function preloadImages() {

// See #1 in the following text


    if (document.images) {

    See #2 in the following text

        var imgFiles = preloadImages.arguments;

        See #3 in the following text

        var preloadArray = new Array();


        See #4 in the following text

        for (var i=0; i < imgFiles.length; i++) {

            // Create a new Image object in the
    // preloadArray array and associate it
    // with a source file, thus loading
            // that image into memory.

            preloadArray[i] = new Image;
            preloadArray[i].src = imgFiles[i];
        }
    }
}
    . . .
// stop hiding -->
</SCRIPT>
</HEAD>

<BODY BGCOLOR="#000000" TEXT="#FFFFFF" LINK="#FFFFFF"
        VLINK="#CCCCFFF" ALINK="#CCCCFFF">
//This second script calls the preloadImages() function
        defined in the first script

<SCRIPT LANGUAGE="JavaScript">
<!--
// Preload all the images used in this file
// (the logo, plus all white and purple
// navigation buttons).

See #5 in the following text
```

(continued)

Listing 9-1 *(continued)*

```
preloadImages('logo.jpg',
'pro_p.gif', 'pub_p.gif', 'mkt_p.gif', 'crs_p.gif',
'res_p.gif', 'who_p.gif', 'pro_w.gif', 'pub_w.gif',
'mkt_w.gif', 'crs_w.gif', 'res_w.gif', 'who_w.gif');
//-->
</SCRIPT>
```

The code in Listing 9-1 begins with the definition of the `preloadImages()` function.

Here's how the JavaScript interpreter steps through this function:

1. **First, the interpreter checks the** `document.images` **property to see if any image placeholders (`<IMG>` tags) appear for this document.**

2. **If one or more `<IMG>` tags exist in this document, the interpreter creates a variable called** `imgFiles` **containing all of the arguments sent to the** `preloadImages()` **function.**

   The `arguments` property is available for every function you create.

3. **Next, the interpreter creates a new variable, called** `preloadArray`, **by calling the** `new` **operator in conjunction with the built-in JavaScript** `Array()` **constructor.**

   The result is an empty array.

4. **Finally, the interpreter fills the empty** `preloadArray` **array (and preloads all the images necessary for this Web page).**

   The interpreter creates new instances of the `Image` object and then immediately associates them with the names of the image files passed into the `preloadImages()` function.

5. **The second script you see in Listing 9-1 — the one placed between the document `<BODY>` . . . `</BODY>` tags — executes as soon as users load the Web page into their browsers.**

   This script calls the `preloadImages()` function, passing to it all of the image files necessary for this page.

You may find it helpful to distinguish your on/off image files by using a simple tagging system in the filenames. The filenames in this example containing _w represent white navigation buttons; _p indicates the purple navigation buttons. So, in this example, pro_p.gif is the name of the *off* image for the E-promotion navigation button, and pro_w.gif is the name of the corresponding *on* image for the E-promotion navigation button.

Setting up the swap meet

As soon as the user's browser loads your rollover images into memory using a scheme like the one you see in the preceding section, you need some way to swap those images out in response to a mouseover event. As you may have guessed if you've glanced through Chapter 7, you do this using the onMouseOver event handler associated with each navigation button. Check out the code in Listing 9-2 to see what I mean! I help you digest this code with plenty of explanation after the listing.

Listing 9-2: **Using the** mouseover **Event to Swap Images**

```
<HEAD>
<SCRIPT LANGUAGE="JavaScript">



//Defining the swap() function
function swap(id, newsrc) {
    var theImage - locateImage(id);
    if (theImage) {
        theImage.src = newsrc;
    }
}

////////////////////////////////////////////////////
// The locateImage() function accepts the name of an
// an image and returns the Image object associated
// with that name.
////////////////////////////////////////////////////

function locateImage(name) {
    var theImage = false;
    if (document.images) {
        theImage = document.images[name];
    }
    if (theImage) {
        return theImage;
    }
    return (false);
}
</SCRIPT>
</HEAD>

<BODY>

    . . .

<A HREF="pro.htm"
onMouseOut="swap('promo_pic','pro_w.gif')"
//Calling the swap() function from an onMouseOver event
        handler
onMouseOver="swap('promo_pic','pro_p.gif')" ><IMG
        NAME="promo_pic" SRC="pro_w.gif" WIDTH="81"
        HEIGHT="12" BORDER="0"></A>
    . . .
```

To help you wade through the code in Listing 9-2, I explain how the swap() function works first; then I explain what happens when you call the swap() function from the onMouseOut and onMouseOver event handlers.

Defining the swap() function

The swap() function you see defined in Listing 9-2 accepts two arguments:

- id, which represents the name of the image you want to swap
- newsrc, which represents the file name of the new image you want to display

Here's what's going on inside the body of the swap() function:

First, a variable called theImage is created and assigned the pre-loaded Image object you want to swap out. (To create theImage, the function locateImage() is used. I explain the inner workings of locateImage() in the next section.)

Second, the file name of theImage is changed, which causes the browser to display the new image. Image swap complete!

```
function swap(id, newsrc) {
    var theImage = locateImage(id);
    if (theImage) {  // if an image was found
        theImage.src = newsrc; // swap it out
    }
}
```

Creating the locateImage() function

If you're interested in how the locateImage() function works, you've come to the right place. As you see in the preceding section, the swap() function uses locateImage() to — well, to locate the image it needs to swap out.

Here's the code for the locateImage() function:

```
function locateImage(name) {
//Start with a blank variable called theImage
    var theImage = false;
//If there are images defined for this document . . .
    if (document.images) {
//Assign the image we're looking for to theImage
        theImage = document.images[name];
    }
//If theImage exists, return it to the calling function
    if (theImage) {
        return theImage;
    }
//Otherwise, return false (0) to the calling function
    return (false);
}
```

Calling the swap ( ) function

To perform a rollover, you must swap out images two different times: when a user mouses onto an image, and when a user mouses off again. You do this by calling the swap() function from both the onMouseOver and onMouseOut event handlers, as shown in the following Listing 9-2 excerpt:

```
// Because the image is implemented as a link, clicking on
// the image automatically loads the pro.htm file.

<A HREF="pro.htm"

onMouseOut="swap('promo_pic','pro_w.gif')"

onMouseOver="swap('promo_pic','pro_p.gif')" ><IMG
          NAME="promo_pic" SRC="pro_w.gif" WIDTH="81"
          HEIGHT-"12" BORDER="0"></A>
```

Notice in this code that the initial value for the E-promotion image source is pro_w.gif (the white button); the name of the image is promo_pic. (You know these things because the SRC attribute of the <IMG> tag is set to pro_w.gif and the NAME attribute of the <IMG> tag is set to promo_pic.)

Now take a look at onMouseOver. This statement swaps the promo_pic image from the white version to pro_p.gif (the purple version).

When the onMouseOut event handler fires, the promo_pic image changes back again to pro_w.gif (back to the white version).

The whole enchilada

Listing 9-3 pulls together all the elements necessary to create rollovers, including the preloadImages() and swap() functions. Take a look!

The example shown in Listing 9-3 — including all of the images and referenced HTML files — is available on the companion CD. Just load list0903.htm in your browser to see this code in action.

Listing 9-3:   Creating Rollovers with preloadImages() **and** swap()

```
<HTML>
<HEAD><TITLE>Mouse rollover example (from JavaScript For
          Dummies, 3rd edition)</TITLE>

<SCRIPT LANGUAGE="JavaScript">
```

(continued)

Listing 9-3 *(continued)*

```
<!-- hide this script from non-Javascript-enabled browsers

///////////////////////////////////////////////////
// The displayMsg() function displays a message at the
// bottom of the browser window.
///////////////////////////////////////////////////

function displayMsg(message) {
    window.status=message
}


///////////////////////////////////////////////////
// The preloadImages() function pre-loads all the
// "flipped" images so that when a user mouses over
// a navigation button, the rollover takes place
// immediately. (If you do not pre-load images,
// the first time a user mouses over each
// navigation button the "mouseover" image must travel
// from the Web server, causing an unattractive delay.
///////////////////////////////////////////////////

function preloadImages() {

    // If there are images embedded in the document . . .

    if (document.images) {

        // Set the imgFiles variable equal to an array of all
            the
        // image files passed as args to the preloadImages()
            function.

        var imgFiles = preloadImages.arguments;

        // Create a new array called preloadArray

        var preloadArray = new Array();

        // For each image file sent as an argument to
        // preloadImages() (all 13 of them) . . .

        for (var i=0; i < imgFiles.length; i++) {

            // Create a new Image object in the
            // preloadArray array
            // and associate it with a source file,
    // thus loading that image into memory.

            preloadArray[i] = new Image;
            preloadArray[i].src = imgFiles[i];
        }
    }
```

```
}


//////////////////////////////////////////////////////
// The swap() function accepts two arguments - the
// name of an Image object, and of an image file -
// and replaces the Image object's old file with the
// new one.
//////////////////////////////////////////////////////

function swap(id, newSrc) {
    var theImage = locateImage(id);
    if (theImage) {
        theImage.src = newSrc;
    }
}


//////////////////////////////////////////////////////
// The locateImage() function accepts the name of an
// an image and returns the Image object associated
// with that name to the calling code.
//////////////////////////////////////////////////////

function locateImage(name) {
    var theImage = false;
    if (document.images) {
        theImage = document.images[name];
    }
    if (theImage) {
        return theImage;
    }
    return (false);
}

// stop hiding -->
</SCRIPT>
</HEAD>
<BODY BGCOLOR="#000000" TEXT="#FFFFFF" LINK="#FFFFFF"
        VLINK="#CCCCFFF" ALINK="#CCCCFFF">

<SCRIPT LANGUAGE="JavaScript">
<!--


preloadImages('logo.jpg', 'pro_p.gif', 'pub_p.gif',
        'mkt_p.gif',
'crs_p.gif', 'res_p.gif', 'who_p.gif', 'pro_w.gif',
        'pub_w.gif',
'mkt_w.gif', 'crs_w.gif', 'res_w.gif', 'who_w.gif');
//-->
</SCRIPT>
```

(continued)

Listing 9-3 *(continued)*

```
<TABLE BORDER="0" CELLPADDING="0" CELLSPACING="0">
<TR>
<TD VALIGN="TOP" ALIGN="LEFT">
<TABLE BORDER="0" CELLPADDING="0" CELLSPACING="0"
          WIDTH="125">

<TR><TD>
<A HREF="index.htm" TARGET="_top" onMouseOver =
          "displayMsg('emilyv.com home'); return true"
          onMouseOut = "displayMsg(''); return true">
<IMG SRC="logo.jpg" WIDTH="92" HEIGHT="18" BORDER="0"></A>
</TD></TR>
</TABLE>
</TD>

<TD VALIGN="CENTER" ALIGN="RIGHT">
<TABLE BORDER="0" CELLPADDING="0" CELLSPACING="0"
          WIDTH="486">

  <TR><!-- Shim row, HEIGHT 1. -->
   <TD><IMG SRC="shim.gif" WIDTH="81" HEIGHT="1"
          BORDER="0"></TD>
   <TD><IMG SRC="shim.gif" WIDTH="6" HEIGHT="1"
          BORDER="0"></TD>
   <TD><IMG SRC="shim.gif" WIDTH="81" HEIGHT="1"
          BORDER="0"></TD>
   <TD><IMG SRC="shim.gif" WIDTH="6" HEIGHT="1"
          BORDER="0"></TD>
   <TD><IMG SRC="shim.gif" WIDTH="72" HEIGHT="1"
          BORDER="0"></TD>
   <TD><IMG SRC="shim.gif" WIDTH="4" HEIGHT="1"
          BORDER="0"></TD>
   <TD><IMG SRC="shim.gif" WIDTH="67" HEIGHT="1"
          BORDER="0"></TD>
   <TD><IMG SRC="shim.gif" WIDTH="7" HEIGHT="1"
          BORDER="0"></TD>
   <TD><IMG SRC="shim.gif" WIDTH="65" HEIGHT="1"
          BORDER="0"></TD>
   <TD><IMG SRC="shim.gif" WIDTH="6" HEIGHT="1"
          BORDER="0"></TD>
   <TD><IMG SRC="shim.gif" WIDTH="89" HEIGHT="1"
          BORDER="0"></TD>
   <TD><IMG SRC="shim.gif" WIDTH="2" HEIGHT="1"
          BORDER="0"></TD>
   <TD><IMG SRC="shim.gif" WIDTH="1" HEIGHT="1"
          BORDER="0"></TD>
  </TR>

  <TR><!-- row 1 -->
```

```
<TD><A HREF="pro.htm" TARGET="_top"
        onMouseOut="swap('promo_pic','pro_w.gif');
        displayMsg(''); return true"
        onMouseOver="swap('promo_pic','pro_p.gif');
        displayMsg('promote your writing online'); return
        true" ><IMG NAME="promo_pic" SRC="pro_w.gif"
        WIDTH="81" HEIGHT="12" BORDER="0"></A></TD>

<TD><IMG NAME="r1_c02" SRC="r1_c02.gif" WIDTH="6"
        HEIGHT="12" BORDER="0"></TD>

<TD><A HREF="pub.htm" TARGET="_top"
        onMouseOut="swap('pub_pic','pub_w.gif');
        displayMsg(''); return true"
        onMouseOver="swap('pub_pic','pub_p.gif');
        displayMsg('is electronic publishing right for
        you?'); return true" ><IMG NAME="pub_pic"
        SRC="pub_w.gif" WIDTH="81" HEIGHT="12"
        BORDER="0"></A></TD>

<TD><IMG NAME="r1_c04" SRC="r1_c04.gif" WIDTH="6"
        HEIGHT="12" BORDER="0"></TD>

<TD><A HREF="mkt.htm" TARGET="_top"
        onMouseOut="swap('mkt_pic','mkt_w.gif');
        displayMsg(''); return true"
        onMouseOver="swap('mkt_pic','mkt_p.gif');
        displayMsg('find paying online markets for your
        work'); return true" ><IMG NAME="mkt_pic"
        SRC="mkt_w.gif" WIDTH="72" HEIGHT="12"
        BORDER="0"></a></TD>

<TD><IMG NAME="r1_c06" SRC="r1_c06.gif" WIDTH="4"
        HEIGHT="12" BORDER="0"></TD>

<TD><A HREF="crs.htm" TARGET="_top"
        onMouseOut="swap('course_pic','crs_w.gif');
        displayMsg(''); return true"
        onMouseOver="swap('course_pic','crs_p.gif');
        displayMsg('take an online writing course');
        return true" ><IMG NAME="course_pic"
        SRC="crs_w.gif" WIDTH="67" HEIGHT="12"
        BORDER="0"></A></TD>
<TD><IMG NAME="r1_c08" SRC="r1_c08.gif" WIDTH="7"
        HEIGHT="12" BORDER="0"></TD>
```

(continued)

Listing 9-3 *(continued)*

```
    <TD><A HREF="res.htm" TARGET="_top"
         onMouseOut="swap('res_pic','res_w.gif');
         displayMsg(''); return true"
         onMouseOver="swap('res_pic','res_p.gif');
         displayMsg('writing-related resources'); return
         true" ><IMG NAME="res_pic" SRC="res_w.gif"
         WIDTH="65" HEIGHT="12" BORDER="0"></a></TD>

    <TD><IMG NAME="r1_c10" SRC="r1_c10.gif" WIDTH="6"
         HEIGHT="12" BORDER="0"></TD>

    <TD><A HREF="who.htm" TARGET="_top"
         onMouseOut="swap('who_pic','who_w.gif');
         displayMsg(''); return true"
         onMouseOver="swap('who_pic','who_p.gif');
         displayMsg('who is emilyv?'); return true" ><IMG
         NAME="who_pic" SRC="who_w.gif" WIDTH="89"
         HEIGHT="12" BORDER="0"></a></TD>
    <TD><IMG NAME="r1_c12" SRC="r1_c12.gif" WIDTH="2"
         HEIGHT="12" BORDER="0"></TD>
    <TD><IMG SRC="shim.gif" WIDTH="1" HEIGHT="12"
         BORDER="0"></TD>
    </TR>

</TABLE>
...
</HTML>
```

Listing 9-3 is a bit daunting when you first look at it. All that code is mighty overwhelming at first glance! But all of it is necessary to create the navigation bar (complete with rollovers) as shown in Figures 9-1 and 9-2.

If you look carefully, you see that the JavaScript statements in Listing 9-3 are the same as those you see in Listing 9-1 and 9-2; what's new in Listing 9-3 are the HTML <TABLE> statements necessary to construct the navigation bar from individual images. (Okay, the displayMsg() function and calls are new in Listing 9-3, too — but they're identical to those I cover in Chapter 8.)

Creating rollovers requires you to define one <IMG> tag, or placeholder, for each rollover. Aligning those <IMG> tags precisely in a row requires the use of <TABLE> statements. (You can find out more about Web graphics placement and manipulation in a good Web design book. One of the best around is "Web Design in a Nutshell," by Jennifer Niederst.)

Toolin' around

Rather than code the necessary HTML statements by hand, you may want to look into one of the many HTML-generating Web development tools on the market, which give you the following capabilities:

- ✔ **Create a handsome navigation bar using a graphics editor.** You can create a navigation bar that runs left to right, like the one shown in this chapter, or top to bottom, or staggered in a pyramid shape, or around in a circle, or whatever else you find appealing. Your only limitations are your imagination and your expertise with the graphics editor you choose!

- ✔ **Slice that navigation bar into individual images.** You end up with a series of navigation buttons, plus a bunch of oddly-shaped images left over from the slicing process. (Slicing images is similar to using a cookie cutter on rolled dough; you're left with the "cookies" — the navigation buttons — as well as the scraps.)

- ✔ **Clone the navigation buttons and change the color of (or otherwise alter) one set.** The result is the collection of identically shaped and sized *on* and *off* images you need to create your rollovers.

- ✔ **Generate the HTML statements necessary to reconstruct the navigation bar and handle the** mouseover **and** mouseout **events.**

Even if you take advantage of a graphics development tool to generate HTML and JavaScript rollover code, however, I recommend keeping this book handy as a reference. Even the best code generation tools don't always do exactly what you want for every project. Using the techniques in this chapter, you can tweak generated code with confidence to make sure your rollover effects behave the way *you* want them to.

If you want to extend this example and add rollover effects to your pages in another way, try combining the techniques from this chapter with the framed table of contents in Chapter 11. You can use a frame to hold the set of links or images and add the rollover effects in the stationary table of contents.

K.I.S.S. (Keep It Simple, Sister!)

The simplest rollover you can create is a text value that changes color in response to a user's mouse. You create this effect by accessing the `style` object associated with an HTML element, as shown here:

```
<OL>
<LI
onMouseOver="this.style.color='
   red'"
onMouseOut="this.style.color='b
   lack'">
Netscape Navigator

<LI
onMouseOver="this.style.color='
   red'"
onMouseOut="this.style.color='b
   lack'">
Microsoft Internet Explorer

<LI
onMouseOver="this.style.color='
   red'"
onMouseOut="this.style.color='b
   lack'">
America Online
```

```
<LI
onMouseOver="this.style.color='
   red'"
onMouseOut="this.style.color='b
   lack'">
Opera
</OL>
```

The code in this sidebar displays a numbered list of Web browsers, from 1 (Netscape Navigator) to 4 (Opera). At runtime, as users mouse over any of the numbered items, that item changes from black to red — then back to black again as the mouse moves away. The JavaScript `this` keyword, as described in Chapter 2, provides a neat shorthand for referring to each HTML element.

To see an example of this code in action, take a look at mouseover.htm, located on the companion CD-ROM.

Chapter 10

Hunting and Gathering (And Validating) User Input

• •

In This Chapter

▶ Getting information from your users

▶ Verifying user input

▶ Giving your users helpful feedback

• •

*I*f you're familiar with HTML fill-in forms, you know how useful they can be. Adding an HTML form to your Web page lets your visitors communicate with you quickly and easily. Users can enter comments, contact information, or anything else into an HTML form. Then, that information is transmitted automatically to you (okay, technically, to your Web server) the instant your users submit the form.

Although HTML forms are great all by themselves, JavaScript makes them even better! Using JavaScript, you can create intelligent forms: forms that instantly correct user input errors, calculate numeric values, and provide feedback. In developer parlance, what JavaScript gives you is a way to perform client-side *data validation* (sometimes referred to as *data scrubbing*) — an essential component of any well-designed piece of software, from simple Web page to full-blown online application!

Forming Opinions (And Other Data)

JavaScript adds two very useful features to plain old HTML forms:

✔ JavaScript lets you examine and validate user input instantly, right on the client.

✔ JavaScript lets you give users instant feedback.

I explain both of these features in the following two sections.

Netscape thoughtfully provides a JavaScript data validation tutorial, complete with sample code you can download and incorporate into your very own scripts. Check it out at

```
http://developer.netscape.com/docs/examples/javascript/regexp
           /overview.html
```

Scrub-a-dub-dub: Scrubbing user input

Back in the old days, Web developers had to write server-side CGI programs to process user input. That approach, which is still in use, is effective — but inefficient.

For example, imagine that you want to allow your visitors to sign up for your monthly e-newsletter, so you create an HTML form containing a single input field called E-mail Address. Then imagine that a visitor accidentally types XYZ into that field (instead of a valid e-mail address such as janedoe@aol.com). The contents of the E-mail Address field have to travel all the way from that user's Web browser to your Web server before your CGI program can examine the information and determine that XYZ is invalid.

Using JavaScript, on the other hand, you can instantly determine whether an input value is valid, right inside the user's browser — saving the user valuable time. (And saving yourself the trouble of having to figure out how to create a CGI program in C, C++, or Perl!)

Input validation generally falls somewhere in one of the following three categories:

✔ **Existence:** Tests whether or not a value exists

✔ **Numeric:** Ensures that the information is numbers only

✔ **Pattern:** Tests for a specific convention, such as the punctuation in a phone number, a social security number, or a date

In Listing 10-1, you see the JavaScript code required to validate the oh-so-common pattern category: an e-mail address. The order form script section in this chapter demonstrates examples of existence and numeric validation, as well as pattern validation.)

Figure 10-1 shows you this code in action; you can experiment with these techniques by loading the list1001.htm file from the companion CD into your Web browser.

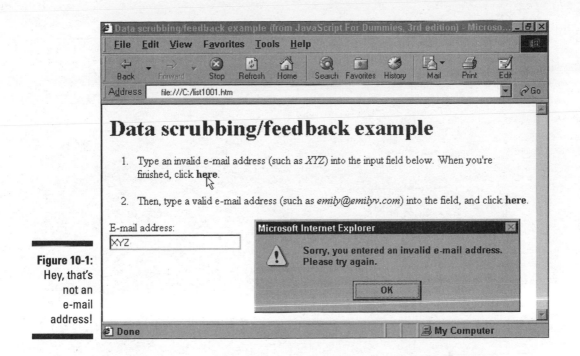

Figure 10-1:
Hey, that's
not an
e-mail
address!

Listing 10-1:   A Script that Validates the E-mail Address Pattern

```
<SCRIPT LANGUAGE="JavaScript">

///////////////////////////////////////////////////
// This function tests for the punctuation characters
// (. and @) found in a valid e-mail address.
///////////////////////////////////////////////////

function isAValidEmail(inputValue) {

    var foundAt = false
    var foundDot = false
    var atPosition = -1
    var dotPosition = -1

    // Step through each character of the e-mail
    // address and set a flag when (and if) an
    // @ sign and a dot are detected.

    for (var i=0; i<=inputValue.length; i++) {
        if (inputValue.charAt(i) == "@" ) {
            foundAt = true
            atPosition = i
        }
```

(continued)

Listing 10-1 *(continued)*

```
        else if (inputValue.charAt(i) == ".") {
            foundDot = true
            dotPosition = i
        }
    }

    // If both an @ symbol and a dot were found, and
    // in the correct order (@ must come first)...

    if ((foundAt && foundDot) && (atPosition < dotPosition))
        {

        // It's a valid e-mail address

        alert("Thanks for entering a valid e-mail address!")
        return true
    }
    else {

        // The e-mail address is invalid

       alert("Sorry, you entered an invalid e-mail address.
            Please try again.")
        return false
    }
}
```

In Listing 10-1, you see that the isAValidEmail() function accepts a single parameter, called inputValue. (I show you an example of calling this function in Listing 10-2.)

Inside isAValidEmail(), the for loop steps through each character of the input e-mail address, one character at a time, looking for an at symbol (@) and a dot (.). If the interpreter finds both of these characters in the input e-mail address — and if the @ symbol appears before the . — that e-mail address passes the test as valid.

If you want to perform additional checks — for example, a check to ensure that at least one character precedes both the @ and the . or one to ensure that the last three characters are com, org, or edu — you can add the additional JavaScript statements to isAValidEmail() to do so. As a developer, the criteria that define a valid pattern are solely up to you. Whether the additional JavaScript statements necessary to catch all conceivable errors are worth the trouble and complexity is your decision, as well. In this example, I figure that the most likely mistake users make is forgetting to type an @ or a period, so the code in Listing 10-1 fits the bill nicely.

Puttin' on the feedback

To someone surfing the Web, few things are more annoying than typing a bunch of information into a form, hitting the form's Submit button, and then — after a lengthy wait — seeing a generic error message that says something like, `You filled something out incorrectly.`

JavaScript lets you check each individual input field, if you like, and pop up instant feedback to let your users know (before they tab clear down to the end of a long form) that they need to make a correction.

In the JavaScript code shown in Listing 10-2, the `isAValidEmail()` function (which I define in Listing 10-1) is called from the HTML `text` element's `onBlur` event handler. The result? Entering an e-mail address into the `text` element and clicking elsewhere on the Web page causes the `isAValidEmail()` function to execute (refer to Figure 10-1).

Listing 10-2: **Calling the** `isAValidEmail()` **Function From an** `onBlur` **Event Handler**

```
<BODY>
<H1>Data scrubbing/feedback example</H1>
<OL>
<LI>Type an invalid e-mail address (such as <I>XYZ</I>) into
          the input field below. When you're finished, click
          <B>here</B>.
<P>
<LI>Then, type a valid e-mail address (such as
          <I>emily@emilyv.com</I>) into the field, and click
          <B>here</B>.
</OL>
<P>
<FORM NAME="myForm">

E-mail address:
<BR>
//Calling isAValidEmail() with the value typed into the
          emailAddress text field.
<INPUT TYPE="text" SIZE="25" NAME="emailAddress"
          onBlur="isAValidEmail(this.value)">
</FORM>

</BODY>
```

Oh, no! Everything's blurry!

The name for the `onBlur` event handler relates to the concept of focus. An object is said to receive focus when you click on it. So, by default, the object becomes *blurry* when you click on something else, and that object *loses* focus.

Here's a quick rundown of when the JavaScript interpreter executes a few common blur-related event handlers:

- `onFocus` executes when an element receives focus (a user tabs to it or clicks on it).

- `onBlur` executes when a user clicks on some element (the element gets focus) and then clicks somewhere else without changing anything (the element loses focus, or *blurs*).

- `onChange` executes when an element loses focus *and* its contents are modified.

- `onSelect` executes when a user selects some or all text (inside a `text` or `textarea` element you specify). The behavior of `onSelect` is similar to `onFocus`, except that `onSelect` occurs when the element receives focus *and* the user also selects text.

Creating the Order Form Script

In the example in this section, you see how to create an intelligent form that validates user data two different ways:

- **At the field level:** You can validate *independent fields* as soon as the user tabs away from them. An independent field is one that you require (such as a credit card number for a credit card purchase), regardless of what a user has types for any other field.

- **At the form level:** You want to validate *dependent fields* when the user clicks the form's Submit button. A dependent field is one that you may or may not validate, depending on what a user types for one or more other fields. For example, you may not require an e-mail address unless your users specify they want to receive your e-mail newsletter.

The example you see here is for a fictitious Web design company called Webmeisters. To allow visitors to request a personalized quote for Web design services, the company decided to create an HTML form and attach JavaScript scripts to meet these design goals:

- **Validate the existence of entries in required fields:** To submit a successful quote request, Webmeister's visitors must enter a service category, a first and last name, and at least one contact method (telephone or e-mail). As you see in Listing 10-3, the `exists()` function implements these validation checks. Existence validation takes place in this example at both the field and form levels.

✔ **Validate two pattern fields:** The scripts must check both phone and e-mail address to ensure they're valid. The isAValidPhoneNumber() and isAValidEmail() functions implement these validation checks, respectively, on a form level.

✔ **Validate numeric fields:** The generic isANumber() function assists in validating phone numbers on a form level.

Figure 10-2 shows you what the completed quote request example looks like.

To see the code responsible for Figure 10-2, list1006.htm, in its entirety, open the file from companion CD-ROM.

Wow! Exist-ential, dude!

You can require that users provide a value for an HTML form field by attaching an existence-validation script to one of that field's event handlers.

In this example, the Wobmcister developers want to ensure that folks requesting a quote enter both their first and last names. Listing 10-3 shows you the JavaScript code necessary to implement this common design requirement.

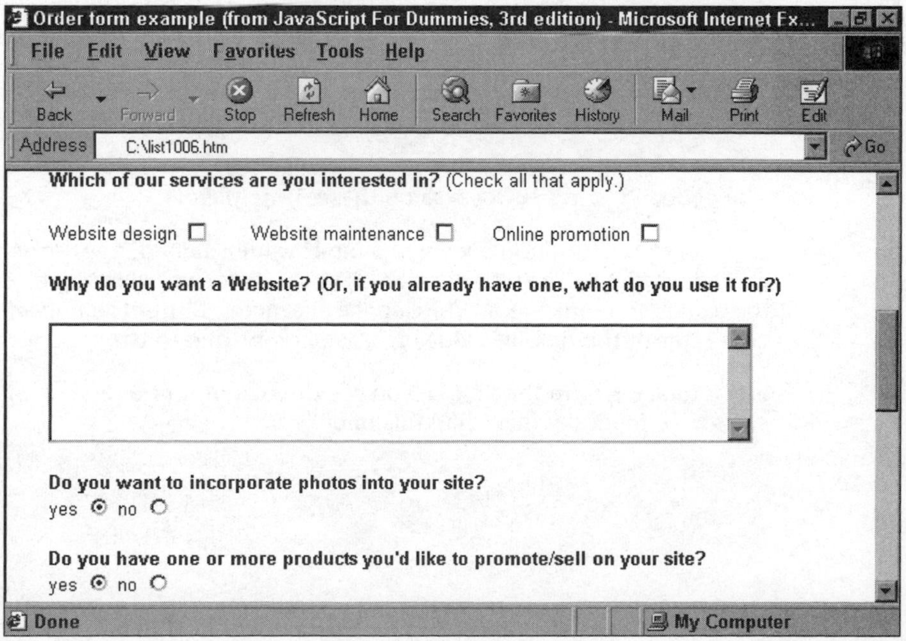

Figure 10-2:
An order form for the fictitious Webmeister company.

Listing 10-3:   Testing for the Existence of an Input Value

```
function exists(inputValue) {

    var aCharExists = false

    // Step through the inputValue, using the charAt()
    // method to detect non-space characters.

    for (var i=0; i<=inputValue.length; i++) {
      if (inputValue.charAt(i) != " " && inputValue.charAt(i)
          != "") {
        aCharExists = true
        break
      }
    }

    return aCharExists
}
...
//The value of the firstName field is sent to the exists()
         function as soon as the user tabs away
<INPUT TYPE="TEXT" NAME="firstName" SIZE="25" onBlur="if
         (!exists(this.value)) { alert('Please enter a
         first name'); }">

//The value of the lastName field is sent to the exists()
         function as soon as the user tabs away

<INPUT TYPE="TEXT" NAME="lastName" SIZE="35" onBlur="if
         (!exists(this.value)) { alert('Please enter a last
         name') }">
```

The code in Listing 10-3 works on these principles:

The `exists()` function accepts an input value (named, appropriately
enough, `inputValue`). As soon as `exists()` receives this value, it checks it
to see if it contains a non-white-space character. Either the non-white-space
character or the default value of `false` is returned to the calling code.

If you look lower in the listing, you see the two input fields that call the
`exists()` function, including this one:

```
<INPUT TYPE="TEXT" NAME="firstName" SIZE="25" onBlur="if
         (!exists(this.value)) { alert('Please enter a
         first name'); }">
```

The preceding JavaScript statement defines a value for the firstName field's onBlur event handler. When a user blurs the firstName field, the value of firstName is passed to exists(). If exists() returns a value of false (the ! operator is shorthand for "if this thing is false") then a pop-up message appears to remind the user to enter a first name. Now, when the user clicks on the Your First Name field and then tabs away without entering a value the code causes a reminder message to appear (see Figure 10-3).

Running numbers

You can require that users provide a valid number for an HTML form field by attaching a numeric validation script to one of that field's event handlers. For an example of the JavaScript code required to perform this validation, take a peek at Listing 10-4.

TECHNICAL STUFF

Numerical assistance

JavaScript offers a handful of built-in functions that help you identify whether or not a value is numeric:

* **parseInt():** Tries to turn a value into an integer; returns either the integer value or false (if the value can't be turned into a number). These two lines illustrate:

```
var result = parseInt("123")
```

result is set to the numeric value 123.

```
var result = parseInt("Emily")
```

result is set to NaN (not a number).

* **parseFloat():** Tries to turn a value into a floating-point (decimal) number; returns either the floating-point value or false (if the value can't be turned into a number). These example show you how:

```
var result = parseFloat("45.6")
```

result is set to the numeric value 45.6.

```
var result = parseInt("grumpy")
```

result is set to NaN.

* **isNaN():** This function, which stands for *is Not a Number*, returns true if the value passed to it is not a number and false if the value passed to it *is* a number. (Yeah, I know — double negatives are confusing, aren't they?) Here are two eamples:

```
var result = isNaN(3)
```

result is set to false, because 3 is a number.

```
var result = isNaN("George
    Clooney")
```

result is set to true, because a string value is not a number.

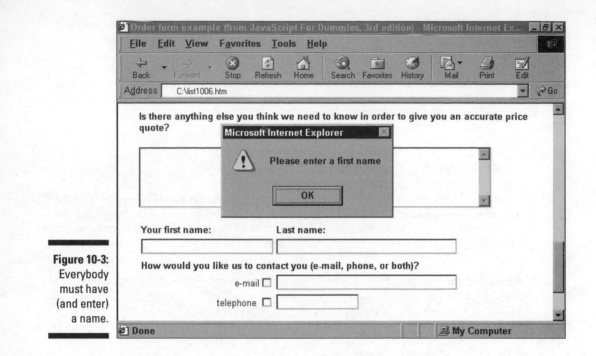

Figure 10-3:
Everybody
must have
(and enter)
a name.

Listing 10-4: Testing to Ensure that a Value Is Numeric

```
//Defining the isANumber() function
function isANumber(inputValue){

    // Assume everything is okay right off the bat
    var result = true

    // If parseFloat() returns false, a non-numeric
    // character was detected in the first position

    if (!parseFloat(inputValue)) {
        result = false
    }

    // Otherwise, we still have to check all the
    // rest of the digits

    else {
    for (var i=0; i<inputValue.length; i++) {
        if (inputValue.charAt(i) != " ") {
            if (!parseFloat(inputValue.charAt(i))) {
                result = false
                break
            }
        }
    }
}
```

```
    }

    // Return true (inputValue is a valid number) or
    // false (it's invalid).

    return result
}

...

function isAValidPhoneNumber(inputValue) {
    ...
    for (var i=0; i<=inputValue.length; i++) {
//Calling the isANumber() function from inside another custom
        function
        if (isANumber(inputValue.charAt(i))) {
            digitsFound++
        }
    }
```

The isANumber() function definition uses the built-in JavaScript function parseFloat() to weed out all values beginning with something other than a number. (parseFloat() returns a value of NaN, if the first character it encounters can't be converted to a number.)

In the event that the first character is a number but subsequent characters aren't (for example, to catch a mistake like 5F5-1212), isANumber() steps through all the remaining characters in inputValue to see if it can detect a non-numeric character.

The last few statements in Listing 10-4 show you an example of how you can call the isANumber() function. In this example, the isAValidPhoneNumber() function (which you get to examine in detail in the next section) calls the isANumber() function as part of its own validation routine.

I think I see a pattern here!

Listing 10-1 earlier in this chapter demonstrates how you may go about validating a very common pattern: the e-mail address. Here, you see an example of another common use for pattern validation: making sure a user types a valid telephone number. Listing 10-5 shows you what I mean.

Listing 10-5:   Validating a Phone Number

```
//Defining the isAValidPhoneNumber() function
function isAValidPhoneNumber(inputValue) {
    var digitsFound = 0

    // Step through the inputValue to see how
```

(continued)

Listing 10-5 *(continued)*

```
    // many digits it contains
    for (var i=0; i<=inputValue.length; i++) {
      if (isANumber(inputValue.charAt(i))) {
          digitsFound++
      }
    }

    // If inputValue contains at least 10
    // digits, assume it is a valid phone number
    if (digitsFound >= 10) {
        return true
    }
    else {
        return false
    }
}
...
//Calling the isAValidPhoneNumber() function
if (!isAValidPhoneNumber(inputValue) {
    alert("We can't contact you via phone unless you give us
            your phone number (make sure to include your area
            code).  Thanks!")
}
```

The code you see in Listing 10-5 checks to see that at a value contains at least ten digits; if so, that value passes the test as a valid telephone number.

Sometimes you want to create more rigid patterns than this. For example, you may want to ensure that users include parentheses and dashes in their telephone numbers. For an example of how to accomplish this (and some caveats), see the sidebar "An alternative approach to pattern-matching" in this section.

An alternative approach to pattern-matching

If you need to define a more rigid pattern than the telephone number example described in Listing 10-5, take a look at the JavaScript code in this sidebar, which requires that users enter a phone number in the following format:

    (512)555-1212

As you see in the following example, the `substring()` method associated with the built-in JavaScript `string` object lets you break a value into chunks and ensure that each chunk is valid. For example, this code instructs the interpreter to extract and inspect the parentheses, area code, exchange, and line portions of the phone number separately.

The benefit to this approach? It ensures that users type exactly what you want them to type in, which reduces the chance of miscommunication. The drawback is that you're expecting a user to type a bunch of characters exactly the way you want them to — a process that is difficult at best!

(Keep in mind that the Web is global, and patterns that may be familiar to you may not be familiar at all to folks in other parts of the world.)

A good design rule to follow is this: If you absolutely must gather information in a specific format, then by all means adapt this example of JavaScript code for your own purposes. But if you can get by with fewer checks (like the phone number validation routine I describe in Listing 10-5), go for it!

```javascript
function isAPhoneNumber(entry){
    if (entry) {
            // Set openParen = to the first character of entry
        var openParen = entry.substring(0,1)


            // Set areaCode = to the next 3 characters
        var areaCode = entry.substring(1,4)


            // Set closeParen = to the 5th character
        var closeParen = entry.substring(4,5)


            // Set exchange = to characters 6, 7, and 8
        var exchange = entry.substring(5,8)


            // Set dash = to the 9th character
        var dash = entry.substring(8,9)


            // Set line = to the 10th through 13th characters
        var line = entry.substring(9,13)


        // The following if statement checks all the pieces,
        // like so:
        // if openParen is not equal to "("
        // OR the areaCode is not a number
        // OR the closeParen is not equal to ")"
        // ... and so on.

        if (
            (openParen != "(")      ||
            (!isANumber(areaCode)) ||
```

(continued)

(continued)

```
                  (closeParen != ")")     ||
                  (!isANumber(exchange)) ||
                  (dash != "-")           ||
                  (!isANumber(line))
               ){
             alert("Incorrect phone number.  Please re-enter in the
following format: (123)456-7890")
            }
        }
}
. . .
<FORM NAME="feedbackForm">
<BR>Please enter your home phone number
<BR>in the following format: (123)456-7890
<INPUT TYPE="text" NAME="homePhone" VALUE="" SIZE=13
onBlur="isAPhoneNumber(this.value)">
. . .
```

Pulling it all together with form-level validation

Sometimes you want to validate fields immediately, as soon as a user enters a value or tabs away from the field. (Listing 10-3 shows you an example of independent field validation.)

But sometimes you want to wait until the user finishes entering information before you begin your validation. For example, the Webmeister form allows users to specify whether they want to be contacted by e-mail or by telephone. At least one option must be selected, but triggering validation the instant a user tabs away from the e-mail field would be useless (and annoying)! After all, that user may very well be intending to select the phone number option; you have no way of knowing until the user finishes filling out the entire form.

A better approach for dependent field validation is to wait until users try to submit their forms before executing your validation scripts, as shown in Listing 10-6. Now, if the user attempts to submit a form without entering either a phone number or an e-mail address, JavaScript generates an error and prevents the form from being submitted. To see how this code behaves at runtime, take a look at Figure 10-4.

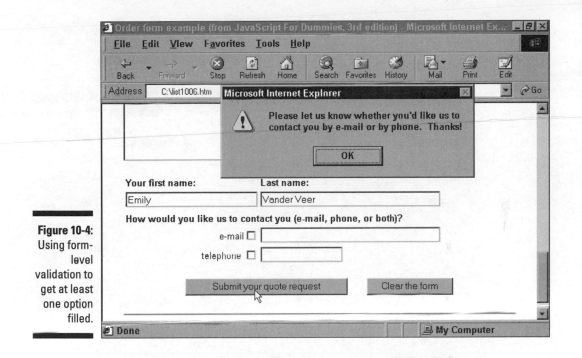

Figure 10-4:
Using form-
level
validation to
get at least
one option
filled.

Listing 10-6:   **Implementing Dependent Validation Checks
via the** validateForm() **Function**

```
<HTML>
<HEAD>
<TITLE>Order form example (from JavaScript For Dummies, 3rd
        edition)</TITLE>

<SCRIPT LANGUAGE="JavaScript">
<!-- hide this script from non-javascript-enabled browsers

//////////////////////////////////////////////////////////
// Checks to see whether a value contains non-numeric data.
//////////////////////////////////////////////////////////
function isANumber(inputValue){

    // Assume everything is okay
    var result = true

    // If parseFloat() returns false, a non-numeric
    // character was detected in the first position
    if (!parseFloat(inputValue)) {
        result = false
    }
```

(continued)

Listing 10-6 *(continued)*

```
        // Otherwise, we still have to check the rest of
        // the digits, so step through the inputValue one
        // character at a time and set result = false
        // if any non-numeric digits are encountered.
        else {
        for (var i=0; i<inputValue.length; i++) {
            if (inputValue.charAt(i) != " ") {
                if (!parseFloat(inputValue.charAt(i))) {
                    result = false
                    break
                }
            }
        }
        }
    }

        // Return true (inputValue is a valid number) or
        // false (it's invalid).

    return result
}

////////////////////////////////////////////////////
// Checks to see whether an input value contains "@"
// and "."
////////////////////////////////////////////////////
function isAValidEmail(inputValue) {

    var foundAt = false
    var foundDot = false

    // Step through the inputValue looking for
    // "@" and "."

    for (var i=0; i<=inputValue.length; i++) {
      if (inputValue.charAt(i) == "@" ) {
          foundAt = true
      }
      else if (inputValue.charAt(i) == ".") {
          foundDot = true
      }
    }

    // If both "@" and "." were found, assume
    // the e-mail address is valid; otherwise,
    // return false so the calling code knows
    // the e-mail address is invalid.

    if (foundAt && foundDot) {
        return true
    }
    else {
        return false
```

```
    }
}

///////////////////////////////////////////////////
// Checks to see if an input value contains 10 or more
// numbers.  This approach lets users type in U.S.-
// style phone formats, such as (123)456-7890,  as
// well as European-style (such as 123.456.7890).
///////////////////////////////////////////////////
function isAValidPhoneNumber(inputValue) {
    var digitsFound = 0

    // Step through the inputValue to see how
    // many digits it contains

    for (var i=0; i<=inputValue.length; i++) {
        if (isANumber(inputValue.charAt(i))) {
            digitsFound++
        }
    }

    // If inputValue contains at least 10
    // digits, assume it is a valid phone number
    if (digitsFound >= 10) {
        return true
    }
    else {
        return false
    }
}

///////////////////////////////////////////////////
// Check for the existence of characters.
// (Spaces aren't counted.)
///////////////////////////////////////////////////
function exists(inputValue) {

    var aCharExists = false

    // Step through the inputValue, using the charAt()
    // method to detect non-space characters.

    for (var i=0; i<=inputValue.length; i++) {
        if (inputValue.charAt(i) != " " && inputValue.charAt(i)
            != "") {
            aCharExists = true
            break
        }
    }

    return aCharExists
}
```

(continued)

Listing 10-6 *(continued)*

```
/////////////////////////////////////////////////////
// Perform cross-field checks that can't be performed
// until all of the data has been entered.
/////////////////////////////////////////////////////

// validateForm() performs all dependent field validation

function validateForm() {

   var rc = true

   // Dependent check #1: ensuring a service category is
          selected

   /////////////////////////////////////////////////
   // Visitors need to check one of the following
   // choices in order to receive an accurate quote:
   // whether they're interested
   // in design, maintenance, or promotion services.
   /////////////////////////////////////////////////

   if (!document.quoteForm.designChoice.checked &&
       !document.quoteForm.maintChoice.checked &&
       !document.quoteForm.promoChoice.checked) {
          alert("Please check whether you're interested in
          our design, maintenance, or promotion services so
          we can give you a more accurate quote.  Thanks!")
       rc = false
   }

   // Dependent check #2: ensuring that a company name exists
          if a
   // user checked "employee"

   /////////////////////////////////////////////////
   // If visitors are employees, they need to specify
   // the name of their company.
   /////////////////////////////////////////////////

   if (document.quoteForm.bizChoice[1].checked) {
       if (!document.quoteForm.corpName.value) {
          alert("You've specified that you're an employee,
          so could you please type in the name of the
          company you work for?  Thanks!")
          rc = false

       }
   }

   // Dependent check #3: double-checking that both first and
```

```
// last names exist

////////////////////////////////////////////////
// Visitors need to include their first and last
// names.
////////////////////////////////////////////////

if (!document.quoteForm.firstName.value ||
    !document.quoteForm.lastName.value) {
    alert("Please type in your entire name (both first and
        last).  Thanks!")
    rc = false
}

// Dependent check #4: ensuring that users enter either an
        e-mail
// address or a phone number


////////////////////////////////////////////////////
// Visitors need to specify either an e-mail
// address or a telephone number.
////////////////////////////////////////////////////
if (!document.quoteForm.emailChoice.checked &&
    !document.quoteForm.phoneChoice.checked) {
    alert("Please let us know whether you'd like us to
        contact you by e-mail or by phone.  Thanks!")
    rc = false
}

// Dependent check #5: ensuring that an e-mail address
        exists
// (if a user chose the e-mail contact option)

////////////////////////////////////////////////////
// If visitors tell us they want us to contact them
// by e-mail, alert them if they haven't put in
// their e-mail address (same with telephone).
////////////////////////////////////////////////////
if (document.quoteForm.emailChoice.checked &&
    !isAValidEmail(document.quoteForm.emailAddr.value)) {
        alert("We can't contact you via e-mail unless you
        give us a valid e-mail address. Thanks!")
    rc = false
}
else {
    if (document.quoteForm.phoneChoice.checked &&

        !isAValidPhoneNumber(document.quoteForm.phoneNumbe
        r.value)) {
```

(continued)

Listing 10-6 *(continued)*

```
            alert("We can't contact you via phone unless you
            give us your phone number (make sure to include
            your area code).  Thanks!")
        rc = false
        }

    }

    if (rc) {
        // If the rc variable is non-zero, then the form data
        // passed with flying colors!
        alert("Thanks! We'll contact you with a quote
            shortly.")
    }
    return rc
}

// -->
</SCRIPT>
</HEAD>

<BODY>
<H1>Order form example</H1>
<HR>

...

<P>
<HR>
<TABLE WIDTH="100%" CELLSPACING="10" CELLPADDING="10"
            BORDER=0>
<TR>
<TD>
<FONT FACE="Helvetica, Arial, Verdana" SIZE="2">
//Dependent validation checks execute when the user attempts
            to submit the form
<FORM NAME="quoteForm" onSubmit="return validateForm();">
<P>
<B>Which of our services are you interested in?</B> (Check
            all that apply.)
<P>
Website design <INPUT TYPE="CHECKBOX" NAME="designChoice"
            VALUE="design">      
Website maintenance <INPUT TYPE="CHECKBOX" NAME="maintChoice"
            VALUE="maint">     
Online promotion
<INPUT TYPE="CHECKBOX" NAME="promoChoice" VALUE="promo">

<P>
<B>Why do you want a Website? (Or, if you already have one,
            what do you use it for?)</B>
<P>
<TEXTAREA NAME="purpose" COLS="60" ROWS="5" WRAP="VIRTUAL">
```

```
</TEXTAREA>
<P>
<B>Do you want to incorporate photos into your site?</B>
<BR>
yes <INPUT TYPE="RADIO" NAME="pixChoice" VALUE="hasPix"
        CHECKED>
no <INPUT TYPE="RADIO" NAME="pixChoice" VALUE="hasNoPix">
<P>
<B>Do you have one or more products you'd like to
        promote/sell on your site?</B>
<BR>
yes <INPUT TYPE="RADIO" NAME="cdChoice" VALUE="hasProducts"
        CHECKED>
no <INPUT TYPE="RADIO" NAME="cdChoice" VALUE="hasNoProducts">
<P>
<B>Are you a small business owner, or do you work for a large
        corporation?</B>
<BR>
small business owner <INPUT TYPE="RADIO" NAME="bizChoice"
        VALUE="isOwner" CHECKED>
employee <INPUT TYPE="RADIO" NAME="bizChoice"
        VALUE="isEmployee">
<P>
<B>If you work for a corporation, what's the name?</B>
<INPUT TYPE="TEXT" NAME="corpName" SIZE="25">
<P>
<B>Is there anything else you think we need to know in order
        to give you an accurate price quote?</B>
<P>
<TEXTAREA NAME="extraInfo" COLS="60" ROWS="5" WRAP="VIRTUAL">
</TEXTAREA>
<P>

<TABLE>
<TR>
<TD>
<FONT FACE="Helvetica, Arial, Verdana" SIZE="2">
<B>Your first name:</B>
</TD>
<TD>
<FONT FACE="Helvetica, Arial, Verdana" SIZE="2">
<B>Last name:</B>
</TD>
</TR>
<TR>
<TD>
<INPUT TYPE="TEXT" NAME="firstName" SIZE="25" onBlur="if
        (!exists(this.value)) { alert('Please enter a
        first name'); }">
</TD>
<TD>
```

(continued)

Listing 10-6 *(continued)*

```
<INPUT TYPE="TEXT" NAME="lastName" SIZE="35" onBlur="if
        (!exists(this.value)) { alert('Please enter a last
        name') }">
</TD>
</TR>
<TR>
</TR>

<TR>
<TD COLSPAN="2">
<FONT FACE="Helvetica, Arial, Verdana" SIZE="2">
<B>How would you like us to contact you (e-mail, phone, or
        both)?</B>
</FONT>
</TD>
</TR>

<TR>
<TD ALIGN="RIGHT">
<FONT FACE="Helvetica, Arial, Verdana" SIZE="2">
e-mail<INPUT TYPE="CHECKBOX" NAME="emailChoice"
        VALUE="email">

</FONT>
</TD>
<TD>

<INPUT TYPE="TEXT" NAME="emailAddr" SIZE="35">
</TD>
</TR>
<TR>
<TD ALIGN="RIGHT">
<FONT FACE="Helvetica, Arial, Verdana" SIZE="2">
telephone <INPUT TYPE="CHECKBOX" NAME="phoneChoice"
        VALUE="phone">

</TD>

<TD>
<INPUT TYPE="TEXT" NAME="phoneNumber" SIZE="15">
</TD>
</TR>
</TABLE>
<P>
<CENTER>
<INPUT TYPE="SUBMIT" VALUE="Submit your quote request">
      <INPUT TYPE="RESET"
        VALUE="Clear the form">
...
</HTML>
```

As you see from the code in Listing 10-6, the `validateForm()` function, which performs five dependent field validation routines, executes when the user attempts to submit the form. (Attaching the `validateForm()` function to the `quoteForm`'s `onSubmit` event handler sees to that!)

TIP

Giving 'em a piece of your mind

Giving users appropriate, timely feedback can be the difference between a confusing Web site and one that is efficient and pleasant to use. Following are a few things to keep in mind as you decide when and how to interact with your users.

DON'T SHOUT!!

Nobody likes being yelled at, and messages THAT ARE IN ALL UPPERCASE LIKE THIS AND END IN EXCLAMATION POINTS ARE YELLS! Say what you need to say; just use normal capitalization and punctuation.

Be specific

Sometimes, you don't particularly care what a user types (for example, if you're asking for free-form comments on your product). At other times, what the user types is crucial. For the times when it's crucial, be sure to let the user know up front, right on the page, what format is expected.

When you *do* need to pop up an error message, make sure that it tells users precisely what's wrong with their input. (`Invalid format. Please retry.` does not count!)

Give your users a break

Just because you're now a card-carrying expert at validating user input doesn't mean you have to pop up an error message *every* time you

detect an error. In some cases, you may be able to *massage* (geek-speak for *modify*) the input data to suit yourself without bugging the user at all. For example, just because you'd like to see a value in uppercase letters doesn't mean the user has to enter it in uppercase letters. Instead of displaying an error and requesting that the user retype the entry, you can just as easily take the input and change it to uppercase yourself using the `toUpperCase()` method of the `string` object.

Pat your users on the back

Don't reserve feedback for only those times when a user enters something incorrectly; reassuring users that things are proceeding as planned is just as useful. For example, let users know when a form passes all validation checks.

Test 'til you drop

Make sure (and this *should* go without saying, but you never know), that you test your form carefully for every conceivable error (and series of errors) that a user might reasonably be expected to make. Few things are more frustrating to users than getting tangled in an endless loop of errors that refuse to go away, even *after* the user has figured out what's wrong and corrected it!

Chapter 11

Framed Again!

In This Chapter

▶ Manipulating frames with JavaScript
▶ Creating a simple JavaScript page map
▶ Creating a collapsible JavaScript site map

Frames let you display multiple HTML documents inside a single browser window. Using JavaScript, you can create all kinds of sophisticated frame effects! Two of the most useful (and most common) frame effects, both of which you see in this chapter's examples, are

✔ Using frames to create a dynamic site map

✔ Using frames to display hyperlinked documents

By the time you finish this chapter, you know enough about how JavaScript interacts with frames to create your own cool frame effects.

Whether or not to include HTML frames in your Web site is a personal design decision. Some folks love frames, because not only do they allow you to create effective navigation structures (like the site map you see in this chapter), they also allow you to provide hyperlinks while discouraging users from surfing off to those hyperlinked sites. The downside? Frames can be complicated to implement, and some people dislike the fact that they "hide" URL information. To see the URL for a link opened in a frame, for example, you can't just click on the link; you must right-click and select Open in New Window (Internet Explorer) or Open Link in New Window (Navigator). If you *do* decide to implement frames, however, JavaScript can help you make the most effective use of them.

One Page at a Time

Scripted frames are a valuable addition to any Web developer's tool belt. Using a combination of HTML frames and JavaScript, you can present a static, clickable table of contents on one side of a page; then, on the other side of the page, you can present the text that corresponds with each table of contents entry. Check out Figures 11-1 and 11-2 to see a table of contents. Figure 11-1 shows my site which has an example of a simple framed table of contents on the left side of the page and content on the right.

One of the benefits of frames is that they allow you to display different HTML files independently from one another. So, for example, as Figure 11-2 shows, the left frame stays visible — even if the user scrolls the right frame. Plus, clicking on a link in the frame on the left automatically loads the appropriate content in the frame you see on the right.

This approach, which I explain in the following sections, helps users navigate through the site quickly and is very useful for organizing small sites — or even larger sites that contain mostly text.

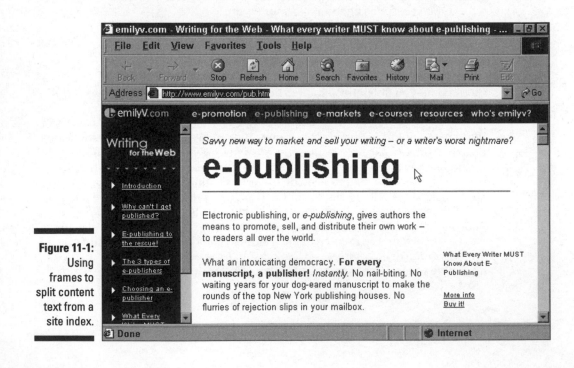

Figure 11-1:
Using frames to split content text from a site index.

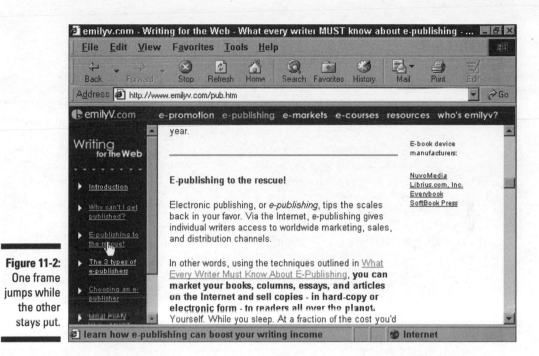

Figure 11-2:
One frame
jumps while
the other
stays put.

Constructing frames

A frame is a special type of window that you create using HTML tags and
manipulate using JavaScript and the document object model. Since this book
doesn't focus on HTML, I don't go into great detail on creating HTML frames;
instead, I show you the basic syntax you need to know to understand how
JavaScript and the document object model fit into the picture. (If you want to
know more about creating HTML frames, you might want to pick up a copy of
HTML for Dummies. I highly recommend it!) Listing 11-1 shows you an excerpt
of the code you need to create frames, using the htm files to hold the two
frames together. list1101.htm pulls together pub_l.htm (left frame's table of
contents) and pub_c.htm (right frame's content).

You can view the complete working example of the code presented in this
section from the companion CD: list1101.htm, pub_l.htm, and pub_c.htm.

Don't fence me in!

Just as you can display other folks' Web pages inside your frames, so those folks can display *your* Web pages inside *their* frames.

But in some cases, you may want to prevent your site from being framed. For example, say you spend weeks creating a beautiful, graphics-rich site optimized for a particular monitor size and screen resolution. Then, say I come along and add a link to your site from mine — but I choose to display your fabulous, pixel-perfect site by squeezing it into a tiny 2" x 2" frame! (Worse yet, I'm a cat lover, so I surround the 2" x 2" frame with an image of my beloved Fifi — so your site appears to be peeking out of my cat's mouth!)

To prevent other sites from displaying your document in a frame, add the short script you see below to your document's head.

```
<HEAD>
 . . .
<SCRIPT LANGUAGE="JavaScript">
<!-- Start hiding from non-
    JavaScript-support browsers
```

```
// The following JavaScript
   code reloads a page so
// that it "breaks out" of its
   container frame, if one
   exists.

// If this page has been loaded
   into a frame...
if (top != self) {
    // Replace the original
    "framing" page with the
    framed page
    top.location.href = loca-
    tion.href;
}
// Stop hiding -->
</SCRIPT>
 . . .
</HEAD>
```

Listing 11-1: HTML Syntax for Creating Index and Content Frames

```
 . . .
<FRAMESET COLS="125, *"
    BORDER="0"
    FRAMESPACING="0"
    FRAMEBORDER="NO">
// Defining the source file, name, and display details
    for the
// left frame
<FRAME SRC="pub_1.htm"
NAME="leftnav"
SCROLLING="AUTO"
NORESIZE MARGINHEIGHT="0"
MARGINWIDTH="0"
LEFTMARGIN="0"
TOPMARGIN="0"
```

```
TARGET="body">
    // Defining the source file, name, and display details
    // for the right frame
    <FRAME SRC="pub_c.htm"
            NAME="content"
            SCROLLING="AUTO"
            NORESIZE
            MARGINHEIGHT="0"
            MARGINWIDTH="0"
            LEFTMARGIN="0"
            TOPMARGIN="0"
TARGET="body">
        </FRAMESET>
    . . .
```

Take a good look at the HTML code in Listing 11-1 to find the two frame definitions:

- ✔ leftnav (which corresponds to the HTML file pub_l.htm)
- ✔ content (which corresponds to the HTML file pub_c.htm)

The file pub_l.htm contains a list of content links (in other words, a table of contents); the file pub_c.htm contains corresponding text. Figures 11-3 and 11-4 show you what these two files look like when loaded separately into Internet Explorer.

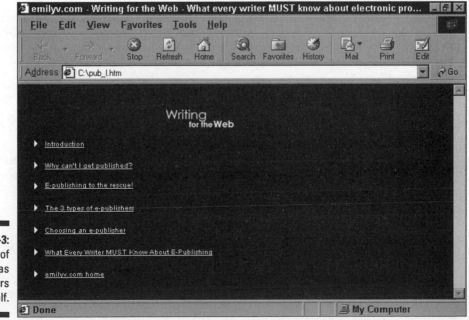

Figure 11-3: The table of contents as it appears by itself.

Looking at pages separately, before you put them into frames, helps you understand how to combine them for the best effect.

In the next section, you see how to connect the two files shown in Figures 11-3 and 11-4.

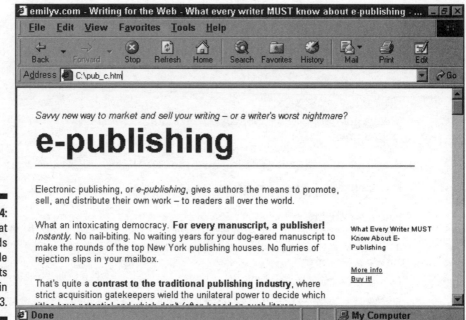

Figure 11-4: The text that corresponds to the table of contents shown in Figure 11-3.

Adding the wiring

In the example in this section, the content in the right frame reloads based on what a user clicks on in the left frame. So, naturally, the code responsible for the text reload can be found in the source code for the left frame, pub_l.htm. Take a look at the pertinent syntax as shown in Listing 11-2. This code snippet, from pub_l.htm, connects the table of contents links to the appropriate content.

Listing 11-2: Connecting the Index Links to the Content Headings

```
// When a user clicks the "Introduction" link,
// the anchor located at pro_c.htm#top loads into the
// frame named content

<A HREF="pro_c.htm#top" TARGET="content"
```

Right on target

When you create a link (or an anchor, area, base, or form) in HTML, you have the option of specifying a value for the TARGET attribute associated with these HTML elements. Valid values for the TARGET attribute include any previously named frame or window, or one of the following built-in values. (Listing 11-2 demonstrates an example of specifying the _top value for the TARGET attribute associated with a link.)

Value	What does it mean?
_blank	Open the link in a brand-new window
_parent	Open the link in this window or frame's parent window/frame
_self	Open the link in <u>this</u> window or frame
_top	Open the link in the root window or frame

```
>Introduction</A>

    . . .

// When a user clicks the "Why can't I get published?" link,
// the anchor located at pro_c.htm#can'tget loads into the
            frame
// named content

<A HREF="pub_c.htm#cantget" TARGET="content"
>Why can't I get published?</A>
    . . .
<A HREF="pub_c.htm#rescue" TARGET="content"
>E-publishing to the rescue!</A>
    . . .
<A HREF="pub_c.htm#types" TARGET="content"
>The 3 types of e-publishers</A>
    . . .
<A HREF="pub_c.htm#choose" TARGET="content"
>Choosing an e-publisher</A>
    . . .
<A HREF="pub_c.htm#epubGuide" TARGET="content"
>What Every Writer MUST Know About E-Publishing</A>
    . . .
// When a user clicks the "emilyv.com home" link, a
// new page (home.htm) replaces the current page

<A HREF="home.htm" TARGET="_top"
>emilyv.com home</A>
```

Each of the links I define in Listing 11-2 contains a value for the TARGET attribute. With one exception, TARGET is set to content — the name of the right frame defined in Listing 11-1. Assigning the name of a frame to the TARGET attribute of a link causes that link to load in the named frame, just as you see in Figure 11-2.

You do need a variation for the exception: At the bottom of Listing 11-2, you see that the last link defined assigns a value of _top to the TARGET attribute. When a user clicks on the link marked emilyv.com home, the page changes to the contents of home.htm.

_top is a built-in value that translates to "whatever the top-level window in this window/frame hierarchy happens to be." (The sidebar "Right on target" in this chapter describes all the built-in values you can specify for the TARGET attribute.)

Specifying a value for TARGET that doesn't match either a) a previously defined frame name, or b) one of the built-in values you see in the sidebar "Right on target" causes the associated link to load into a brand-new window. So if you expect a link to open in a frame and it pops up in a new window instead, check your source code; odds are you've made a typo!

The example in this section shows you how to load the contents of one frame based on a user clicking a link in another. To load two frames based on a user clicking a link, you can create a JavaScript function similar to the following:

```
function loadTwoFrames(leftURL, contentURL) {

    // Loads the first URL passed in
    // into the container frame previously defined
    // as "leftNav" in an HTML file such as the one
    // you see in Listing 11-1

    parent.leftNav.location.href=leftURL

    // Loads the second URL passed in
    // into the container frame previously defined
    // as "content"

    parent.content.location.href=contentURL
}
```

Then pass the loadTwoFrames() function two URL strings; for example:

```
<A HREF="javascript:loadTwoFrames('some.htm',
         'another.htm')">
```

or

```
<INPUT TYPE="button" VALUE="Load Two Frames"
        onClick="loadTwoFrames('some.htm',
        'another.htm')">
```

Creating Collapsible Indexes

Anyone who's used the Windows Explorer utility (see Figure 11-5) knows how useful a collapsible table of contents can be.

Clicking on any of the plus-sign icons shown in Figure 11-5 expands the associated directory; clicking on a minus-sing icon collapses the associated directory. The collapsible list shown on the left side of Figure 11-5 is a nifty, useful way to organize and present a lot of information in a logical, hierarchical manner.

Using a combination of free, pre-built JavaScript *libraries* and HTML frames, you can create similar collapsible lists for your Web site.

Checkin' out the library

When computer programmers talk about libraries, they don't mean quiet buildings where you can go to check out books! In programming parlance, a *library* is a bunch of functions — sometimes free, sometimes not — that you can reference and call from your own code.

To implement JavaScript libraries, you use them as .js files that you include in your own files with the help of the SOURCE attribute of the <SCRIPT> tag, as shown below (a complete working example can be seen in Listing 11-3):

```
//Including a JavaScript library with the SRC attribute
<SCRIPT LANGUAGE="JavaScript"
        SRC="someFile.js">
</SCRIPT>
```

```
<SCRIPT LANGUAGE="JavaScript">
 . . .
// someFunction is defined in someFile.js
// so it's available for use here
// Calling a function defined by the someFile.js library
someFunction()
 . . .
```

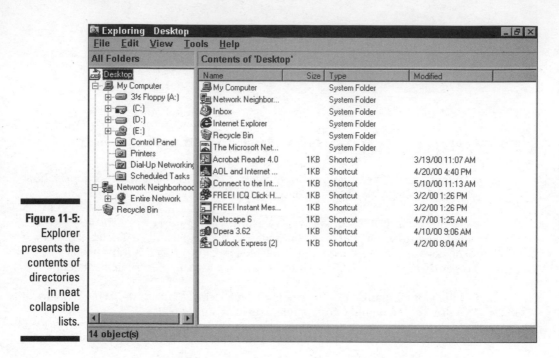

Figure 11-5:
Explorer
presents the
contents of
directories
in neat
collapsible
lists.

The first script declaration in the preceding code, incorporates the file `someFile.js` into the HTML document. The second script declaration shows how to make a call to a function called `someFunction()`— a function defined by the `someFile.js` library. Organizing generic JavaScript code into reusable libraries offers these benefits:

✔ **Cuts down on errors.** After a JavaScript library is fully tested, you can reuse it with confidence. (Compare *that* to cutting and pasting JavaScript functions into each HTML file where you want to call those functions!)

✔ **Improves performance time.** A single copy of a JavaScript library downloads into memory where the JavaScript interpreter can access it, no matter how many pages (one document or a dozen) reference that library.

The good folks at Netscape have a library, list.js, currently available that offers collapsible list creation functions. (You see how to create a full-scale collapsible table of contents later in this chapter, in the "Outlining your site contents" section.) You can download a copy of list.js for free from the following site:

```
http://developer.netscape.com/docs/technote/dynhtml/collapse/
                           index.html
```

Calling all code

Using a library can be simple or difficult, depending on how well the library developer documents the library!

Netscape documents fairly well the library example I demonstrate in this section, list.js. Listing 11-3 shows you an example of how you incorporate list.js and use the JavaScript functions it contains to create a collapsible list.

Listing 11-3:   Using Netscape's list.js Library to Create a Collapsible List

```
<HTML>
<HEAD><TITLE>Creating collapsible lists with Netscape's
          list.js (from JavaScript For Dummies, 3rd
          edition)</TITLE>

// Including the list.js library
<SCRIPT LANGUAGE="JavaScript1.2" SRC="list.js"></SCRIPT>

<SCRIPT LANGUAGE="JavaScript">
function init() {

    // Specify the list dimensions
    var width = 350, height = 22;

    // Create a new list!
    // List() function is defined and documented in list.js
    myList = new List(true, width, height, "#CCCCCC");

    // Add two items to the list
    myList.addItem("Computer");
    myList.addItem("Text editor");

    // Create a "sub" list
    subList = new List(false, width, height, "#CCCCCC");


    // Add three items to the new (sub) list
    subList.addItem("Netscape Navigator");
    subList.addItem("Internet Explorer");
    subList.addItem("America Online");

    // Attach the sub-list to the original list and
    // give it an entry.
    myList.addList(subList, "Browsers");
```

(continued)

Listing 11-3 *(continued)*

```
        // The list (complete with a sub-list) now exists
        // in memory, so display it on the screen
        myList.build(100,20);


}
</SCRIPT>
</HEAD>
<BODY ONLOAD="init();">
</BODY>
</HTML>
```

If you're new to working with code libraries, your first question is probably "How the heck do I know what the names of the functions are? Or what they do? Or what kind of values do I need to pass to them?"

The answer is you don't — unless the library developer tells you! Most code libraries have an accompanying text file that explains the functions that the library defines, how to call them, and a few working examples. In this case, Netscape kindly provides online examples and documentation (which you can find at the same site as the library itself):

```
http://developer.netscape.com/docs/technote/dynhtml/collapse/
            index.html).
```

Take a look at Figures 11-6 and 11-7 to see what the code in Listing 11-3 looks like in a back-level (4.0x) version of Netscape Navigator. When the user clicks on the right arrow next to Browsers, the code expands the list (in other words, displays the attached sub-list). The user can click the down arrow to collapse the list.

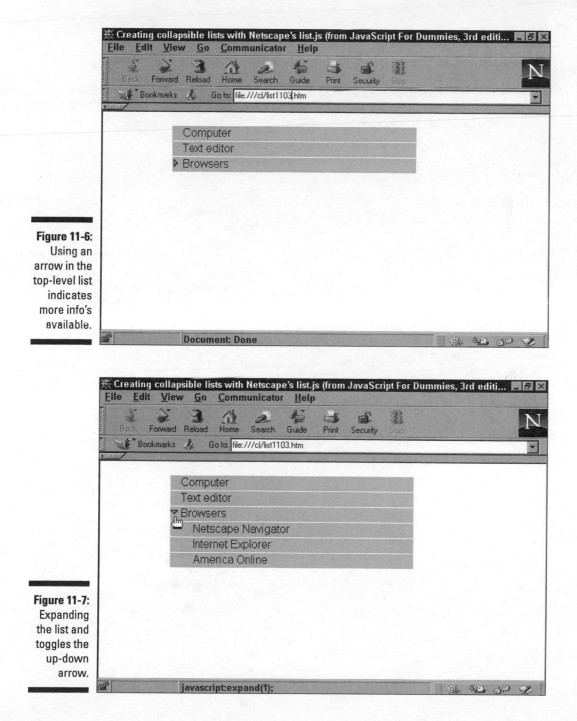

Figure 11-6:
Using an
arrow in the
top-level list
indicates
more info's
available.

Figure 11-7:
Expanding
the list and
toggles the
up-down
arrow.

Part IV
Automating Your Web Site

The 5th Wave   By Rich Tennant

"I couldn't get this 'job skills' program to work on my PC, so I replaced the motherboard, upgraded the BIOS, and wrote a program that links it to my personal database. It told me I wasn't technically inclined and should pursue a career in sales."

In this part . . .

Part IV is jam-packed with information you can use to
make Web pages so cool you just may shock yourself!
Here you'll see how to create sophisticated-looking page
layouts with dynamic HTML, the very latest in JavaScript
technology. You also discover little-known tricks such as
how to keep track of how long users spend on your Web
pages, how to password-protect your pages, and how to
create dynamic effects such as automatic scrolling of page
content and digital clocks. You also find out how to embed
Java applets, Netscape plug-ins, and ActiveX components
into your Web pages — and manipulate the components
you embed with JavaScript statements.

Chapter 12

DHTML Dyn-o-mite!

In This Chapter

▶ Getting familiar with dynamic HTML (DHTML)

▶ Manipulating images and arrays

▶ Creating simple animations and slide shows

Dynamic HTML, or *DHTML*, refers to the collection of client-side languages and standards you use to create Web pages that change appearance dynamically, after they're loaded into a user's Web browser.

The languages and standards that contribute to DHTML include

✔ HTML (of course!)

✔ JavaScript

✔ Cascading style sheets

✔ The document object model (DOM)

Because this is a book about JavaScript, my focus in this chapter is on JavaScript and the document object model and how they combine to contribute to DHTML — in short, how you can use JavaScript to access and manipulate the DOM and create cool dynamic effects, including slide shows and simple animations.

 While the examples in this chapter include HTML and cascading style sheet code, I don't spend a lot of time describing these two languages in-depth. If you're interested in finding out more about DHTML, including HTML and cascading style sheets, you might want to check out a good book devoted to these subjects. One worth checking out is "*Dynamic HTML For Dummies, 2nd Edition,*" by Michael Hyman (IDG Books Worldwide, Inc.).

Chapter 3 describes the document object model and shows you how to access it; Appendix C presents both Internet Explorer's and Netscape Navigator's document object models.

Animation Sensation

Typically, when you see a cool animation on a Web page, you're looking at one of the following:

- ✔ **A Java applet:** Java applets are small software applications written in the Java programming language that your browser downloads from a Web server to your machine when you load a page.

- ✔ **A plug-in:** A plug-in is special software you can download that "plugs in" to your browser and allows an application to execute inside a Web page. Flash is one popular animation plug-in (from the good folks at Macromedia).

- ✔ **An animated GIF:** GIF stands for *graphics interchange format,* and it describes a special way of compressing image files. Regular GIF files are used to transfer images on the Web. Animated GIFs are a bunch of regular GIFs packaged together — much like those cartoon flip-books you may have had as a child, where each page contains a separate drawing. When you flip the flip-book pages (or load an animated GIF) those separate images flow from one to another to create an animated effect. Animated GIFs are a popular choice for Web-based animations because most browsers support them, no separate download is required (unlike plug-ins), and because they don't hog a lot of client resources (unlike some Java applets).

Having said all that, you can create simple animations with JavaScript, as well. You might want to do so for two very good reasons:

- ✔ Creating JavaScript animations saves your users time. (JavaScript animations don't require any downloads, either up-front or during animation execution, unlike plug-ins and applets, respectively).

- ✔ Creating JavaScript animations saves *you* the trouble of figuring out another programming language, such as Java, or learning how to use an animation construction tool, such as Macromedia's FireWorks.

The downside? Because JavaScript wasn't designed specifically to create animations, it isn't optimized for this purpose — meaning that specially-built functions and the compression techniques necessary for hard-core animation execution don't exist in JavaScript. In other words, JavaScript animations are best kept simple. Fortunately, many times, simple animations are all you need!

Another downside to using JavaScript to create animations lies in the incompatibilities between Netscape Navigator's and Internet Explorer's document object models — the very object models you must manipulate with JavaScript to create your animated effects. Netscape has announced changes in the way Navigator supports the animation-related portion of the DOM to coincide more closely with Internet Explorer's and the World Wide Web Consortium's standards, but to be sure your examples will work, you may want to test these in several versions of Navigator. The examples you see in this chapter work just fine in Internet Explorer. For more information on using the DOM and targeting dynamic HTML techniques for display in Navigator, visit DevEdge Online at this site

```
http://developer.netscape.com/docs/technote/
```

In this example, I show you how to create the simplest animation of all: an image that changes from its original view and then changes back again. Take a look at Figures 12-1 and 12-2 to see how my smiley changes, thanks to the recursive invocation of setTimeout().

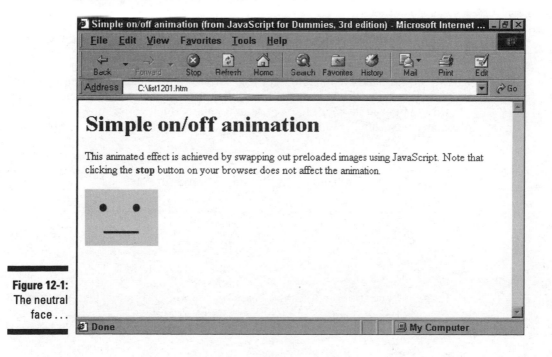

Figure 12-1:
The neutral
face . . .

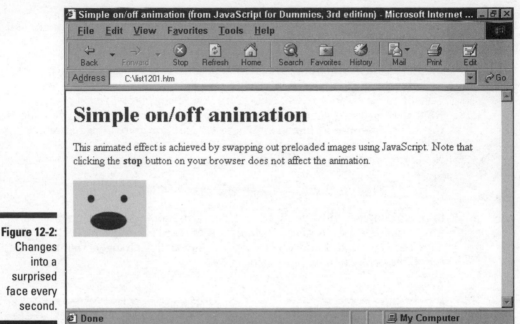

Figure 12-2:
Changes
into a
surprised
face every
second.

The relevant code responsible for this simple animation is shown in Listing 12-1. Check out the simple on/off animation using image manipulation and the built-in JavaScript setTimeout() function. If you want to load and experiment with the animation example, load the file list1201.htm from the companion CD.

Listing 12-1: Creating a Simple Animation with JavaScript's setTimeout() Function

```
. . .
//Global variable declarations
var whichImg = 1
var nextImage


/////////////////////////////////////////////////
// The swap() function replaces the image
// associated with the first input
// parameter (id) with the image specified
// for the second input parameter (newSrc)
/////////////////////////////////////////////////

function swap(id, newSrc) {
    var theImage = findImage(document, id, 0);
    if (theImage) {
        theImage.src = newSrc;
```

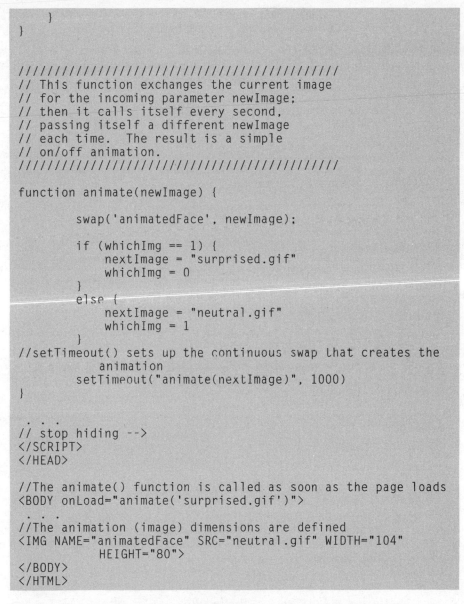

```
        }
}


/////////////////////////////////////////////
// This function exchanges the current image
// for the incoming parameter newImage;
// then it calls itself every second,
// passing itself a different newImage
// each time.  The result is a simple
// on/off animation.
/////////////////////////////////////////////

function animate(newImage) {

        swap('animatedFace', newImage);

        if (whichImg == 1) {
            nextImage = "surprised.gif"
            whichImg = 0
        }
        else {
            nextImage = "neutral.gif"
            whichImg = 1
        }
//setTimeout() sets up the continuous swap that creates the
            animation
        setTimeout("animate(nextImage)", 1000)
}


   . . .
// stop hiding -->
</SCRIPT>
</HEAD>

//The animate() function is called as soon as the page loads
<BODY onLoad="animate('surprised.gif')">
   . . .
//The animation (image) dimensions are defined
<IMG NAME="animatedFace" SRC="neutral.gif" WIDTH="104"
            HEIGHT="80">
</BODY>
</HTML>
```

The JavaScript code in Listing 12-1 depends on two image files to create the animation:

✔ neutral.gif — This image of a yellow square contains two black "eyes" and a straight line for a mouth for the neutral look.

✔ surprised.gif — The image of the surprised "face." (Okay, okay, it's just a smiley face with a big circle for a mouth instead of a straight line. Artist's rendition! Artist's rendition!)

Here's the order in which JavaScript interpreter steps through the code in Listing 12-1 — a peek inside the interpreter's mind, as it were:

1. **The HTML `<IMG>` tag names and defines the animation placeholder frame (the spot on the page where the images appear alternately during the animation).**

   In the `<IMG>` tag, the name is `animatedFace`, and the dimensions are 80 x 104.

2. **As soon as the page loads, the `onLoad` event handler executes the `animate()` function and sends it the name of a source file (`surprised.gif`, to be exact).**

3. **The `animate()` function calls the `swap()` function to swap out the source file associated with the `animatedFace` placeholder frame.**

   Now, instead of the original `neutral.gif`, `animatedFace` holds `surprised.gif`.

4. **Using the globally defined variables `whichImg` and `nextImage`, the `animate()` function logs which image it just swapped out and queues up the next image by calling the `setTimeout()` function.**

   `setTimeout()` calls `animate()` every second, alternately passing `animate()` the `neutral.gif` and `surprised.gif` filenames.

Tickets to a Slide Show

Sometimes you want to set up a slideshow using JavaScript: a way for your users to click a button and see a different image, or "slide," without necessarily popping to another Web page.

Figures 12-3 through 12-5 show you the process of clicking a button to change the image from one view to the other.

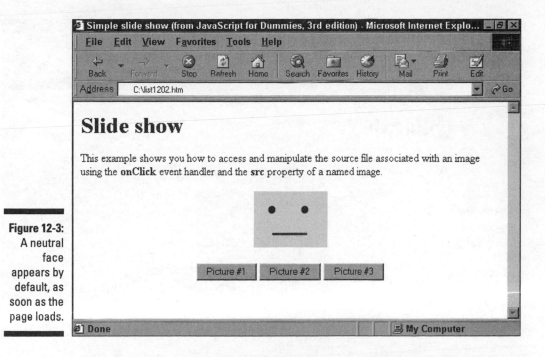

Figure 12-3:
A neutral face appears by default, as soon as the page loads.

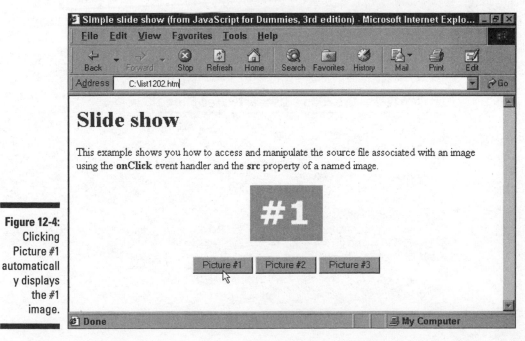

Figure 12-4:
Clicking Picture #1 automatically displays the #1 image.

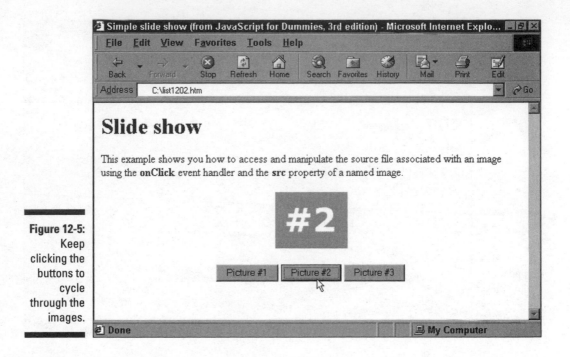

Figure 12-5: Keep clicking the buttons to cycle through the images.

The JavaScript code necessary to create the simple slide show example appears in Listing 12-2.

The code in Listing 12-2 is located on the companion CD in list1202.htm.

Listing 12-2:   Creating a User-activated Slide Show

```
   . . .

//////////////////////////////////////////////
// This swap() function constructs a file name
// based on the input parameter and then sets
// the slideshow image's source to that
// file name.
//
// Note: the initial image determines the size
// of the slideshow "frame".  Swapping to
// a larger image causes that larger image to
// be squeezed to fit the initial image "frame".
//////////////////////////////////////////////
function swap(newImage) {
```

```
        var fileName = newImage.toString() + ".gif"
        document.all.slideshow.src = fileName
}

// stop hiding -->
</SCRIPT>
</HEAD>

<BODY>
<H1>Slide show</H1>
This example shows you how to access and manipulate the
            source file associated with an image using the
            <B>onClick</B> event handler and the <B>src</B>
            property of a named image.
...

<!-- The initial image (a face) to display is specified
            here. -->

<IMG NAME="slideshow" SRC="neutral.gif" WIDTH="104"
            HEIGHT="80">


<P>

<!-- These three onClick event handlers call the swap()
            function to display the user-selected image -->

<INPUT TYPE="button" VALUE="Picture #1" onClick="swap('1')">
<INPUT TYPE="button" VALUE="Picture #2" onClick="swap('2')">
<INPUT TYPE="button" VALUE="Picture #3" onClick="swap('3')">
..
```

See the <IMG> tag near the bottom of the Listing 12-2 code listing? That <IMG> tag defines the initial image that displays when this page first appears, as shown in Figure 12-3, and names the placeholder for that initial image slideshow.

When a user clicks on any of the buttons — Picture #1, Picture #2, or Picture #3 — that button's onClick event handler springs into action and calls the swap() function, passing the swap() function the appropriate number: 1, 2, or 3. Inside the swap() function are just two lines of JavaScript code:

```
var fileName = newImage.toString() + ".gif"
document.all.slideshow.src = fileName
```

The first line creates a variable called fileName and then assigns to fileName a string based on the parameter sent to swap() from the onClick event handler. (You must use the `toString()` method to convert the value of `newImage` to a string before you can tack on the ".gif.") After the JavaScript interpreter interprets this first line, `fileName` contains one of the following string values: `1.gif`, `2.gif`, or `3.gif`. (These file names correspond to actual GIF files located on the companion CD.) The second line of the `swap()` function assigns this new `fileName` to the built-in `src` property of the slideshow placeholder. (You specify a specific image placed in a document by navigating from the `document` object to the `all` object to the named `Image` object.)

Now You See It ... Now You Don't!

A variation on the slide show example you see in the previous section is the ability to present an image to a user and then give that user the ability to hide the image. Hiding and showing images is easy using the built-in `visibility` property, as you see in Listing 12-3.

Listing 12-3:   Giving Users the Option to Hide Images

```
. . .

var showing = true

//////////////////////////////////////////////////
// The toggle() function alternately hides and
// shows an element.
//////////////////////////////////////////////////
function toggle() {
// If the image is visible, hide it
    if (showing == true) {
        document.all.toggledImg.style.visibility = "hidden"
        showing = false
    }
// Otherwise, the image is hidden, so show it
    else {
        document.all.toggledImg.style.visibility = "visible"
        showing = true
    }

    return true
}

// stop hiding -->
</SCRIPT>
```

```
</HEAD>

<BODY>
. . .
// You use the SPAN tag to create hide-able/show-able
          elements
<SPAN ID="toggledImg">
<IMG NAME="animatedFace" SRC="neutral.gif" WIDTH="104"
          HEIGHT="80">
</SPAN>
<P>
<INPUT TYPE="button" VALUE="toggle visible/invisible"
          onClick="toggle()">
</BODY>
</HTML>
```

To see what the code in Listing 12-3 looks like in action, see Figure 12-6, which shows the image using the `toggle()` function at `visibility = "visible"`.

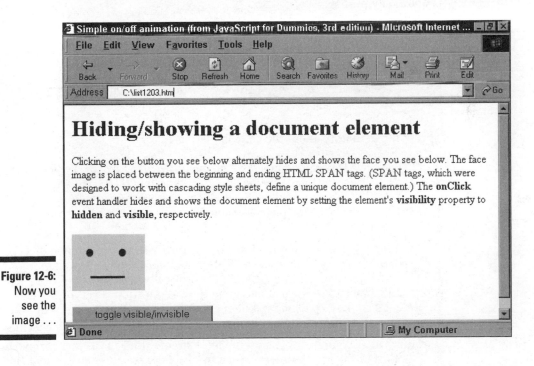

Figure 12-6:
Now you see the image . . .

Figure 12-7 shows the opposite effect with `visibility = "hidden"`.

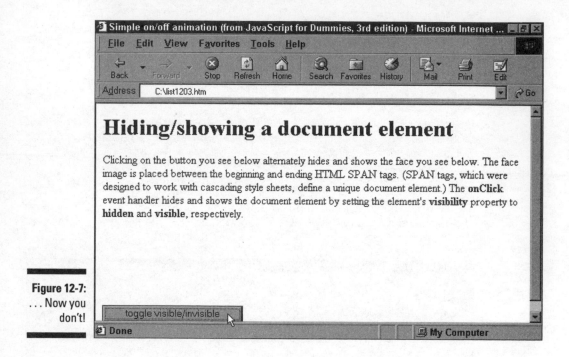

Figure 12-7:
... Now you
don't!

Three things to note about the code in Listing 12-3:

✔ The image is wrapped in a `span` element. (In other words, I place the the HTML `<IMG>` tag inside the beginning and ending HTML `<SPAN>` . . . `</SPAN>` tags.) The `span` element gives you the ability to show and hide the contents of a Web page — using the `span` element's `visibility` property.

✔ Changing an element's `visibility` property to `visible` immediately redisplays that element. Acceptable values for the visibility property are `visible`, `hidden`, and `inherit`. (Theoretically, a value of `inherit` tells the browser to use whatever visibility configuration is set for the element's containing element, but support for this property is not provided in the latest browsers.)

✔ Internet Explorer's object model implements the `visibility` property as part of the `style` object, which in turn is part of a `span` element (in this case, the `span` element named `toggledImg`), which in turn is part of the `all` object, which in turn is embedded in a `document`:

```
document.all.toggledImg.style.visibility
```

(If you find the preceding line of code a bit daunting, don't worry! I discuss the `style` object further in the next section, and you can find out more about the document object model in general — including how to navigate it using dots, as shown above — in Chapter 3.)

You're Really Stylin' Now!

Cascading style sheets allow Web developers to separate the way information is presented (bold, underlined, red, green, centered, and so on) from the information itself. And because the presentation properties you define using cascading style sheets become a part of the browsers' document object models, you can manipulate those properties dynamically using JavaScript. Listing 12-4 shows you how!

Listing 12-4:   Manipulating Cascading Style Sheet Properties

```
. . .
<SCRIPT LANGUAGE="JavaScript">

function changeColor(newColor) {
// Changing text color by referencing the UPCTR ID selector
    document.all.UPCTR.style.color = newColor
}

</SCRIPT>

//Defining a cascading style sheet
<STYLE TYPE="text/css">

/* =================================================
Define an ID selector called UPCTR that centers
associated text and displays it in all uppercase.
================================================= */

//Defining the UPCTR ID selector
#UPCTR {
    color= red;
    text-align: center;
    text-transform: uppercase;
}
```

(continued)

Listing 12-4 *(continued)*

```
</STYLE>
</HEAD>

<BODY>

<H1>Changing CSS properties dynamically</H1>

<P ID="UPCTR">
By default, this paragraph displays red, centered, and all
          uppercase because it's associated with a specially
          defined ID selector (called UPCTR).<BR>
</P>
Clicking the buttons changes the value for the color property
          associated with the UPCTR ID selector.
<P>
<INPUT TYPE="button" VALUE="Change text color: green"
onClick="changeColor('green')">
<INPUT TYPE="button" VALUE="Change text color: red"
onClick="changeColor('red')">
  . . .
```

In this example, the text you display on a Web page changes from green to red based on whether a user clicks the Change text color: green or Change text color: red button.

Most of the code you see in Listing 12-4 is HTML and cascading style sheet declarations. The JavaScript code you want to take a look at is the changeColor() function:

```
document.all.UPCTR.style.color = newColor
```

This line of JavaScript changes the color of the displayed text by assigning a new color (the color selected by the user and transmitted to changeColor() by the onClick event handler) to the text element's color property.

Chapter 13

Timing Is Everything

● ●

In This Chapter

▶ Getting familiar with JavaScript's built-in time methods and functions

▶ Scheduling functions to execute at a later time

▶ Creating a stopwatch to time user activities

▶ Refreshing Web content automatically and on-demand

● ●

*T*he more sophisticated your Web pages, the more likely you are to need JavaScript's built-in time functions and methods. These functions and methods let you schedule common tasks for automatic execution. For example, you can automatically refresh Web page content or display a reminder after a predetermined period of time.

You can also use JavaScript's built-in time functions and methods to keep track of the time your users spend on different activities on your page — a useful feature for Web developers interested in understanding how folks use their site.

Ready, Set, Go! Keeping Track of Time In JavaScript

In addition to the Date() function, which you use to calculate the current date and time, JavaScript provides a handful of time-related methods associated with the Window object. Check out Table 13-1 for an overview of these methods.

Table 13-1	Built-in Time-Related Window Methods
Name	**Description**
`setInterval(code, interval)`	Executes code every `interval` (`interval` must be in milliseconds); returns an id
`clearInterval(id)`	Stops executing code scheduled with `setInterval()`
`setTimeout(code, interval)`	Executes code after timeout (`interval` must be in milliseconds); returns an id
`clearTimeout(id)`	Stops executing code scheduled with `setTimeout()`

You get to see these methods at work, along with the `Date()` function, in the following sections.

The Stopwatch Script

Logging the elapsed time between two JavaScript events — for example, between the time a document loads (the `load` event) and the time a user clicks a button (the `click` event) is easy! As you see in Listing 13-1, all you need to do is follow these steps:

Time well spent

Why keep track of the time your users spend on your Web pages? To gauge the effectiveness of your pages, of course! Some examples:

- Determining how long the average user takes to read a product description before hitting the Buy It Now! button

- Determining how much time the average user spends typing in feedback comments

- Determining how much time the average user spends reading a newsletter description

before opting to subscribe (or choosing *not* to)

To analyze the time data you gather using JavaScript, you want to send the details to a Web server (through hidden input fields or some other mechanism) so you can combine and examine statistics from a bunch of users all at once.

1. **Call the built-in** Date() **function in the** onLoad **event handler to log the precise time the document loads.**

2. **Call** Date() **again in the** onClick **event handler to log the precise time a user clicks a button.**

3. **Determine the difference between the two times.**

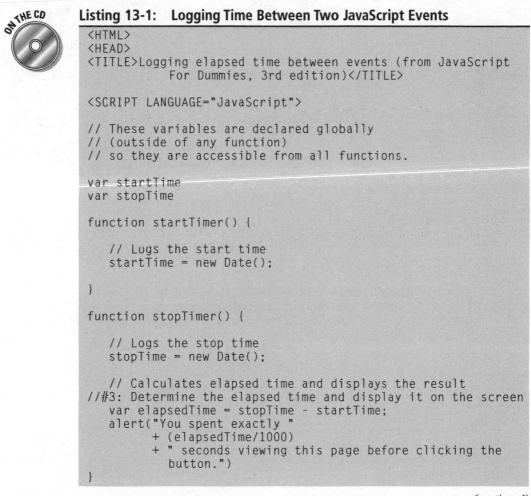

Listing 13-1: Logging Time Between Two JavaScript Events

```
<HTML>
<HEAD>
<TITLE>Logging elapsed time between events (from JavaScript
        For Dummies, 3rd edition)</TITLE>

<SCRIPT LANGUAGE="JavaScript">

// These variables are declared globally
// (outside of any function)
// so they are accessible from all functions.

var startTime
var stopTime

function startTimer() {

    // Logs the start time
    startTime = new Date();

}

function stopTimer() {

    // Logs the stop time
    stopTime = new Date();

    // Calculates elapsed time and displays the result
//#3: Determine the elapsed time and display it on the screen
    var elapsedTime = stopTime - startTime;
    alert("You spent exactly "
        + (elapsedTime/1000)
        + " seconds viewing this page before clicking the
          button.")
}
```

(continued)

Listing 13-1 *(continued)*

```
</HEAD>
// #1: call startTimer() to start the clock ticking
<BODY onLoad="startTimer()">
<H1>Timing actions in JavaScript</H1>
This script tracks how long it takes you to click the
button you see below (the clock starts when the page
loads).
<P>
Sending the contents of the <B>elapsedTime</B>
variable back to the Web server (in a hidden HTML
field, for example) allows you to process and chart
how long your visitors are spending on your Web site.
<FORM>
<INPUT
TYPE="button"
//#2: As soon as a user clicks the button, the stopTimer()
          function executes
VALUE="Click here to stop the timer"
onClick="stopTimer()">
</FORM>
</BODY>
</HTML>
```

The code in Listing 13-1 is fairly straightforward. The Date() function, which you see called from the onLoad event handler, logs the split second when the page loads into a user's Web browser.

The second call to the Date() function executes when a user clicks the "Click here to stop the timer" button. The code you see in the stopTimer() function takes the difference between these two times and displays that difference in a pop-up alert box, as shown in Figure 13-1.

The Date() function returns the current date and time in milliseconds (thousands of a second). The code in Listing 13-1 divides the elapsed time by 1000 in order to calculate the number of seconds elapsed.

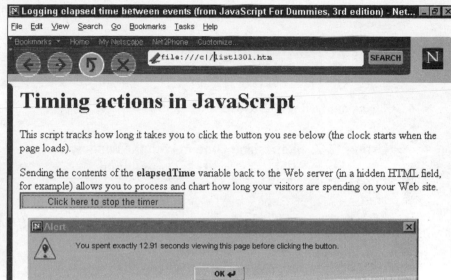

Figure 13-1:
Clicking the
button stops
the timer
and displays
the elapsed
time.

The Pause That Refreshes (Content, That Is!)

Sometimes you find it useful to refresh Web page content every so often automatically. For example, if the price of the widgets you sell on your Web site is very volatile, you might want to refresh those prices every so often to make sure your users have the most current purchasing information possible.

The JavaScript code you see in Listing 13-2 refreshes content automatically every ten seconds using the setInterval() method associated with the Window object.

The setInterval() method is similar to the setTimeout() method you see demonstrated in Listing 13-3, with one difference. These snippets illustrate:

setTimeout() waits the amount of time you specify and then calls the designated code just once.

```
// someFunction() is called after one
// minute (60,000 milliseconds)
var timerId = setTimeout("someFunction()", 60000)
```

setInterval() repeatedly calls the code you specify after every interval you specify.

```
// otherFunction() is called every 10
// seconds (10,000 milliseconds)
var timerId = setInterval("otherFunction()", 10000)
```

Check out Listing 13-2 to see setInterval() in action.

Listing 13-2: Refreshing Content with the Window Object's setInterval() Method

```
<HTML>
<HEAD><TITLE>Refreshing content automatically (from
          JavaScript For Dummies, 3rd edition)</TITLE>
<SCRIPT LANGUAGE="JavaScript">

// This global variable is shared by the two functions
// defined below.

//Declare a global variable called timerId
var timerId
</SCRIPT>
</HEAD>

// As soon as the page loads, setInterval() schedules the
          page
// to reload every 10 seconds.  It does this by calling the
          reload()
// method of the this window's location object.  (The
          location object
// represents the URL of this page.)
<BODY onLoad="timerId = setInterval('self.location.reload()',
          10000)">

<H1>Refreshing content automatically</H1>
This page will refresh automatically every ten seconds
(just as though you clicked the <B>Refresh button</B>
on the button bar every ten seconds).
<P>
To stop refreshing, click the link below.
<P>
When a user clicks the "Stop" button, clearInterval() clears
          the interval (and stops the  reload() method from
          being called again)
<A HREF="javascript:clearInterval(timerId)">Stop automatic
          refresh</A>
</FORM>
</BODY>
</HTML>
```

setInterval() expects two variables: the code you want to execute, and the number of milliseconds you want the JavaScript interpreter to wait before executing that code. In this case, the reload() method is executed every 10,000 milliseconds (every 10 seconds).

In addition, as you can see in the code above, the value javascript:clearInterval(timerId)" assigned to the HREF attribute of the <A> tag. This value uses the javascript: protocol to call the clearInterval() function from inside an <HTML> tag.

If you take a close look at Listing 13-2, you see setInterval() and clearInterval() being called.

setInterval() is assigned to the onLoad event handler, so it executes as soon as the document loads into a browser. setInterval() tells the JavaScript interpreter to execute the reload() method associated with the location object every 10 seconds until the end of time. setInterval() returns a unique identifier (based on the current date and time, if you must know!) that is stored in the globally declared timerId variable. You need to hold onto this identifier in order to clear the interval (and stop the automatic execution of the reload() method).

clearInterval() executes as soon as a user clicks the Stop Automatic Refresh link. Because clearInterval() is passed timerId, it knows to clear the unique interval established by the setInterval() call.

You can use setInterval() and clearInterval() to automatically execute any method or function you like; you're not limited to refreshing Web page content.

Never META minute I didn't like

The approach you see in Listing 13-2 represents just one way to refresh Web content. Another way is via the HTML <META> tag, as shown below. (The code below works even if users have turned JavaScript support off in their browsers, unlike Listing 13-2. The approach you choose is up to you!)

```
<HEAD>
<!-- Refresh content every 10
     seconds -->
<META http-equiv="refresh" con-
     tent="10">
</HEAD>
```

Refreshing content on demand is even simpler; in fact, technically, you can allow users to refresh content using a simple HTML link — without using JavaScript at all!

The code in Listing 13-3 shows you two approaches: using a simple HTML link, and using `setTimeout()` to call the `reload()` method. Figure 13-2 shows you how the code in Listing 13-3 appears when loaded into Navigator.

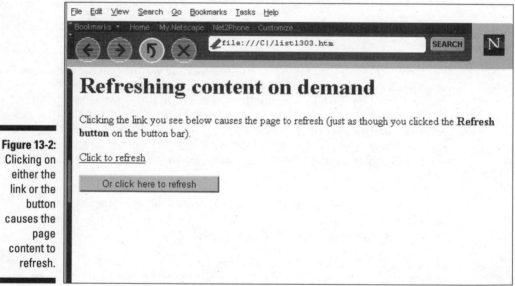

Figure 13-2:
Clicking on either the link or the button causes the page content to refresh.

Listing 13-3:   **Refreshing Content on Demand with** `setTimeout()`

```
<HTML>
<HEAD><TITLE>Refreshing content on demand (from JavaScript
          For Dummies, 3rd edition)</TITLE>
</HEAD>
<BODY>
<H1>Refreshing content on demand</H1>
Clicking the link you see below causes the page to
refresh (just as though you clicked the
<B>Refresh button</B> on the button bar).
<P>
//When clicked, this link causes the page to reload
          immediately
<A HREF="list1303.htm">Click to refresh</A>
<P>
<FORM>
```

```
//When clicked, this button causes the page to reload in one
        millisecond
<INPUT TYPE="button" VALUE="Or click here to refresh"
onClick="setTimeout('self.location.reload()', 1)">
</FORM>
</BODY>
</HTML>
```

If you work with HTML, the code to create a link (`<A HREF="list1303.htm">Click to refresh</A>`) is probably very familiar to you. The second approach to refreshing automatically, however, may not be familiar to you:

```
onClick="setTimeout('self.location.reload()', 1)"
```

`setTimeout()` expects two variables: the code you want to execute, and the number of milliseconds you want the JavaScript interpreter to wait before executing that code. The preceding JavaScript statement attaches the `setTimeout()` method of the `Window` object to the `onClick` event handler. So when a user clicks the button, the JavaScript interpreter waits one millisecond and then executes the `reload()` method associated with this window's `location` object. (`location` refers to the URL of the currently loaded page.)

You can use `clearTimeout()` method to halt a scheduled execution if you need to. In this example, you could provide users a way to stop the page from automatically being reloaded. You do this by assigning the value returned from `setTimeout()` to a variable, and then passing that variable to `clearTimeout()`, as shown in Listing 13-4.

Because users can potentially have very different browser configurations, interests, and temperaments, giving users as much control over automatic functions as possible is a good approach to Web page design. For example, users with very slow Internet connections (or those who read slowly) might appreciate being able to prevent a potentially intrusive automatic event such as a page reload.

Listing 13-4: Stop the Presses! with `setTimeout()`

```
// Schedule someFunction() to be executed in
// exactly 2 minutes

var timerId = setTimeout("someFunction()", 120000)

...

// Cancel the timeout so that someFunction() is NOT
// called
clearTimeout(timerId)
```

Chapter 14

JavaScript Tricks

In This Chapter

▶ Displaying a "site last updated" message

▶ Kicking off Java applets

▶ Password-protecting your site

▶ Creating new browser windows

▶ Detecting browser plug-ins

▶ Automatically scrolling text

▶ Letting users customize the way they view your pages

You can't use JavaScript to access a user's hard drive (without going through the browser's secure cookie mechanism, which you find out about in Chapter 6). You also can't use JavaScript to transfer information back to a Web server. (If you need to transmit information back to a Web server, you can set up an HTML form; when users submit the forms, the form data uploads to a Web server for inspection and processing.)

The actual transmittal of form data to a Web server is the province of HTML, not JavaScript. For details on how the form submission process works, check out a good HTML book, such as *HTML For Dummies*.

Other than that, you can do pretty much whatever you like with JavaScript. Especially these days: with every new browser version, both the JavaScript language and the document object model with which it interacts have become more and more sophisticated.

In this chapter, you see a handful of cool, useful effects you can create with JavaScript. From interacting with Java applets to password-protecting your Web site, this chapter contains something for everyone — whether you create Web pages for fun or profit. Use these examples as-is in your own development efforts, or let them inspire you to create your own knock-out JavaScript effects!

Dated for Freshness

Folks in cyberspace are spoiled: They expect the Web pages they visit to offer fresh content. ("Fresh" often means updated daily!)

The easiest way to let visitors know how current your Web site is is to append a Site Last Updated message to your content.

Many of the tools you use to create your Web site add such a message to your Web pages automatically. If yours doesn't (or if you just want to display the current date, to give the illusion of fresh content), all you have to do is drop in a few lines of JavaScript code similar to what I show you in Listing 14-1.

Before you add this code, though, take a look at Figure 14-1, which shows you how the JavaScript code in Listing 14-1 appears in Internet Explorer.

Listing 14-1: Adding a Fresh Date

```
<SCRIPT LANGUAGE="JavaScript">
<!-- Hide from browsers that do not support JavaScript
//This example uses the current date to "date" the site
// Get the current date
today = new Date();

// Get the current month
month = today.getMonth();

// Attach a display name to the month number
//The switch() statement assigns a display month to the
            generically formatted month returned by getMont()
switch (month) {
    case 0 :
        displayMonth = "January"
        break
    case 1 :
        displayMonth = "February"
        break
    case 2 :
        displayMonth = "March"
        break
    case 3 :
        displayMonth = "April"
        break
    case 4 :
        displayMonth = "May"
        break
    case 5 :
        displayMonth = "June"
```

```
            break
      case 6 :
          displayMonth = "July"
          break
      case 7 :
          displayMonth = "August"
          break
      case 8 :
          displayMonth = "September"
          break
      case 9 :
          displayMonth = "October"
          break
      case 10 :
          displayMonth = "November"
          break
      case 11 :
          displayMonth = "December"
          break

      default: displayMonth = "INVALID"
}

// To hard-code the date your site was last
// updated, simply pass the date string you
// want to use to writeln(), like this:
// document.writeln("Site last updated: May 20, 2000")
//Display the date on the Web page
document.writeln("Site last updated: "
    + displayMonth
    + " "
    + today.getDate()
    + ", "
    + today.getYear());

// -->
</SCRIPT>
```

The script in Listing 14-1 displays the current date on the Web page, as you see in Figure 14-1. (This approach is convenient if you do, in fact, update your Web site every day.)

To display a specific date, you can simply pass a date string to the writeln() method shown near the bottom of the script. For example:

```
document.writeln("Site last updated Monday, August 28, 2000")
```

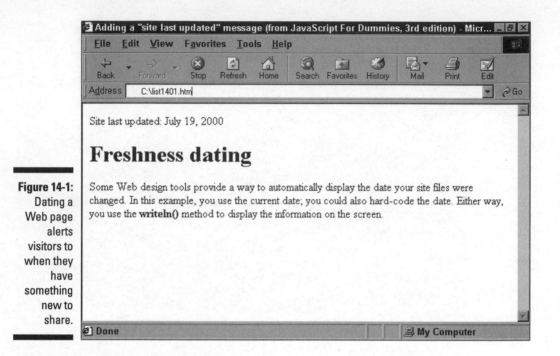

Figure 14-1:
Dating a
Web page
alerts
visitors to
when they
have
something
new to
share.

Applet-y Good

Java applets are programs written in the Java programming language that you can embed in your Web pages. At runtime, Java applets stream from a Web server to the user's browser and execute right there, in the browser's Java execution environment.

Java-supporting browsers such as Internet Explorer and Netscape Navigator come complete with a Java execution environment, commonly referred to as a Java virtual machine, or *JVM* for short.

You embed Java applets in a Web page using HTML tags — either <APPLET> or <OBJECT>. But after you embed them in your page, you can interact with them — for example, call the methods they define or access the properties they expose — by using JavaScript. Listing 14-2 shows you how.

Listing 14-2: Calling a Java Applet's Methods Using JavaScript

```
<BODY>
<!--
This Java applet is freely available from JavaSoft.
For more info, visit
http://www.javasoft.com/openstudio/index.html
```

```
-->
<H1>Interacting with applets</H1>
You can call any method defined for a Java applet once that
           applet is embedded in a Web page.  By convention,
           all applets support the <B>start()</B> and
           <B>stop()</B> methods; most support others, as
           well.
<BR>
<P>
//Embeds a Java applet into the Web page. The browser looks
           for the Java code file JavaClock.class in the
           subdirectory "classes"
<APPLET CODEBASE="classes" CODE="JavaClock.class" WIDTH="150"
           HEIGHT="150" >
<PARAM     NAME="bgcolor" VALUE="FFFFFF">
<PARAM     NAME="border"      VALUE="5">
<PARAM     NAMF="ccolor"      VALUE="dddddd">
<PARAM     NAME="cfont"       VALUE="TimesRoman|BOLD|18">
<PARAM     NAME="delay"       VALUE="100">
<PARAM     NAME="hhcolor" VALUE="0000FF">
<PARAM     NAME="link"       VALUE="http://java.sun.com/">
<PARAM     NAME="mhcolor" VALUE="00FF00">
<PARAM     NAME="ncolor"      VALUE="000000">
<PARAM     NAME="nradius" VALUE="80">
<PARAM     NAME="shcolor" VALUE="FF0000">
</APPLET>

<P>
<FORM>
//Invokes the applet's stop() method, which stops the clock
<INPUT TYPE="button" VALUE="Stop the clock"
           onClick="document.applets[0].stop()">

//Invokes the applet's start() method, which restarts the
           clock a'ticking
<INPUT TYPE="button" VALUE="Start the clock"
           onClick="document.applets[0].start()">

</FORM>

</BODY>
```

Figure 14-2 demonstrates how the code in Listing 14-2 works. In a nutshell, the clock applet defines two methods: stop() and start(). Invoking these methods from JavaScript — in this case, from the onClick event handlers associated with the Stop the Clock and Start the Clock buttons — causes the Java-implemented clock to stop and start, respectively:

```
...
onClick="document.applets[0].stop()"
...
onClick="document.applets[0].start()"
```

The built-in `applets[]` array contains a list of all the applets embedded in a document. So `document.applets[0]` refers to the first — and, in this case, only — Java applet embedded in this document. A second embedded applet would be represented by `document.applets[1]`; a third, by `document.applets[2]`; a fourth, by `document.applets[3]`; and so on.

By definition, all Java applets define the `start()` and `stop()` methods, but most applets define many more, as well. The total number and type of methods implemented depends completely on the applet developer. A calculator applet, for example, might support methods such as `add()`, `subtract()`, `multiply()`, and `divide()`.

How do you know the names of the methods an applet defines — let alone the number of parameters each method expects? By asking the applet developer, of course! Applet developers must document the methods and properties their applets support and make that documentation available along with their applet code.

The applet you see demonstrated in this section was implemented and made freely available by the good folks at JavaSoft. To experiment with this code, download the JavaClock example from the JavaSoft site:

```
http://www.javasoft.com/openstudio/index.html
```

Beneath whatever directory you install list1402.htm, install the necessary Java files in a subdirectory called CLASSES).

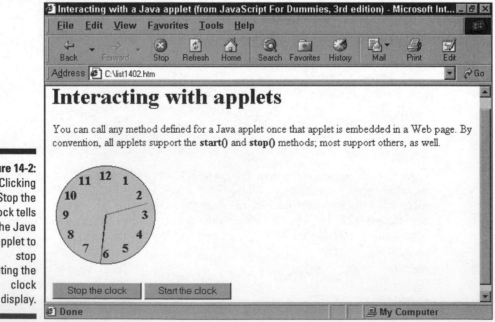

Figure 14-2: Clicking Stop the Clock tells the Java applet to stop updating the clock display.

Psst! Pass It Along!

Security on the Web is of enormous importance, for obvious reasons!
Developers whose Web applications absolutely, positively must be secure
typically turn to intranets (internal, company-wide networks that don't connect directly to the Internet), firewalls (computers that sit between the
Internet to provide a physical layer of security), and other heavy-duty security measures to safeguard and restrict access to their data.

But in certain situations, you may not need heavy-duty security measures.
For some Web applications, you might be satisfied with the cyber-equivalent
of a "Beware of dog" sign: a password protection scheme that *can* be circum-
vented — but that will deter most (if not all) of the mischievous folks who
visit your site.

Using JavaScript, you can create your own virtual bulldog! Take a look at
Listing 14-3 to see what I mean.

Listing 14-3: `prompt()` **and** `onLoad` **Combine to Form
a Simple Password-Protection Scheme**

```
<HTML>
<HEAD><TITLE>Password-protecting a site with JavaScript (from
          JavaScript For Dummies, 3rd edition)</TITLE>

<SCRIPT LANGUAGE="JavaScript">

function getPassword() {
//The window.prompt() method lets users type in a value

    var password = prompt("Please enter a password:
          \('secret'\)", "xxxxx")
//Checking the password to see if it's the correct one (in
          this case, the correct password is "secret")

    if (password == "secret") {
//The password is correct, so display the site.
        document.writeln("<BODY><H1>Congratulations!</H1>Your
          password was accepted.  Please enjoy our
          site.</BODY>")
    }
    else {
//The password is incorrect, so display an error message
          instead of the "real" site.
        document.writeln("<BODY><H1>Sorry!</H1>You attempted
          to access our site with an incorrect password.
          Please hit the <B>back</B> button on your browser
          and try again.</BODY>")
```

(continued)

Listing 14-3 *(continued)*

```
      }
}

</SCRIPT>

</HEAD>
//The getPassword() function is called as soon as a user
           tries to load the page
<BODY onLoad="getPassword()">
</BODY>
</HTML>
```

Executing the code in Listing 14-3 pops up the display you see in Figure 14-3. The input field you see in Figure 14-3 is preloaded with a bunch of x's by the parameters passed to the prompt() method (which you can see in Listing 14-3). To input a password value, users can delete or just type over these x's.

Figure 14-3:
Users must
type a valid
password to
see the
restricted-
access Web
page.

Explorer User Prompt	☒
Script Prompt:	OK
Please enter a password: ('secret')	Cancel
xxxxx	

If the user types in a valid password (which, in this case, is secret), that user gets to see a password-restricted page, such as the one shown in Figure 14-4.

As you can see in Figure 14-3, in this example, the correct password — secret — appears in the text of the prompt. I do this so that if you're experimenting with the code in Listing 14-3 and accidentally lose your place in this book, you'll know what the correct password is so that you can run the example! In a real-life situation, of course, you would not display the correct password this way.

If, on the other hand, the user types in an incorrect password, a different (error-bearing) Web page appears — like the one shown in Figure 14-5

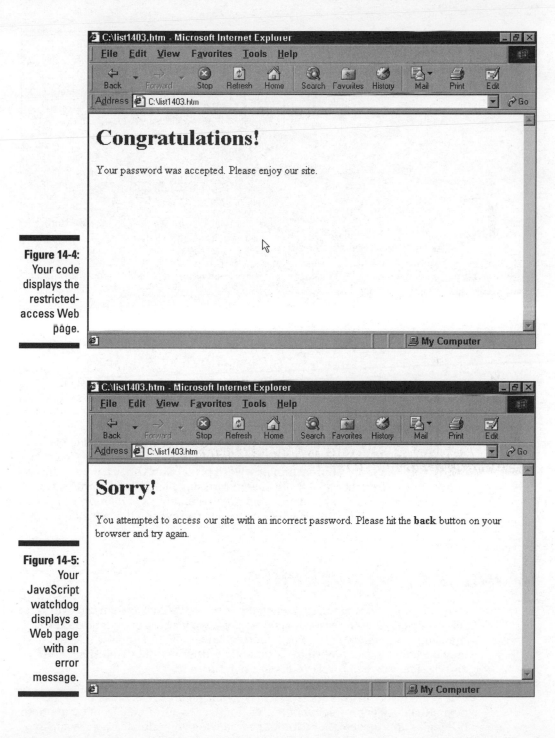

Figure 14-4:
Your code
displays the
restricted-
access Web
page.

Figure 14-5:
Your
JavaScript
watchdog
displays a
Web page
with an
error
message.

Security blanket

HTML forms can contain an input element called a `password` element. You create a password element like this:

```
<FORM>

...

<INPUT TYPE="password" ...>

</FORM>
```

The password element — just like the password-protection example I demonstrate in this chapter — represents a quick and dirty way of implementing security on a Web site. Neither approach is bulletproof, however. For example, although the `password` element doesn't appear on the screen as a user types it in, it isn't encrypted when it's sent to a Web server.

Likewise, the example I show you in this chapter is appropriate for some applications, but not for those that require strict security measures. (JavaScript is incapable of encrypting password information.)

If you need real, robust security measures, you need to bypass JavaScript's so-so security in favor of solutions that

- ✔ Encrypt password information as that information travels from client to server

- ✔ Allow you to approve or deny access on the Web server (before sending protected information to the browser)

Technically, the approach you see here is considered a relatively insecure solution. Why? Because the code containing the secret password is stored in text format in the HTML file (just as you see in Listing 14-3) and is downloaded to the browser. Although the average surfer can't see the secret password, unscrupulous hacker-types can. Still, this approach is quick, easy, and effective for restricting access to non-life-threatening secret information. (In other words, the JavaScript approach to password protection you see here is fine if you're putting together a Web site of embarrassing high school pictures for a college reunion and want to restrict access to alumni; it's *inappropriate* for highly sensitive information such as company secrets and financial data.)

Window of Opportunity

One popular school of thought when it comes to Web design is to do everything you can (within reason, of course!) to keep visitors at your site after they find it. For example, adding hypertext links to your site — while useful — may backfire by scooting your visitors off to other people's Web sites. After all, who knows when (or if) your visitors return?

One remedy for this situation is to make your page's HTML links open the next site in a new browser window. Visitors get to surf freely from your site to others, as appropriate, but without ever leaving your site. It's a win-win situation! Take a look at Figures 14-6 and 14-7 to see what I mean.

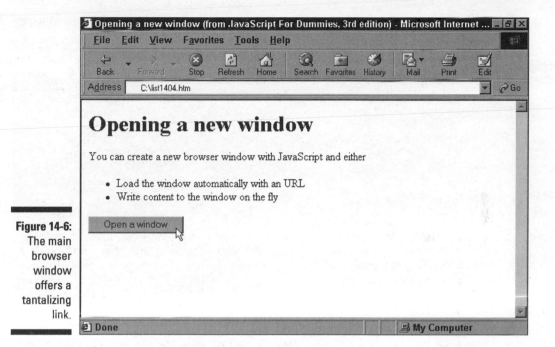

Figure 14-6:
The main
browser
window
offers a
tantalizing
link.

In Figure 14-7 you see how creating a new window to display a link leaves the original browser window intact.

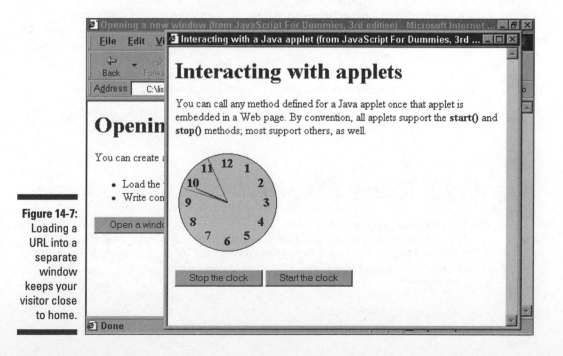

Figure 14-7:
Loading a
URL into a
separate
window
keeps your
visitor close
to home.

Creating such a new window is mighty easy in JavaScript. Listing 14-4 shows you how!

Listing 14-4:   Loading a URL into a New Browser Window

```
<SCRIPT LANGUAGE="JavaScript">

function popItUp() {
//Creating a new window and loading it with applet.htm
    var newWindow = open("list1402.htm", "secondWindow",
           "scrollbars,resizable,width=500,height=400");
}

</SCRIPT>
```

To create a new browser window and load it with a new document automatically, you need to use the `open()` method associated with the `window` object as shown in Listing 14-4. As you can see, the `open()` method accepts three parameters:

- The URL you want to load into the new window (in this case, `list1402.htm`)
- The name for this new window (in this example, the name of the new window is `secondWindow`)
- A string of configuration options

  In this example, the window you create has scrollbars, has a user-resizing option, and appears with initial dimensions of 500 x 400 pixels. (A quick peek at Figure 14-7 shows you the visible scrollbars; you can verify the other characteristics by loading the file LIST1404.HTM from the companion CD in your own browser.)

To see a full description of the `open()` method, check out:

```
http://developer.netscape.com/docs/manuals/js/client/jsref/wi
        ndow.htm#1202731.
```

Are Your Users Plugged In?

In Navigator, plug-ins are referred to (oddly enough!) as plug-ins. To plug non-HTML content into a document for display in Navigator, you use the HTML `<EMBED>` tag. To see that plugged-in content, users must first download the correct plug-in and install it into their version of Navigator.

Internet Explorer, not surprisingly, supports a different plug-in scheme. Rather than embed objects using an <EMBED> tag, Internet Explorer embeds non-HTML content called *ActiveX objects* via the HTML <OBJECT> tag.

Both browsers support the embedding of a specialized type of non-HTML content — Java applets — via the HTML <APPLET> tag.

HTML 4.0 favors the <OBJECT> tag over <APPLET>. What this means is that you can use the <OBJECT> tag to embed applets, just as you can the <APPLET> tag. However, the specialized <APPLET> tag may not be supported in future browser versions, so it's a good idea to start using the <OBJECT> tag.

How do you determine, at runtime, whether a user has specific plugged-in content? JavaScript offers two different ways:

- **Navigator:** The navigator.plugins[] array contains a list of all the plug-ins Navigator supports. (Popular plug-ins include Adobe Acrobat and Macromedia Flash.) The navigator.mimeTypes[] array contains a list of all of the MIME types supported by Navigator. (MIME, which stands for *Multipurpose Internet Mail Extension*, refers to the file types that Navigator can understand and display. Examples of popular MIME types include Adobe's portable document framework (pdf) and Real.com's RealAudio (ram).

- **Both Navigator and Internet Explorer:** The document.embeds[] array contains a list of all of the objects embedded in a document via the <OBJECT> tag (Internet Explorer) and the <EMBED> tag (Netscape Navigator). The document.applets[] array contains a list of all of the applets embedded in a document via the <APPLET> tag.

In Internet Explorer, the navigator.plugins[] and navigator.mimeTypes[] arrays are always null, because Internet Explorer implements embedded ActiveX objects in place of plug-ins. To detect embedded content in documents viewed in Internet Explorer, access the document.embeds[] array.

Detecting plugged-in content can be a little tricky. Fortunately, the code you see in Listing 14-5 helps you understand the differences between embedded objects and plug-ins.

Before scanning the code listing, though, first take a look at Figures 14-8 and 14-9, which show the code in Listing 14-5 loaded in Netscape Navigator and Internet Explorer, respectively. You can click on the Detect Plug-Ins button to display all the plug-ins installed in the user's version of Netscape Navigator.

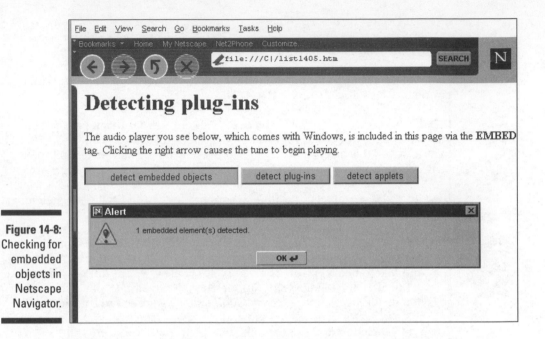

Figure 14-8:
Checking for
embedded
objects in
Netscape
Navigator.

Figure 14-9 shows how clicking the Detect Embedded Objects button displays the total number of `<EMBED>` and `<OBJECT>` tags in this document. You can click OK to cycle through each button and message. (Clicking Detect Plug-Ins displays the number of plug-ins you have downloaded and installed on your own machine; clicking Detect Applets displays the number of Java applets embedded in the document — which is none, since no `<APPLET>` tags are included in the code in Listing 14-5.)

The same code — Listing 14-5 — executed in Internet Explorer appears a bit differently, but it works the same. The only difference in behavior, in fact, is that when you click on the `Detect Plug-Ins` button, the number of plug-ins detected is always *none*, because Internet Explorer does not recognize or implement plug-ins.

Now take a look at Listing 14-5. As you skim through the code, notice the similarities in detecting different kinds of embedded content. In each case, you examine the `length` property associated with a built-in array (`navigator.plugins.length`, `document.embeds.length`, and `document.applets.length` to detect plug-ins, embedded objects, and embedded applets, respectively).

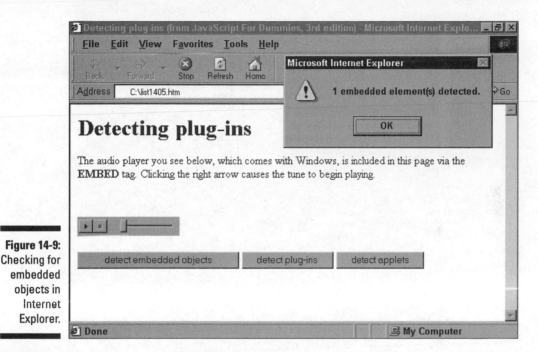

Listing 14-5:   Detecting Plugged-in Content

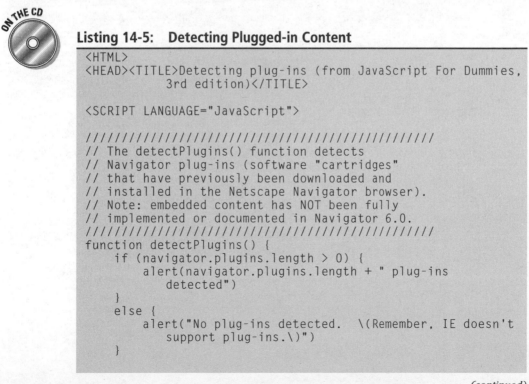

```
<HTML>
<HEAD><TITLE>Detecting plug-ins (from JavaScript For Dummies,
          3rd edition)</TITLE>

<SCRIPT LANGUAGE="JavaScript">

///////////////////////////////////////////////
// The detectPlugins() function detects
// Navigator plug-ins (software "cartridges"
// that have previously been downloaded and
// installed in the Netscape Navigator browser).
// Note: embedded content has NOT been fully
// implemented or documented in Navigator 6.0.
///////////////////////////////////////////////
function detectPlugins() {
    if (navigator.plugins.length > 0) {
        alert(navigator.plugins.length + " plug-ins
            detected")
    }
    else {
        alert("No plug-ins detected.  \(Remember, IE doesn't
            support plug-ins.\)")
    }
```

(continued)

Listing 14-5 *(continued)*

```
        // Another way to detect Navigator plug-ins is
        // to examine the mimeTypes[] array, like this:
        // if (navigator.mimeTypes["application/pdf"]
        //      != null) ...
        //
        // You can also query for a particular plug-in
        // like so:
        // if (navigator.plugins["Shockwave"] != null)...

}

/////////////////////////////////////////////////
// The detectEmbeds() function detects content
// embedded in a Web page via the EMBED
// or OBJECT tag.
//
// The length of the document.embeds array
// represents the number of objects embedded
// in a Web page.
//
// The existence of additional embeds[]
// properties depends on the implementation
// of each embedded object.
/////////////////////////////////////////////////
function detectEmbeds() {

    if (document.embeds.length > 0) {
        alert(document.embeds.length + " embedded element(s)
            detected.")

        // Because this embedded object defined a
        // value for the SRC attribute, you can
        // examine the src property if you like,
        // like so:
        //
        // document.embeds[0].src
    }
    else {
        alert("No embedded elements detected.")
    }
}


/////////////////////////////////////////////////
// The detectApplets() function detects Java
// applets embedded in a Web page via the
// APPLET tag.
//
// The length of the document.applets array
// represents the number of objects embedded
// in a Web page.
//
```

```
// The existence of additional applets[]
// properties and methods depends on the
// implementation of each individual applet.
//////////////////////////////////////////////////
function detectApplets() {
    if (document.applets.length > 0) {
        alert(document.applets.length + " Java applets
            detected.")

    }
    else {
        alert("No Java applets detected.")
    }
}


</SCRIPT>

</HEAD>
<BODY>
<H1>Detecting plug-ins</H1>
The audio player you see below, which comes with Windows, is
            included in this page via the <B>EMBED</B> tag.
            Clicking the right arrow causes the tune to begin
            playing.
<P>
<!-- ATTENTION Windows NT and Win 2K users:

Substitute "c:\winnt\media\canyon.mid: for the SRC value
            below

-->
<EMBED SRC="c:\windows\media\canyon.mid" CONTROLS="console"
            HEIGHT="60" WIDTH="145"></EMBED>

<P>
<FORM>
<INPUT TYPE="button" VALUE="detect embedded objects"
            onClick="detectEmbeds()">

<INPUT TYPE="button" VALUE="detect plug-ins"
            onClick="detectPlugins()">

<INPUT TYPE="button" VALUE="detect applets"
            onClick="detectApplets()">
</FORM>
</BODY>
</HTML>
```

Keep in mind that you can use two ways to detect Netscape Navigator plug-ins: by examining the `navigator.plugins[]` array and by examining the `navigator.mimeTypes[]` array, as shown in Listing 14-5. Because Internet Explorer does not support plug-ins, however, (instead, Internet Explorer supports embedded ActiveX controls), these two arrays are *always* empty in Internet Explorer.

Objects embedded using either the `<EMBED>` or `<OBJECT>` tag are added to the `document.embeds[]` array.

`document.plugins[]` is a synonym for the `document.embeds[]` array, but because `document.plugins[]` appears so similar to `navigator.plugins[]` — an array that holds an entirely different kind of object — I suggest sticking with `document.embeds[]` when you want to determine the number of embedded `<OBJECT>` and `<EMBED>` tags contained in a document.

Just Scrollin' Along

For certain applications, scrolling text (either horizontal or vertical) can provide a sophisticated, eye-catching change from static text.

An option is to use the HTML `<MARQUEE>` tag, which allows you to create horizontally scrolling text effects. Unfortunately, only Internet Explorer supports the `<MARQUEE>` tag.

To create the scrolling text effect, you follow this plan:

1. **Use the** `scrollTo()` **method associated with the** `window` **object to scroll the text to a specified spot on the screen.**

2. **Use the** `setTimeout()` **and** `clearTimeout()` **methods associated with the** `window` **object to call** `scrollTo()` **over and over.**

   The repeated calling of `scrollTo()` is what creates the continuous scrolling effect.

In the example you see in Listing 14-6, a document begins auto-scrolling vertically the instant it's loaded into a browser. This presents an effect as if a user is dragging the right scroll bar slowly down.

Listing 14-6:   Auto-Scrolling Page Content

```
...
<SCRIPT LANGUAGE="JavaScript">

var position = 0

/////////////////////////////////////////////////////////
```

```
// Scroll vertically 1,000 pixels (which is enough
// times to display the content for this page when
// viewed in a standard-sized window.)
//////////////////////////////////////////////////
//The scrollIt() function
function scrollIt() {
    if (position != 1000) {
        position++;

        // Since we want to scroll vertically only
        // in this case, we continue to pass 0 to
        // the scrollTo() function but bump up the
        // value of the position variable each time
        // we call scrollTo().  This makes the
        // scroll effect appear to be very smooth.
//Scroll the window vertically
        window.scrollTo(0, position);
        clearTimeout(timer);
//Call the scrollIt() function again
        var timer = setTimeout("scrollIt()", 25);
    }
}
</SCRIPT>
</HEAD>
//As soon as the page loads, call the scrollIt() function
<BODY onLoad="scrollIt()">
. . .
```

For a detailed description of the `scroll()To`, `setTimeout()`, and `clearTimeout()` methods, visit

```
http://developer.netscape.com/docs/manuals/js/client/jsref/bk
         last.htm
```

Different Strokes for Different Folks

Using JavaScript, you can offer your users the opportunity to view your Web site the way *they* want to view it. How? By triggering a `prompt()` method on the `onLoad` event handler and using the user's response to build the `<BODY>` section of an HTML document. Listing 14-7 shows you a simple example.

Listing 14-7:   Customizing Page Appearance On the Fly

```
<SCRIPT LANGUAGE="JavaScript">

//////////////////////////////////////////////////
// You can use JavaScript to determine
```

(continued)

Listing 14-7 *(continued)*

```
// user preferences before the page
// loads -- and then use those
// preferences to display Web page content
// appropriately.
//////////////////////////////////////////

// Ask the user for a color preference
var displayColor = prompt("What background color do you
          want?", "red")

// The default text color is black
var textColor = "black"

// If the user chooses a black background, change
// the text to white so it is visible

if (displayColor == "black" || displayColor == "#000000" ||
          displayColor == null) {
    textColor = "white"
}

// Display page content
//The BODY tag and document content are generated by the
          writeln() method
document.writeln("<BODY BGCOLOR=" + displayColor + " TEXT=" +
          textColor + ">You chose " + displayColor +
          "</BODY>")

</SCRIPT>
```

Figure 14-10 shows you how users can type the name of a color to select a background, which appears in the next page, as shown in Figure 14-11.

Figure 14-10:
Red, black, yellow, blue . . . Pick a color, any color!

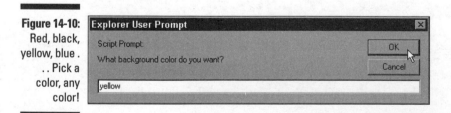

Customizing page display (from JavaScript For Dummies, 3rd edition) - Microsoft Intern...

File   Edit   View   Favorites   Tools   Help

Back   Forward   Stop   Refresh   Home   Search   Favorites   History   Mail   Print   Edit

Address C:\list1407.htm   Go

You chose yellow

Figure 14-11:
This user
chose a
blinding
yellow
background.

Done   My Computer

When you place the script in Listing 14-7 between the beginning and ending
HTML `<HEAD>...</HEAD>` tags, the script statements execute right away —
before the Web page loads. The `prompt()` method prompts the user to enter a
favorite color; that color is then used to construct and display the document
body. (If the user clicks Cancel, the default color scheme, white text on a black
background, appears.)

Insert, stage left

Theoretically, another way to incorporate
JavaScript-gathered user input into HTML tags
(besides the approach shown in Listing 14-7) is
to use *JavaScript entities*. A JavaScript entity is
a JavaScript statement enclosed on the left by
an ampersand and an open curly brace, and
enclosed on the right by a closing curly brace
and a semicolon, like this:

```
&{    };
```

JavaScript entities let you assign the results of
JavaScript statements to HTML attributes.
Here's an example of a JavaScript entity:

```
<BODY
    BGCOLOR="&{getBackgroundCol
    or();};">
```

Unfortunately, while JavaScript entities are supported by some older versions of Internet
Explorer and Netscape Navigator, the latest versions do not yet fully support JavaScript entities.

Part V
The Part of Tens

The 5th Wave — By Rich Tennant

"You're part of an 'Insect-Clothing Club' on the Web? Neat! Where do you get buttons that small?"

In this part . . .

Part V begins with a list of some great JavaScript-related Web sites that are full of useful information about all aspects of JavaScript. If you feel the need to communicate with real live people about your JavaScript scripts, Chapter 15 even provides you with a list of some user groups that enable you to do just that.

These online resources are followed by a chapter explaining the most common mistakes you're likely to run into when you implement your Web pages (along with tips on how to avoid them). And finally, no programming book worth its salt would be complete without at least a few handy debugging techniques. Chapter 17 provides you with lots of bug-related tips that make debugging — if not downright pleasant — at least entirely bearable!

Chapter 15

Top Ten (Or So) Online JavaScript Resources

In This Chapter

▶ Finding and using JavaScript tutorials

▶ Reading up on the JavaScript FAQs

▶ Finding cool JavaScript examples online

▶ Taking advantage of the essential JavaScript related newsgroups

Getting help on how to do something has never been easier than it is right now. Why? The Internet, of course! From its roots in government and university installations, the Internet remained a close-knit, mostly academic community until as recently as a few years ago. Inevitably, commercialism reared its ugly head and has had a tremendous effect — and not all bad, either — on all things Net. (For example, the commercialism of the Internet is directly responsible for the proliferation of Web tools and languages such as JavaScript.)

Although marketing and advertising have become common on the Internet, the spirit of sharing and intellectual collaboration hasn't been snuffed out. Helping other people (and maybe showing off a little in the process) is a fundamental joy. And because access to the Internet is relatively cheap and easy, everybody and their dog indulges — as you see when you visit the URLs and newsgroups listed in this chapter.

Ten Web Sites to Check Out

With no further ado, then, on to the good stuff: a list of irresistibly good JavaScript-related Web resources. You'll find tips, tricks, tutorials, examples, and up-to-the- minute documentation. The site's URL follows a description of the goodies offered.

Netscape

Netscape's JavaScript Developer Central contains a wealth of information on getting started with JavaScript, including a complete language reference, how-to articles, and sample code. It also offers a list of known JavaScript bugs (for Navigator releases).

```
http://developer.netscape.com/tech/javascript/
```

Microsoft

Microsoft maintains an information-packed site devoted to their JavaScript-compatible language, JScript. Documentation, tutorials, sample code, and access to JScript-related newsgroups are just some of the great resources you find here.

```
http://msdn.microsoft.com/scripting/jscript/default.htm
```

CNET

Dubbed "Spotlight on JavaScript," CNET Builder.com's JavaScript section features tips and tutorials in addition to cut-and-paste JavaScript code.

```
http://builder.cnet.com/Programming/JsSpotlight/
```

ZDNet

ZDNet maintains a killer JavaScript Developer section with tutorials, in-depth articles (many on form validation techniques), downloadable JavaScript development tools, and an archive of JavaScript code — all free for the taking.

```
http://www.zdnet.com/devhead/filters/javascript
```

Project Cool's JavaScript Zone

Project Cool's JavaScript Zone offers hands-on JavaScript tutorials. From basic to advanced, all are organized into neat, bite-sized chunks perfect for beginning JavaScript programmers.

```
http://www.projectcool.com/developer/jsz/index.html
```

Gamelan

Gamelan's JavaScripts.com offers tutorials, online discussion groups, a free weekly JavaScript-intensive newsletter, and a huge (6,000 and counting) repository of cut-and-paste scripts.

```
http://javascripts.earthweb.com/toc.cfm
```

About.com

About.com's "Focus on JavaScript" contains articles, tutorials, and download-able scripts on every conceivable JavaScript related topic — including my personal favorite, cross-browser compatibility.

```
http://javascript.about.com/compute/javascript/
```

Netscape's DevEdge FAQ

Not just a list of helpful questions and answers, Netscape's DevEdge FAQ for JavaScript includes direct access to a JavaScript newsgroup as well as to a handful of real, live JavaScript gurus.

```
http://developer.netscape.com/support/faqs/champions/
            javascript.html
```

WebReference.com

WebReference.com's homegrown JavaScript resource list contains links to online JavaScript magazines, script archives, and much more.

```
http://www.webreference.com/programming/javascript.html
```

ScriptSearch.com

ScriptSearch.com maintains a giant database of JavaScript scripts, from ad banners to visual effects.

```
http://www.scriptsearch.com/pages/14.shtml
```

Stop, thief!

Most of the sites I describe in this chapter are commercial sites, and without exception, the JavaScript source code they offer is clearly marked "for free download." (You may have to register your e-mail address before you can download, though, so these companies can stick you on their electronic mailing lists.)

But if you're looking for scripts, you're not limited to commercial sites. As you may know, you can cut and paste embedded JavaScript source code from *any* site, with or without that Webmaster's permission, simply by clicking

View⇨Source (from Internet Explorer) or View⇨Page Source (Navigator). (This is one reason why password protection and other highly sensitive features aren't typically implemented in JavaScript!)

One caveat: If you run across source that includes a copyright notice, contact the author or Webmaster and ask for permission before using it. (It never hurts to ask!) If in doubt, don't copy a file line for line; instead, take a look at how the programmer solved the problem and base your solution on the overall approach.

Not-to-Be-Missed Newsgroups

The Web sites listed in the preceding section are a great source of information. Sometimes, though, you just have to send a message to a real live person and ask a point-blank question. Newsgroups can be a great timesaver, especially when it comes to researching specific how-to's and known bugs.

To access newsgroups, you need to have a news server defined. Generally, you set up both a Web server and a news server as part of the browser installation and configuration process, but you can always add news support later.

To participate in a user group, either by viewing other peoples' messages or by posting your own, you need to switch from surfing the Web to perusing the news. To do this, choose Tasks⇨Newsgroups from the Navigator menu or Tools⇨Mail and News⇨Read News if you're an Internet Explorer fan.

For detailed instructions on configuring your browser software to access newsgroups, check with your browser provider (in other words, contact technical support at either Microsoft or Netscape) or check out a good book on the topic, such as *The Internet For Dummies*, by John R. Levine, Carol Baroudi, and Margaret Levine Young (IDG Books Worldwide, Inc.).

Collectively, newsgroups are known as *Usenet*. For more information about newsgroups — including where to find news, how to write effective posts, and even how to create your own — visit Usenet.org at

`www.usenet.org/.`

Although user groups come and go, the following have established themselves as *the* place to be for JavaScript-related development:

- If you only follow one user group, make it the following one. This group is very well attended and is currently the premier JavaScript information group, for newbies and advanced scripters alike:

  `comp.lang.javascript`

  (`it.comp.lang.javascript` and `de.comp.lang.javascript` are high-traffic Italian- and German-language versions.)

- Get answers to HTML questions answered here:

  `comp.infosystems.www.authoring.html`

- Microsoft's public scripting newsgroup focuses on JScript tips and questions:

  `microsoft.public.scripting.jscript`

- JavaScript "champions" monitor Netscape's scripting newsgroup. (This newsgroup can be accessed only through a special, secure news server. For simple instructions on how to access this news group, visit http://developer.netscape.com/support/faqs/champions/javascript.html.)

  netscape-devs.javascript

Chapter 16

Ten (Or So) Most Common JavaScript Mistakes (And How to Avoid Them)

In This Chapter

▶ Typographical errors

▶ Unmatched pairs

▶ Putting scripting statements between HTML tags

▶ Nesting quotes incorrectly

▶ Treating numbers like strings

▶ Treating strings like numbers

▶ Logic errors

*E*very JavaScript author makes mistakes. (Actually, I like to think of it in the reverse — it's the JavaScript *interpreter* that makes the mistakes by not figuring out what we humans mean by something. Yeah! That's it!) Most of the time, the errors you make fall into one of the categories listed in this chapter. The good news is, the errors are all easy to correct. The better news is, JavaScript tells you quickly — and in no uncertain terms — when it encounters an error.

Check out this book's companion CD to see the sample listings scattered throughout this chapter. I've named the files after the listings so you can find them easily. For example, you can find Listing 16-1 in the file list1601.htm.

Typing-in-a-Hurry Errors

Spelling and capitalization errors easily take first prize for being the most common mistakes all JavaScripters make, from the greenest beginner to the most highly seasoned veteran.

HTML woes

Because JavaScript statements are embedded in HTML files, some of the mistakes you may find are actually HTML mistakes. For example, the following is an HTML error (TYE="button" should be TYPE="button"):

```
<INPUT TYE="button" NAME="testButton" VALUE="test"
onClick='test()'>
```

In this case, the JavaScript interpreter won't display an error message because the error doesn't concern it. What *will* happen is that your button element won't display properly.

If your page doesn't behave as expected and JavaScript doesn't alert you, you're probably dealing with an HTML error. If this happens (and you can't find the solution in this chapter), check out a good HTML reference such as *HTML For Dummies,* 3rd Edition, by Ed Tittel and Steve James (published by IDG Books Worldwide, Inc.).

The JavaScript interpreter is a stickler for correct spelling: you simply can't access an object, property, method, variable, or function unless you spell its name properly. For example, the following generates an error:

```
var identification = "ABC"
alert("The id number is " + identificatoin) // error:
        misspelled variable
```

The JavaScript interpreter is also case-sensitive, which means you can't substitute upper-case letters for lower-case letters in object, property, method, variable, or function names:

```
alert("Broadcast network ID = " +
        identification.TOLOWERCASE() // error: correct
        method name is toLowerCase()
```

To detect and correct these errors:

- ✔ Be aware, as you write your JavaScript code, that consistency in spelling and capitalization is essential to bug-free statements

- ✔ Take advantage of any spell checking utilities or point-and-click method name insertion utilities your text editor provides

Breaking Up a Happy Pair

JavaScript scripts are typically rife with pairs: pairs of opening and closing tags (courtesy of HTML), pairs of parentheses and curly braces, pairs of quotes and double quotes. The JavaScript interpreter treats the stuff between the pairs as one entity, so if one half of the pair is missing, the interpreter gets confused — mighty confused, in some cases!

Following are specific examples of happy couples you don't want to break up in JavaScript.

Lonely angle brackets

Looking at the following code, you'd think that the display would include two text elements: one to hold a first name, and one to hold a last name. It doesn't, though, because a closing angle bracket is missing.

```
<FORM NAME="myForm">
. . .
First name: <INPUT TYPE="text" NAME="firstName" LENGTH=15
//missing an angle bracket after LENGTH-15
Last name: <INPUT TYPE="text" NAME="lastName" LENGTH=30>
. . .
```

If a text element doesn't appear — no error message, no nothing, just blank space where the element should have appeared — immediately suspect a missing angle bracket on the line right before the invisible text element.

Lonely tags

The code you see in Listing 16-1 depicts a tiny little script, perhaps a first attempt at a JavaScript-enabled Web page. At first blush, perhaps you don't see anything amiss. If you were to load this script, though, you'd see that something is *definitely* amiss!

Listing 16-1:   Source Containing a Missing Tag

```
. . .
<HEAD>
<SCRIPT LANGUAGE="JavaScript">
function test() {
    var aString = "some text"
    alert("aString is " + aString)
}
```

(continued)

Listing 16-1 (continued)

```
//The closing </SCRIPT> tag that should be here is missing.
</HEAD>
<BODY>
<FORM NAME="myForm">
<INPUT TYPE="button" NAME="testButton" VALUE="test"
onClick='test()'>
<P>
First name: <INPUT TYPE="text" NAME="firstName" LENGTH=15>
Last name: <INPUT TYPE="text" NAME="lastName" LENGTH=30>
</FORM>
</BODY>
</HTML>
```

The absence of the closing </SCRIPT> tag in the preceding code snippet causes the page to display nothing — zip, nada, zilch — instead of the button and text elements you expect.

Whenever elements refuse to appear, check your HTML statements to see if an opening two-part tag, such as <TITLE> . . .</TITLE>, <SCRIPT> . . . </SCRIPT>, or <BODY> . . .</BODY>, is missing its closing half.

Lonely parentheses

When you look closely at the body of the test() function in the following example, you can easily spot the missing parenthesis on line three. As your JavaScript skills increase, though, you may find yourself putting together whopping long statements. And, each of these may contain many pairs of parentheses, often nested a few layers deep — and that's when you're most likely to make this kind of mistake.

```
function test() {
    var aString = "some text"
    alert("aString is " + aString
//A closing parenthesis should end the previous statement
}
```

Unless the editor you use to create your script provides an automatic parentheses pair checking utility, you need to eyeball your code to catch and correct this mistake.

Lonely quotes

Take a good look at the following example:

```
<INPUT TYPE="button" NAME="testButton" VALUE="test"
onClick='test("hello)'>
```

The mistake here is that no closing double quote appears after the word `hello`.

Unmatched quotes manifest themselves differently in Internet Explorer 5.5 and Netscape Navigator 6.0. In Internet Explorer, the preceding code generates an `unterminated string constant` error. In Navigator, the code doesn't generate an error at all — it just disables the `testButton`'s `onClick` event handler.

Here's how the corrected statement looks:

```
<INPUT TYPE="button" NAME="testButton" VALUE="test"
onClick='test("hello")'>
```

Putting Scripting Statements in the Wrong Places

When you're new to JavaScript, remembering the order of things may be a little difficult. For example, JavaScript statements are valid only when they're placed between the `<SCRIPT>` . . .`</SCRIPT>` tags or as values assigned to event handlers. If you forget and place them somewhere else, you're bound to get an unexpected result.

The good news is, you find out as soon as you load your page and take a look at it that something is amiss — because your source code appears right there on the page! Check out the source shown in Listing 16-2 to see what I mean.

Listing 16-2: Source Containing Misplaced Scripting Statements

```
<SCRIPT LANGUAGE="JavaScript">
function test(inputValue) {
    alert("Wow, I sure do love JavaScript!" +
      "\nHere's what the public is saying about JavaScript: "
        +
        inputValue)
}
</SCRIPT>
// The addNumbers() function is incorrectly defined below the
            closing </SCRIPT> tag
function addNumbers(numberOne, numberTwo) {
    return numberOne + numberTwo
}
</HEAD>
 . . .
```

When you execute the code in Listing 16-2, you don't see a JavaScript error, but you do see the text of the `addNumbers()` function displayed on the screen. (You don't see a JavaScript error because the JavaScript interpreter can't access any statement outside of the beginning and ending `<SCRIPT>` tags — *unless* that statement is a value for an event handler.)

Moving the `</SCRIPT>` tag just after the closing brace of the `addNumbers()` function fixes this script, causing the JavaScript interpreter to interpret `addNumbers()` as JavaScript code.

Anytime that you see your well-crafted JavaScript statements displayed in living color appear on your page, you can be pretty sure that the problem is that your statements are outside the bounds of the `<SCRIPT> . . .</SCRIPT>` tags. Move the statements back to where they belong and they should behave.

Nesting Quotes Incorrectly

Nesting single and double quotes together, like so, is perfectly legitimate:

```
onClick="alert('This is an example of nested quotes.')"
```

or

```
onClick='alert("This is another example of nested quotes.")'
```

Just make sure that you don't nest double quotes inside double quotes, or single quotes inside single quotes, like this:

```
onClick="alert("Oops! These incorrectly nested quotes
            generate a syntax error!')'
```

Treating Numbers as Strings

Humans tend not to make a big fuss over the difference between text and numbers — at least not in most contexts. For example, when you write a sentence in English, you don't need to do anything different to include a number. (Even if you write 333 of them!)

Numbers and text strings are two very different things to most programming languages, though, and that includes JavaScript. In JavaScript trying to treat a number as a string, as shown in Listing 16-3, generates an error every time.

Listing 16-3: Source Containing Statement that Treats a Number Like a String

```
. . .
<SCRIPT LANGUAGE="JavaScript">
function testIt(inputValue) {
//The bold() method you see in the next line is associated
          with the string object (not the Number object)
    document.write(inputValue.bold())
    document.close()
}
</SCRIPT>

. . .
<FORM NAME="myForm">
//The following onClick event handler sends the number 2 to
          the testIt() function
<INPUT TYPE="button" NAME="testButton" VALUE="test"
onClick='testIt(2)'>
```

The problem occurs when the number 2 is passed from the definition of the onClick event handler to the testIt() function, which isn't set up to handle numbers. If you look at the testIt() function, you can see that it's taking whatever the input value is (in this case, the number 2) and trying to call the string object's bold() method on it. And that ain't flying. The only thing that you can call a string function on is a string, and 2 isn't a string! (If you'd like more information on what a string is, take a look at Chapter 3.)

Sometimes you *are* going to want to send a number to a function and have that function deal with it as a string. In these cases, all you need to do is add lines like the following to your function:

```
function testIt(inputValue) {
    // Set up a temporary string variable
    var aString = ""

    // Place the input value into the temporary
    // string variable
    aString += inputValue

    // Call the bold() method on the string version of
    // the inputValue
    document.write(aString.bold())

}
```

Now you can send whatever value you like to the testIt() function, and testIt() will behave nicely!

Treating Strings as Numbers

The preceding section shows what happens when you treat numbers as strings. As you may guess, the reverse — treating strings like numbers — also causes grief in JavaScript. Let me explain by way of the code snippet shown in Listing 16-4.

Listing 16-4: Source Containing Statement that Treats a String Like a Number

```
function calculateTax(inputNumber) {
    return inputNumber * .50
}
 . . .
<INPUT TYPE="button" NAME="calculateTaxButton"
    VALUE="Calculate"
onClick='alert("The tax is " + calculateTax("baked"))'>
 . . .
```

When you click the Calculate button, the string baked goes to the calculateTax() function, where it's immediately multiplied by .50. Now, if you can tell me what the result of baked times .50 is, you're a better mathematician than I'll ever be. (Okay, so maybe it's half-baked!) JavaScript doesn't know, either, so it displays a built-in value, NaN, which stands for "I don't know what the heck this is, but I do know it's Not A Number!)

Once again, in JavaScript as in life, you can do pretty much anything you like — *if* you know how to go about doing it! If you want to create a function that expects a number but can deal gracefully with a string (in programming circles, *gracefully* is a euphemism meaning "doesn't blow up in your face"), all you need to do is add a few lines to the very top of your function. Listing 16-5 shows you how.

Listing 16-5: Source for a Function that Expects a Number but Deals with a String

```
function calculateTax(inputNumber) {
    // myNumber will be false if inputNumber is a string
    var myNumber = parseFloat(inputNumber)

    // If the inputNumber was, in fact, a number,
    // perform the necessary calculation.
    if (myNumber) {
        return myNumber * .50
    }
    // Otherwise, display an error
    else {
        alert("A non-numeric value was passed to a function
            that expected a number")
```

```
        return inputNumber
    }
}
. . .
<INPUT TYPE="button" NAME="calculateTaxButton"
VALUE="Calculate"
onClick='alert("The tax is " + calculateTax("baked"))'>
    . . .
```

In this new, improved, better-tasting version, the first thing the calculateTax() function does is see whether it can convert whatever value it receives into a number. If it can, it converts the value, if necessary, and then goes on to perform its calculations on the converted value. For example, you can pass a number or a string, such as *1234.56*, to calculateTax() instead of the string baked. If the calculateTax() function can't make a conversion (what number does "baked" convert to?), it recognizes that it can't convert this value and doesn't bother to perform any calculations.

Missing the Point: Logic Errors

Logic errors are the most difficult errors to track down because they don't generate one specific type of error message. (You never see the JavaScript interpreter spit out a Clearly, that is not how you calculate the interest on a 20-year loan! message, for example.)

How could the JavaScript interpreter possibly know what you're logically trying to do? It can't read your code, analyze it, and confer with other interpreters to figure out if it accomplishes some reasonable task, the way a human can. JavaScript just skims your code for syntax errors. If you want to give your users the option to submit a form, but then not actually submit the form when they indicate Yes — that's up to you. JavaScript is not your mother!

The only way to track down logic errors is the old-fashioned way: by studying your code, displaying the contents of variables, making changes, and re-testing.

Neglecting Browser Incompatibility

Few things are more frustrating than spending hours creating a fantastic, impressive script, posting it to your Web server, and then having someone who visits your Web site e-mail you with the bad news: *It doesn't work in my Web browser!*

JavaScript support varies not just between Internet Explorer and Navigator, but among versions of these browsers, as well. If a script behaves as expected in one browser but tanks in another, you've run into the dreaded browser incompatibility problem. Here are three suggestions for overcoming this bane of every Web developer's existence:

1. **Always test your scripts in multiple browsers before going "live."**

   Before you actually post your JavaScript-enabled pages to your Web server (thereby exposing them for all the world to see) make sure you test them in as many browsers as possible.

   Although the America Online browser has a fairly large market share, it's often overlooked by JavaScript developers. You can download your own free copy of this browser from `http://free.aol.com`

   Rather than downloading and installing multiple browsers, you can take advantage of an online service, such as Net Mechanic, to help you spot cross-browser bugs at this site:

   `http://www.netmechanic.com/cobrands/zdnet/browsercheck/`

2. **Check the documentation.**

   The only way you know which JavaScript statements are supported by a browser and which are not is to take a look at that browser's technical documentation.

   • Netscape's client-side JavaScript language reference:

   `http://developer.netscape.com/docs/manuals/js/client/jsre
          f/objintro.htm`

   • Microsoft's JavaScript-compatible JScript language reference:

   `http://msdn.microsoft.com/scripting/jscript/default.htm`

3. **Include browser sniffer code.**

   Chapter 4 shows you how to create a script that detects a visitor's browser on the fly and behaves differently based on different browser capabilities.

Chapter 17

Ten (Or So) Tips for Debugging Your Scripts

- -

In This Chapter

▶ Comparing code to design specifications

▶ Tracking down bugs with alerts

▶ Getting help from online resources

▶ Watching the code in process

▶ Breaking up functions

▶ Turning user errors into useful information

- -

In Chapter 16, you see some of the most common mistakes (or *bugs*) JavaScript authors tend to make. This chapter expands on that theme by showing you the quickest, most direct ways to pinpoint and correct any bugs you happen to introduce into your code. Many language compilers and interpreters come complete with tools for debugging; unfortunately, few debugging tools exist for JavaScript just yet. That means that for now, you have to rely on your wits — and the advice in this chapter.

Debugging is sort of like doing dishes. Neither chore is exactly a ton of fun, but both are necessary, and you always feel better when they're finished! Debugging doesn't have to be a *dreaded* chore, though. You may find that, with a little help (like the tips presented in this chapter) and a little experience, the job gets easier and easier.

Microsoft provides a free script debugger you can download separately and use in conjunction with Internet Explorer to step through, examine, and debug your JavaScript scripts. For more information, visit this page:

```
http://msdn.microsoft.com/scripting/default.htm?/scripting/de
       bugger/default.htm
```

Netscape also provides a freely downloadable script debugger. Unfortunately, you may find that this debugging tool is *not* compatible if you download a beta version of Navigator. For details on compatibility as well as the latest full version, visit

```
http://developer.netscape.com/software/tools/index.html
```

JavaScript Reads Your Code, Not Your Mind!

Strangely enough, the first step in successful bug extermination involves determining whether you've actually encountered one! If your JavaScript script doesn't behave the way that you expect it to, you could be dealing with a bug. Or your script may be working as designed, and the problem is in your understanding of how the script is *supposed* to work.

In the old days, programmers created *flow charts:* pages and pages of little symbols and lines that described how they wanted their programs to behave at runtime. Flow charts have fallen out of favor — not because they were a bad idea, but because they were nearly as time-intensive to create as the programs themselves.

These days, most programmers find it helpful to write *pseudo-code* as part of the design process. Then, during testing, these programmers have something to refer back to — a touchstone, as it were, to help them clarify whether a potential bug lies in their JavaScript code or in their programming logic.

Pseudo-code is a shorthand combination of JavaScript and the programmer's natural language. Because this tool is designed to be as easy and natural for programmers as possible, no hard-and-fast rules define precisely how to write pseudo-code.

Say, for example, that your goal is to calculate the total price (including sales tax, if any) for international orders placed through your Web site. Here's an example of the process your pseudo-code might take:

1. **As soon as the user hits the Submit button . . .**

2. **If U.S. order {calculate the tax (look up the tax rate based on** `myForm.state`**) and stick it in** `totalTax`**}**

   `else` {What to do if non-U.S. orders?!}

3. **Multiply the number of widgets (**`myForm.numWidgets`**) ordered by the price (**`myForm.price`**) . . . .**

As useful as writing pseudo-code is to helping you clarify the requirements of a Web page, you find it absolutely indispensable when it comes to tracking down bugs in your logic after you've finished implementing your Web page.

Don't keep your comments to yourself

Getting into the habit of commenting your JavaScript code as you write it can be a great help when it comes time to debug that code. (It's surprising how much you can forget between the time you create a script and the time, weeks or even months down the line, when your code misbehaves!)

If you create pseudo-code to help you plan and design your scripts, try using that pseudo-code as the basis for your JavaScript comments. Doing so helps the future you (or someone else to whom the task of debugging your script has fallen) understand precisely what the code is trying to accomplish.

Isolating the Bug

If you've encountered a genuine bug, you need to try to hone in on it and identify precisely which lines of code are affected. Here are some examples to help you work backward from the clues:

- ✔ Does the problem occur the instant the page loads? If so, the problem is probably either HTML-related or in the code you set up to handle the onLoad event.

- ✔ Does it occur when users type text in an input field? Check the onChange and onBlur event handlers associated with that field.

- ✔ When users push a button, do things go haywire? Check that button's onClick event handling code.

- ✔ Does something go wrong when users close the window? The culprit is probably lurking in your onUnload event handling statements.

First, decide on a place to begin your search — say, with the function that's called from one of your onClick event handlers (I'll call it buggyFunction()). The next step, then, is to dig a little deeper. For example, try adding a test button to your JavaScript code that exercises that same function, as the following one does:

```
<INPUT TYPE="button" NAME="testButton" VALUE="Test"
onClick="buggyFunction(123, "abc")
```

In the first line, you're sending the buggy function numeric and string literals. This process helps you determine whether the function itself is buggy — or if the problem lies with the variables that your original code is passing to the function.

Then pass the offending function some hard-coded parameters (that is, string or numeric literals instead of variables). See what happens. If the function still fails, you know that the bug is in your function. If it behaves correctly, you need to check the parameters that the original onClick is sending to the function. (See the "Displaying Variable Values" section later in this chapter.)

Setting up a special function to test your code is a good idea, because that way you don't end up altering your real code. Until you find and correct the mistake (or "bag it and tag it," as a friend of mine used to say), your goal is to change as little source code as possible so that you don't introduce new bugs into your file while you're eliminating old ones.

Another strategy along these lines is to make a copy of your original HTML file before you make *any* changes. Few things are more frustrating than modifying a file beyond recognition, only to have it perform even worse than when you started — and then forgetting how the code originally looked!

If buggyFunction(), in turn, calls other functions, apply the same strategy. From the onClick event handler attached to your test button, call each of the other functions in turn, one after the other, and see if *they* perform as expected. Step by step is the only way to track those wily bugs down.

Consulting the Documentation

The *Client-Side JavaScript Guide* is the most up-to-date resource available regarding the JavaScript language as Netscape implements it. Bookmarking this guide in your browser helps ensure it's at your fingertips when you need it!

```
http://developer.netscape.com/docs/manuals/js/client/jsguide/
         contents.htm
```

Internet Explorer, as you may know, implements JavaScript via the Microsoft scripting language JScript. Check out the following URL for a complete description of all things JScript-related:

```
http://msdn.microsoft.com/scripting/jscript/default.htm
```

Displaying Variable Values

A useful debugging technique involves displaying the values of variables at various stages in their little lives. For example, suppose you have a function whose job is to calculate the total cost of an order. Based on your understanding of the way the total should be calculated, you've determined that this function always returns an incorrect value; you just don't know *why*.

Seeing what JavaScript *thinks* is going on at every stage in the process (from the beginning of the function right down to the statement that calculates the return value) is easy to do with the debugging statements you see in Listing 17-1.

Listing 17-1:   Tracking Down a Bug with Alert Display Statements

```
. . .

var price=3.50

function calculatePrice(numberWidgets) {
// Examine variable at the beginning of the function
    alert("Inside calculatePrice, numberWidgets is " +
            numberWidgets)

    var totalPrice = 0

    // No tax calculated on orders of 100 or less
    if (numberWidgets >= 10) {
// Test to see that the "if" statement is coded correctly
        alert("Apparently numberWidgets is 11 or higher")
        var tax = calculateTax(numberWidgets * price)
        totalPrice = tax + (numberWidgets * price)
    }

    else {
        alert("numberWidgets is 10 or less so no tax
            calculated")
        totalPrice = numberWidgets * price
    }
// Displaying all the values that contribute to a calculation
            helps you spot errors
    alert("totalPrice is $" + totalPrice +  " based on a per-
            item price of $" + price)
    return totalPrice

}
```

The code in Listing 17-1 contains four `alert()` calls. Each `alert()` displays the values of variables at different points in the `calculatePrice()` logic, as shown in the following series of figures. Alert number one shows you what the value of the `numberWidgets` variable is at the beginning of the `calculatePrice()` function, as shown in Figure 17-1. Alert number two, shown in Figure 17-2, helps you determine whether your `if` statement is coded correctly. Alert number three lets you examine several values at a single point in the code (see Figure 17-3).

Figure 17-1:
Getting the
initial
value in
`calculate Price()`.

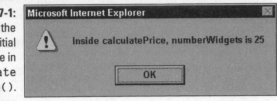

The more knotty and complex your logic, the more this technique can help you pinpoint your bug. But whatever answers you find, keep one thing in mind: After you track down the bugs in your script, make sure you remember to remove the alert statements. Forgetting to do so can be embarrassing!

Figure 17-2:
Checking
the `if`
statement's
performance.

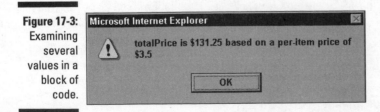

I once worked with a programmer who thought he'd removed all his debug statements, but missed one. The condition causing the debug statement to appear occurred so infrequently, he forgot all about it! Until, that is, dozens of folks — including the programmer's boss, his boss's boss, and the company's most important clients — were evaluating the application in a meeting. You guessed it: up popped the debug statement! This most unfortunate — and embarrassing — situation can be avoided if you search for all the occurrences of alert in your script using the search/replace function available in your text editor.

Figure 17-3:
Examining
several
values in a
block of
code.

Breaking Large Blocks of Statements into Smaller Functions

Limiting the size of the functions you create to about a screenful of text is good design practice. (You don't have to take my word for it, though. A time or two debugging a complex, monster-huge function should convince you!)

Limiting function size gives you these breathing-easier advantages:

- **Increases your ability to reuse code.** The smaller and more discrete a function is, the more likely you are to be able to reuse that function in another context. For example, say you write a large function called `isAPhoneNumber()` to determine whether an input value is a valid phone number or not. Removing the statements that deal with numeric validation and organizing those statements into a separate function, called `isANumber()`, gives you a generic function you can call not just from `isAPhoneNumber()`, but from any other function that requires numeric validation (such as `isAValidCreditCardNumber()`, `isAValidAge()`, and so on.)

- **Decreases your frustration level.** Small functions are much easier to debug than large functions, simply because small functions are easier for humans to step through mentally and comprehend than their outsized counterparts.

Functions too big to fit on the average monitor display tend to be poorly designed from a standpoint of reuse. That is, usually (and I say *usually* because this is just a general rule) when a function gets that big, it's that big because you're trying to make it perform more than one conceptual task. Ideally, a function is an implementation of just *one* conceptual task.

Honing the Process of Elimination

When you're chasing bugs, sometimes figuring out what *isn't* causing the problem is just as important as figuring out what *is*. For example, if you have a bug in your HTML code, no amount of searching and testing your JavaScript code is going to help you correct the problem.

Although I can't tell you *exactly* how to pinpoint your errors (if I could, I'd be rich!), I can tell you that good programmers have a general pattern they follow when they're debugging:

1. **Create several *test cases*.**

   A test case is a single, real-life scenario that describes how a user might reasonably interact with your pages. For an educational site, for example, your test cases might include

   - A student searching for a specific piece of information
   - A teacher posting lesson plans
   - A parent interested in school grading policies

2. **For each test case (make sure you have several), load your pages and interact with them.**

   Note the way your site behaves, and compare what happened to what you expected would happen for that test case.

If you see a difference between what you expect and what actually happens, the first thing to do is to try to figure out whether the problem is related to your browser, JavaScript script, or HTML statements.

Debugging browser problems

A problem with your browser is unlikely to occur unless you've just downloaded and installed a new version or have been doing something in another application that may have altered the way that your browser works.

Symptoms:

Your browser doesn't come up. Or it does come up, but you can't get it to load any local files (as opposed to it being able to load every file but the file that you're testing).

Hone-in strategy:

If you've just reinstalled your browser, try reinstalling it again. If you still have problems, browse the technical help or contact the technical support line.

Tracking HTML bugs

If you're new to JavaScript or HTML, you're likely to make a few HTML errors before you get the hang of it. Not to worry, though . . . HTML is one well-documented animal!

Symptoms:

Your Web page displays only part of what you think it should display (buttons or other elements that you can see defined in your HTML source are missing). Or conversely, your Web page displays more than you expected. (For example, some of your JavaScript statements are splashed on the screen.)

Hone-in strategy:

Note exactly what displays (or what doesn't). If only the first two elements that you defined appear, check the source code that defines the second element — and every statement after that line of source code. If the second element is contained within a tag set (for example, between the `<BODY>` . . . `</BODY>` tags), check to see that the closing tag is placed and spelled correctly.

If JavaScript statements appear that shouldn't, note the very first word in the statement that's showing. Then find that word in the .HTML source file and check the preceding line.

Checking the JavaScript code

As a JavaScript programmer, you're likely to make most of your mistakes in — well, in your JavaScript code.

Symptoms:

Any bug that shows its face before a form is submitted is almost certainly a JavaScript bug. Pre-form-submittal bugs can occur either in response to a user event (clicking a button, for example, or typing text), or in the course of calculating some numbers.

Hone-in strategy:

Here's where your skills at displaying variable values and breaking up functions really pay off. After you've traced a bug to an event or calculation, try to isolate that event or calculation. Create a test button that exercises the functions involved.

Exercising a function means calling it with a variety of parameters to see what happens in each case. If a function is long, break it up and exercise each resulting function separately.

Taking Advantage of Others' Experience

When you hit a hard-shelled bug, you really come to appreciate the Usenet user groups (called *newsgroups*) listed in Chapter 15. Not only can you browse the groups to see whether someone else has already encountered the problem you're struggling with, but you can also post a message that contains a section of code and a description of the error. Many newsgroup contributors pride themselves on their abilities to debug others' code, and technical support people (including some Netscape gurus) often monitor the newsgroups as part of their jobs.

Keep in mind that no matter how frustrated you are or how urgent your problem is, you should check through the newsgroups archives for a problem similar to your own before posting. Chances are good that some similar problem has been posted at least once (and maybe a dozen times), and your group mates will appreciate your adapting existing posts before opening a new debate.

Exercising the Time-Honored Trial-and-Error Approach

When all else fails, just do something — anything. Make a change to your code, note the change, and then load the page and see what happens. The JavaScript interpreter makes testing out things both quick and easy for you. If the code change doesn't work, put the code back the way it was and try again. Whatever you do, don't be afraid to try something. The worst thing you can do is crash your browser — and believe me, browser crashes are not fatal. (If they were, I sure wouldn't be alive to write this book!)

If you tend, like me, to be on the conservative side, make a habit of copying your source code file to a safe place as soon as it begins to behave and at regular intervals thereafter. That way, if the unthinkable happens and you accidentally mangle the file while you're editing it, you can always drop back to your last good copy.

The best advice I can give you is to enjoy yourself. The more mistakes you make, the more you can figure things out on your own — and the easier creating your *next* JavaScript-enabled Web page will be.

Just Try and Catch Me Exception Handling!

Support for *exception handling* — a technique for anticipating and recovering gracefully from errors that has long been supported in languages like C++ — was finally implemented for JavaScript in the 5.x and 6.x versions of Internet Explorer and Navigator, respectively.

Technically, an exception is any unexpected condition, good or bad, that occurs during the processing of a script. In reality, however, an exception is virtually always an error. (No news is good news, after all!) Exceptions can result directly from a JavaScript error, an unanticipated user input error, or from a problem with a user's browser, operating system, or even hardware configuration. Trying to make your code access objects (an array element, a property, or a file, and so on) that don't exist is a common source of exceptions that may occur while your JavaScript code is executing in someone's browser.

If you're creating a commercial JavaScript application, you want to make liberal use of JavaScript's exception handling abilities. Allowing your users to view cryptic, system-generated errors such as File Not Found or No Such Object just plain makes you look bad! While anticipating and handling those errors using try and catch blocks might not prevent the errors from occurring, it does give you the opportunity to

✔ Reassure users. You can use JavaScript's exception handling functions to display a message telling users that an error has occurred, but is being handled appropriately. (This approach is much better than allowing a cryptic system message or blank screen to confuse and alarm users.)

✔ Provide users with helpful, appropriate suggestions. You can explain the cause of the error and provide users with tips for avoiding that error in the future.

You handle exceptions by creating two special JavaScript functions, or blocks: a *try* block and a *catch* block. Then, in any statement that might possibly generate an error, you use the keyword throw to throw an error. The code in Listing 17-2 shows you how.

Listing 17-2: Handling Exceptions with try . . . catch **and** throw

```
. . .
<SCRIPT LANGUAGE="JavaScript">

function getMonthName (monthNumber) {

    // JavaScript arrays begin with 0, not 1, so
    // subtract 1
    monthNumber = monthNumber - 1

    // Create an array and fill it with 12 values
    var months = new
        Array("Jan","Feb","Mar","Apr","May","Jun","Jul",
                        "Aug","Sep","Oct","Nov","Dec")

    // If a month array element corresponds to the
    // number passed in, fine; return the array
    // element.

    if (months[monthNumber] != null) {
        return months[monthNumber]
    }

    // Otherwise, an exception occurred, so throw
    // an exception.

    else {
```

(continued)

Listing 17-2 *(continued)*

```
// This statement throws an error directly to the catch
        block.
    throw "InvalidMonthNumber"
    }
}


///////////////////////////////////////////////////
// The "try" block wraps around the main JavaScript
// processing code. Any JavaScript statement inside
// the try block that generates an exception will
// automatically throw that exception to the
// exception handling code in the "catch" block.
///////////////////////////////////////////////////

// The try block
try {

    // Call the getMonthName() function with an
    // invalid month # (there is no 13th month!)
    // and see what happens.

    alert(getMonthName(13))

    alert("We never get here if an exception is thrown.")

}

// The catch block
catch (error) {

    alert("An " + error + " exception was encountered.
          Please contact the program vendor.")

    // In a real-life situation, you might want
    // to include error-handling code here that
    // examines the exception and gives users specific
    // information (or even tries to fix the problem,
    // if possible.)
}
```

Take a look at Figure 17-4 to see the error that running the code in Listing 17-2 generates in Internet Explorer.

The first code executed in Listing 17-2 is the code you see defined in the try block:

```
alert(getMonthName(13))
```

Figure 17-4:
The catch
block
handles all
exceptions
generated in
the try
block.

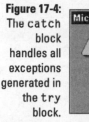

Microsoft Internet Explorer

⚠ An InvalidMonthNumber exception was
encountered. Please contact the program
vendor.

OK

Because only twelve months are defined in the months array, passing a value
of 13 to getMonthName() causes an exception ("InvalidMonthNumber") to be
thrown, as shown below:

```
function getMonthName(monthNumber) {
    . . .
    throw "InvalidMonthNumber"
```

All thrown exceptions are processed automatically by whatever code exists
in the catch block, so the message you see in Figure 17-4 appears automatically when the exception is thrown.

If you want to write truly airtight JavaScript code, you need to identify all of
the events that could possibly cause an exception in your particular script
(such as actions the user could take, or error conditions the operating
system could generate, and so on), and implement a try/catch block for each.

Depending on your application, you may want to include more processing
code in the catch block than the simple pop-up message shown in Figure
17-4. For example, you may want to include JavaScript statements that examine the caught exception, determine what kind of exception it is, and process
it appropriately.

You aren't limited to a string literal when it comes to identifying a thrown
exception. Instead of InvalidMonthNumber, you can create and throw an
elaborate custom exception object (using the function and new operators, I
describe in Chapter 3).

For more information on how Netscape implements exception handling
(including examples), visit

```
http://developer.netscape.com/docs/manuals/js/core/jsguide/st
        mtsov.htm#1011537
```

To see how Microsoft does the same for Internet Explorer, check out this page:

```
http://msdn.microsoft.com/scripting/JScript/doc/
        jsstmtrycatch.htm
```

Part VI
Appendixes

The 5th Wave   By Rich Tennant

"I don't know how it happened, but there's an applet in the toaster and some guy in Norway keeps burning my toast."

In this part . . .

I've included a number of resources to help you develop more complex and exciting scripts. Here, you'll find words you can't use in your code, and plenty of short-cuts and objects that you're sure to incorporate.

JavaScript reserves certain words that you don't want to use as variables or other user-defined elements in your code and gives you a couple of options for making sure the colors you want in your pages appear the way you intend (or close to it).

Although I haven't included every possible explanation for every possible object, you can find nearly all the objects you're sure to need in the near future with their respective methods and properties, as well as some tips on which ones are browser-conscious. And, finally, you can use the special characters in this section to make sure your web pages comply with the demands of the global marketplace and the languages of your users.

Appendix A

JavaScript Reserved Words

The words listed in this appendix mean something special to the JavaScript interpreter implemented in the current versions of Navigator and Internet Explorer (or are reserved for future versions). If you try to use any of these words to do anything other than what they are designed to do, the JavaScript interpreter generates an error when you try to run the script. For example, don't try to use any of these words to name a variable, a function, a method, or an object.

abstract	final	public
boolean	finally	return
break	float	short
byte	for	static
case	function	super
catch	goto	switch
char	if	synchronized
class	implements	this
comment	import	throw
const	in	throws
continue	instanceof	transient
debugger	int	true
default	interface	try
delete	label	typeof
do	long	var
double	native	void
else	new	volatile
enum	null	while
export	package	with
extends	private	
false	protected	

Appendix B

JavaScript Color Values

● ●

*F*ollowing is an alphabetical listing of all predefined colors available to you in JavaScript. When you refer to a color in JavaScript code, you can use either the human-readable color names (for example, aliceblue) or their hexadecimal equivalents (F0F8FF). For example, the following two JavaScript statements are equivalent:

```
document.write(someTextString.fontcolor("aqua"))
document.write(someTextString.fontcolor("00FFFF"))
```

Keep in mind, however, that only those colors shown in bold are considered absolutely Web safe. Those ten colors — aqua, black, blue, cyan, fuchsia, lime, magenta, red, white, and yellow — appear the same on virtually all computer monitors, and I've marked them with an asterisk (*). The remaining 130 colors, when viewed on some older computer monitors, may not display correctly. The upshot? Some color combinations might look great in *your* Web browser, but be hard to read (or even invisible!) on others.

To be on the safe side, make sure you test your Web pages on as many computer configurations as possible before releasing them for all the world to see.

Color	Hexadecimal	Color	Hexadecimal
aliceblue	F0F8FF	blue*	0000FF
antiquewhite	FAEBD7	blueviolet	8A2BE2
aqua*	00FFFF	brown	A52A2A
aquamarine	7FFFD4	burlywood	DEB887
azure	F0FFFF	cadetblue	5F9EA0
beige	F5F5DC	chartreuse	7FFF00
bisque	FFE4C4	chocolate	D2691E
black*	000000	coral	FF7F50
blanchedalmond	FFEBCD	cornflowerblue	6495ED

Color	Hexadecimal	Color	Hexadecimal
cornsilk	FFF8DC	gainsboro	DCDCDC
crimson	DC143C	ghostwhite	F8F8FF
cyan*	00FFFF	gold	FFD700
darkblue	00008B	goldenrod	DAA520
darkcyan	008B8B	gray	808080
darkgoldenrod	B8860B	green	008000
darkgray	A9A9A9	greenyellow	ADFF2F
darkgreen	006400	honeydew	F0FFF0
darkkhaki	BDB76B	hotpink	FF69B4
darkmagenta	8B008B	indianred	CD5C5C
darkolivegreen	556B2F	indigo	4B0082
darkorange	FF8C00	ivory	FFFFF0
darkorchid	9932CC	khaki	F0E68C
darkred	8B0000	lavender	E6E6FA
darksalmon	E9967A	lavenderblush	FFF0F5
darkseagreen	8FBC8F	lawngreen	7CFC00
darkslateblue	483D8B	lemonchiffon	FFFACD
darkslategray	2F4F4F	lightblue	ADD8E6
darkturquoise	00CED1	lightcoral	F08080
darkviolet	9400D3	lightcyan	E0FFFF
deeppink	FF1493	lightgoldenrodyellow	FAFAD2
deepskyblue	00BFFF	lightgreen	90EE90
dimgray	696969	lightgrey	D3D3D3
dodgerblue	1E90FF	lightpink	FFB6C1
firebrick	B22222	lightsalmon	FFA07A
floralwhite	FFFAF0	lightseagreen	20B2AA
forestgreen	228B22	lightskyblue	87CEFA
fuchsia*	FF00FF	lightslategray	778899

Color	Hexadecimal	Color	Hexadecimal
lightsteelblue	B0C4DE	palegoldenrod	EEE8AA
lightyellow	FFFFE0	palegreen	98FB98
lime*	00FF00	paleturquoise	AFEEEE
limegreen	32CD32	palevioletred	DB7093
linen	FAF0E6	papayawhip	FFEFD5
magenta*	FF00FF	peachpuff	FFDAB9
maroon	800000	peru	CD853F
mediumaquamarine	66CDAA	pink	FFC0CB
mediumblue	0000CD	plum	DDA0DD
mediumorchid	BA55D3	powderblue	B0E0E6
mediumpurple	9370DB	purple	800080
mediumseagreen	3CB371	red*	FF0000
mediumslateblue	7B68EE	rosybrown	BC8F8F
mediumspringgreen	00FA9A	royalblue	4169E1
mediumturquoise	48D1CC	saddlebrown	8B4513
mediumvioletred	C71585	salmon	FA8072
midnightblue	191970	sandybrown	F4A460
mintcream	F5FFFA	seagreen	2E8B57
mistyrose	FFE4E1	seashell	FFF5EE
moccasin	FFE4B5	sienna	A0522D
navajowhite	FFDEAD	silver	C0C0C0
navy	000080	skyblue	87CEEB
oldlace	FDF5E6	slateblue	6A5ACD
olive	808000	slategray	708090
olivedrab	6B8E23	snow	FFFAFA
orange	FFA500	springgreen	00FF7F
orangered	FF4500	steelblue	4682B4
orchid	DA70D6	tan	D2B48C

Color	Hexadecimal
teal	008080
thistle	D8BFD8
tomato	FF6347
turquoise	40E0D0
violet	EE82EE
wheat	F5DEB3
white*	FFFFFF
whitesmoke	F5F5F5
yellow*	FFFF00
yellowgreen	9ACD32

Appendix C

Document Object Model Reference

● ●

*Y*ou can think of this appendix as an alphabetical cheat sheet that lists all of the objects, properties, methods, and event handlers that make up the document object model you interact with in JavaScript. (The built-in functions available to you in JavaScript are also listed in the second half.)

The folks who implemented the document object model — Netscape and Microsoft — surely had their reasons for beginning some, but not all, object names with uppercase letters! JavaScript is a case-sensitive language, which means that if an object begins with a lowercase (or uppercase) letter, you must access it that way.

The Document Object Model

I've organized the document object model alphabetically, by object; if you need to look up a particular property or method — say, `prompt()` — and don't know what object it belongs to, take a quick peek at the index you find at the back of this book.

This appendix is as up-to-date as is humanly possible, but because new browser versions appear regularly (each of which may implement a slightly different document object model), you may find some minor differences between the object model your browser supports and the one listed here. In fact, both Netscape and Internet Explorer have pledged their intention to continue modifying their object models until that happy day when they both match the ECMA standard and developers can count on the same object existing, and behaving identically, in both browsers! So for the last word in object implementation, including detailed descriptions of any of the elements you find in this appendix, visit Netscape and Microsoft online.

Internet Explorer's document object model:

```
http://msdn.microsoft.com/workshop/author/dhtml/reference/
              objects.asp
```

Netscape Navigator's document object model:

```
http://developer.netscape.com/docs/manuals/js/client/jsref/
              partobj.htm
```

Because all of the objects in the document object model derive from the `Object` object (try saying *that* three times fast!), all JavaScript objects inherit the `Object` object's properties and methods. (I tell you this, instead of listing those few properties and methods associated with the `Object` object over and over again for every other object, in the interest of saving space.)

Anchor

Description: The target of a hyperlink.

What creates it: `<A NAME="`*anchorName*`">` or
`String.anchor("`*anchorName*`")`

How to access it: `document.anchors[`*i*`]` (individual anchor) or
`document.anchors.length` (number of anchors in a document)

Properties: `name`, `text`, `x`, `y`

Methods: None

Event handlers: None

Applet

Description: A reference to a Java applet in a Web page.

What creates it: `<APPLET NAME="`*appletName*`">`

How to access it: `document.applets[`*i*`]` or `document.`*appletName*

Properties: Depends on applet

Methods: Depends on applet (`start()` and `stop()` supported by convention)

Event handlers: None

Area

Description: Defines an area of an image as an image map.

See Link

arguments

Description: A collection of the arguments passed into a function.

What creates it: `function functionName() { functionStatements }`

How to access it: `arguments` (from inside a function body)

Properties: `callee`, `caller`, `length`

Methods: None

Event handlers: None

Array

Description: A collection of objects.

What creates it:

`arrayName = new Array(arrayLength)` **or**

`arrayName = new Array(element0, element1, . . ., elementN)`

How to access it: `arrayName[i]`

Properties: `constructor`, `index`; `input`, `length`, `prototype`

Methods: `concat()`, `join()`, `length()`, `pop()`, `push()`, `reverse()`, `shift()`, `slice()`, `sort()`, `splice()`, `toSource()`, `toString()`, `unshift()`, `valueOf()`

Event handlers: None

Boolean

Description: A boolean (true/false) value.

What creates it:

booleanName = new Boolean(*value*) (constructor) **or**

booleanName = Boolean(*value*) (conversion function)

How to access it: *booleanName*

Properties: constructor, prototype

Methods: toSource(), toString(), valueOf()

Event handlers: None

Button

Description: A push button included in an HTML form.

What creates it: <FORM NAME="*formName*"> . . . <INPUT TYPE="button" NAME="*buttonName*" . . . ></FORM>

How to access it: document.*formName*.*buttonName* **or** *formName*.elements[i]

Properties: form, name, type, value

Methods: blur(), click(), focus(), handleEvent()

Event handlers: onBlur, onClick, onFocus, onMouseDown, onMouseUp

Checkbox

Description: A checkbox included in an HTML form. (A checkbox is a toggle switch that lets the user click a value on or off.)

What creates it: <FORM NAME="*formName*"> . . . <INPUT TYPE="checkbox" NAME="*checkboxName*" . . . ></FORM>

How to access it: document.*formName*.*checkboxName* **or** *formName*.elements[i]

Properties: checked, defaultChecked, form, name, type, value

Methods: blur(), click(), focus(), handleEvent()

Event handlers: onBlur, onClick, onFocus

clientInformation

Description: Describes browser configuration details; supported only by Internet Explorer. (Internet Explorer also supports the navigator object.)

What creates it: Automatically created by Internet Explorer

How to access it: window.clientInformation (or just clientInformation)

Properties: appCodeName, appMinorVersion, appName, appVersion, browserLanguage, cookieEnabled, cpuClass, onLine, platform, systemLanguage, userAgent, userLanguage, userProfile

Methods: javaEnabled(), taintEnabled()

Event handlers: None

crypto

Description: This object defines two cryptography-related methods that developers can use to implement digital signatures; supported only by Netscape Navigator.

What creates it: Automatically created by Netscape Navigator

How to access it: window.crypto (or just crypto)

Properties: None

Methods: random(), signText()

Event handlers: None

Date

Description: An object that lets you create, manipulate, and format date and time values.

What creates it: *aDate* = new Date()
aDate = new Date(*milliseconds*)
aDate = new Date(*dateString*)
aDate = new Date(*yr_num, mo_num, day_num*
[, *hr_num, min_num, sec_num, ms_num*])

How to access it: aDate

Properties: constructor, prototype

Methods: getDate(), getDay(), getFullYear(), getHours(),
getMilliseconds(), getMinutes(), getMonth(), getSeconds(),
getTime(), getTimezoneOffset(), getUTCDate(), getUTCDay(),
getUTCFullYear(), getUTCHours(), getUTCMilliseconds(),
getUTCMinutes(), getUTCMonth(), getUTCSeconds(), getYear(),
parse(), setDate(), setDay(), setFullYear(), setHours(),
setMilliseconds(), setMinutes(), setMonth(), setSeconds(),
setTime(), setUTCDate(), setUTCFullYear(), setUTCHours(),
setUTCMilliseconds(), setUTCMinutes(), setUTCMonth(),
setUTCSeconds(), setYear(), toGMTString(), toLocaleString(),
toSource(), toString(), toUTCString(), UTC(), valueOf()

Event handlers: None

document

Description: The currently loaded HTML document; provides methods for displaying HTML output to the user.

What creates it: <BODY> . . . </BODY>

How to access it: window.document (or just document)

Properties: alinkColor, anchors[], applets[], bgColor, cookie, domain,
embeds, fgColor, formName, forms[], images[], lastModified,
linkColor, links[], plugins[], referrer, title, URL, vlinkColor

Properties (Netscape Navigator only): classes, height, ids, tags, width

Properties (Internet Explorer only): activeElement, all[], charset,
children[], defaultCharset, expando, parentWindow, readyState

Methods: `close()`, `handleEvent()`, `open()`, `write()`, `writeln()`

Methods (Netscape Navigator only): `captureEvents()`, `contextual()`, `getSelection()`, `releaseEvents`, `routeEvent()`

Methods (Internet Explorer only): `elementFromPoint()`

Event handlers: `onClick`, `onDblClick`, `onKeyDown`, `onKeyPress`, `onKeyUp`, `onMouseDown`, `onMouseUp`

elements[]

Description: A collection of the form elements included in an HTML document.

What creates it: `<FORM NAME="formName">` . . . `</FORM>`

How to access it: `document.formName.elements[]`

Properties: `checked`, `defaultChecked`, `defaultValue`, `form`, `length`, `name`, `options[]`, `selectedIndex`, `type`, `value`

Methods: `blur()`, `click()`, `focus()`, `select()`

Event handlers: `onBlur`, `onChange`, `onClick`, `onFocus`

event

Description: One of several pre-defined occurrences in JavaScript, such as a mouse click, a text entry, or a document load. This object is passed as an argument to an event handler automatically when an event occurs.

What creates it: Automatically created by browser.

How to access it: `window.event` (or just `event`)

Properties (Netscape Navigator only): `data`, `height`, `modifiers`, `pageX`, `pageY`, `screenX`, `screenY`, `target`, `type`, `which`, `width`

Properties (Internet Explorer only): `altKey`, `button`, `cancelBubble`, `clientX`, `clientY`, `ctrlKey`, `fromElement`, `keyCode`, `offsetX`, `offsetY`, `reason`, `returnValue`, `screenX`, `screenY`, `shiftKey`, `srcElement`, `srcFilter`, `toElement`, `type`, `x`, `y`

Methods: None

Event handlers: None

FileUpload

Description: A file upload element on an HTML form. (A file upload element lets users select or specify a file as input to a Web application.)

What creates it: `<FORM NAME="formName">` . . . `<INPUT TYPE="file" NAME="fileUploadName" . . . ></FORM>`

How to access it: `document.formName.fileUploadName` or `formName.elements[i]`

Properties: `form, name, type, value`

Methods: `blur(), focus(), handleEvent(), select()`

Event handlers: `onBlur, onChange, onFocus`

Form

Description: An HTML form. HTML forms let users input text and interact with such elements as checkboxes, radio buttons, and selection lists. Forms can be configured to post data to a Web server automatically on submit.

What creates it: `<FORM NAME="formName">` . . . `</FORM>`

How to access it: `document.formName`

Properties: `action, elements[], encoding, length, method, name, target`

Methods: `handleEvent(), reset(), submit()`

Event handlers: `onReset, onSubmit`

Frame

Description: An HTML display frame.

What creates it: `<FRAME>` . . . `</FRAME>`

(*See Window*)

Function

Description: A chunk of JavaScript code to be pre-processed by the JavaScript interpreter.

What creates it:

```
new Function ([arg1[, arg2[, . . . argN]],] functionBody)
```

```
function functionName([param[, param[, . . . param]]])
{ statements }
```

How to access it: *functionName*

Properties: arguments[], arity, caller, length, prototype

Methods: apply(), call(), toSource(), toString(), valueOf()

Event handlers: None.

Hidden

Description: A non-displayed HTML form field useful for holding and trans-mitting calculated values to a Web server.

What creates it: <FORM NAME="*formName*"> . . . <INPUT TYPE="hidden" NAME="*hiddenName*" . . . ></FORM>

How to access it: document.*formName*.*hiddenName* or *formName*.*elements*[i]

Properties: form, name, type, value

Methods: None

History

Description: A collection of URLs that a user has visited.

What creates it: Automatically created by browser.

How to access it: window.history, frame.history, **or just** history)

Properties: curent, length, next, previous

Methods: back(), forward(), go()

Event handlers: None

Image

Description: An image included in an HTML document.

What creates it: <IMG NAME="*imageName*">

How to access it:

document.*imageName*

document.images[i]

document.images.length

Properties: border, complete, height, hspace, lowsrc, name, src, vspace, width

Methods: handleEvent()

Event handlers: onAbort, onError, onKeyDown, onKeyPress, onKeyUp, onLoad

java

Description: A top-level object used to access any Java class in the package java.*.

What creates it: Automatically created by Java-supporting browser.

(*See* packages.java)

JavaArray

Description: The JavaScript representation of a Java array.

What creates it: Any Java method that returns an array.

How to access it: By calling a method defined by an individual Java applet.

Properties: length

Methods: toString()

Event handlers: None

JavaClass

Description: JavaScript representation of a Java class.

What creates it: Automatically created by Java-supporting browser.

(*See* packages.JavaClass)

JavaObject

Description: JavaScript representation of a Java object.

What creates it: Any Java method that returns an object type.

How to access it: By calling a method defined by an individual Java applet.

Properties: Determined by individual Java applet/method.

Methods: Determined by individual Java applet/method.

Event handlers: None

JavaPackage

Description: JavaScript representation of a Java package.

What creates it: Automatically created by Java-supporting browser.

How to access it: Packages.JavaPackage

Properties: Determined by individual Java package.

Methods: Determined by individual Java package.

Event handlers: None

Link

Description: A hypertext link included in an HTML document.

What creates it: `<A>`, `<AREA>`, or `String.link()`

How to access it: `document.links[i]` (individual link)or `document.links.length` (number of links in a document)

Properties: `hash`, `host`, `hostName`, `href`, `pathname`, `port`, `protocol`, `search`, `target`, `text`, `x`, `y`

Methods: `handleEvent()`

Event handlers: `onDblClick`, `onMouseOut`, `onMouseOver` (`<AREA>`)

`onClick`, `onDblClick`, `onKeyDown`, `onKeyPress`, `onKeyUp`, `onMouseDown`, `onMouseOut`, `onMouseUp`, `onMouseOver` (`<A>` **or** `String.link()`)

Location

Description: The currently loaded URL.

What creates it: Automatically created by browser.

How to access it: `window.location` (or just `location`)

Properties: `hash`, `host`, `hostname`, `href`, `pathname`, `port`, `protocol`, `search`

Methods: `reload()`, `replace()`

Event handlers: None

Math

Description: A built-in object containing properties and methods for mathematical constants and functions.

What creates it: Automatically created by browser.

How to access it: `Math`

Properties: `E`, `LN10`, `LN2`, `LOG10E`, `LOG2E`, `PI`, `SQRT1_2`, `SQRT2`

Methods: `abs()`, `acos()`, `asin()`, `atan()`, `atan2()`, `ceil()`, `cos()`, `exp()`, `floor()`, `log()`, `max()`, `min()`, `pow()`, `random()`, `round()`, `sin()`, `sqrt()`, `tan()`

Event handlers: None

MimeType

Description: A MIME type (Multipart Internet Mail Extension, such as `pdf`) supported by the browser.

What creates it: Automatically created by Netscape Navigator.

How to access it:

`navigator.mimeTypes[i]`

`navigator.mimeTypes["type"]`

`navigator.plugins[i].mimeTypes[j]`

`navigator.mimeTypes.length`

Properties: `description`, `enabledPlugin`, `suffixes`, `type`

Methods: None

Event handlers: None

navigator

Description: Browser configuration details.

What creates it: Automatically created by browser.

How to access it: `window.navigator` **(or just** `navigator`**)**

Properties: `appCodeName`, `appName`, `appVersion`, `language`, `mimeTypes`, `platform`, `plugins`, `userAgent`

Methods: `javaEnabled()`, `plugins.refresh()`, `preference()`, `savePreferences()`, `taintEnabled()`

Event handlers: None

netscape

Description: A top-level object used to access any Java class in the package `netscape.*`.

What creates it: Automatically created by Netscape Navigator.

(*See* `Packages.JavaClass`)

Number

Description: A JavaScript object wrapper for primitive numeric values.

What creates it: `aNumber = new Number(value)`

How to access it: `aNumber`

Properties: `constructor, MAX_VALUE, MIN_VALUE, NaN, NEGATIVE_INFINITY, POSITIVE_INFINITY, prototype`

Methods: `toSource(), toString, valueOf()`

Event handlers: None

Object

Description: The primitive JavaScript object type from which all other objects derive.

What creates it:

`anObject = new Object()`

`anotherObject = new Object(anObject)`

How to access it: *anObject, anotherObject*

Properties: `constructor, prototype`

Methods: `eval(), toSource(), toString(), unwatch(), valueOf(), watch()`

Event handlers: None

Option

Description: An option in an HTML select list.

What creates it: `<FORM NAME="`*formName*`"><SELECT NAME="`*selectName*`"><OPTION></SELECT></FORM>`

```
new Option([text[, value[, defaultSelected[,
    selected]]]])
```

How to access it: `document.`*formName*`.`*selectName*`.options[`*i*`]`

Properties: `defaultSelected, index, length, selected, text, value`

Methods: None

Event handlers: None

Packages

Description: A top-level object used to access Java classes from within JavaScript code.

What creates it: Automatically created by Java-supporting browsers.

How to access it: Depends on Java package.

Properties: `className, java, netscape, sun`

Methods: Depends on Java package.

Event handlers: None

Password

Description: A password field included in an HTML form. When a user enters text into a password field, asterisks (*) hide that text from view.

What creates it: `<FORM NAME="`*formName*`">` . . . `<INPUT TYPE="password" NAME="`*passwordName*`"` . . . `></FORM>`

How to access it:

`document.`*formName*`.`*passwordName*

formName`.elements[i]`

Properties: `defaultValue, form, name, type, value`

Methods: `blur(), focus(), handleEvent(), select()`

Event handlers: `onBlur, onFocus`

Plugin

Description: A plug-in application module installed in Netscape Navigator.

What creates it: Netscape Navigator (on browser plug-in install).

How to access it: `navigator.plugins[i]`

Properties: `description, filename, length, name`

Methods: None

Event handlers: None

Radio

Description: A radio button in a set of radio buttons included in an HTML form. The user can use a set of radio buttons to choose one item from a list.

What creates it: `<FORM NAME="`*formName*`"> . . . <INPUT TYPE="radio" NAME="`*radioName*`" . . . ></FORM>`

How to access it: `document.`*formName*`.`*radioName* **or** *formName*`.elements[i]`

Properties: `checked, defaultChecked, form, name, type, value`

Methods: `blur(), click(), focus(), handleEvent()`

Event handlers: `onBlur, onClick, onFocus`

RegExp

Description: Contains the pattern of a regular expression. This object provides properties and methods for using that regular expression to find and replace matches in strings.

What creates it:

```
/pattern/flags
```

```
new RegExp("pattern"[, "flags"])
```

How to access it: Regular expressions are tricky animals. You use regular expressions for pattern-matching applications. The following gives an example:

```
<SCRIPT LANGUAGE="JavaScript1.2">
aRegularExpression = /(\w+)\s(\w+)/;
oldString = "John Smith";
newString=oldString.replace(aRegularExpression, "$2, $1");
document.write(newString)
</SCRIPT>
```

(This script displays Smith, John.)

For more information, visit this page:

```
http://developer.netscape.com/docs/manuals/js/client/jsref/re
              gexp.htm
```

Properties: $1, . . . , $9, $_, $*, $&, $+, $`, $', constructor, global, ignoreCase, input, lastIndex, lastMatch, lastParen, leftContext, multiline, prototype, rightContext, source

Methods: compile(), exec(), test(), toSource(), toString(), valueOf()

Event handlers: None

Reset

Description: A reset button on an HTML form. This button resets all elements in a form to their defaults.

What creates it: <FORM NAME="formName"> . . . <INPUT TYPE="reset" NAME="resetName" . . . ></FORM>

How to access it: document.formName.resetName or formName. elements[i]

Properties: form, name, type, value

Methods: blur(), click(), focus(), handleEvent()

Event handlers: onBlur, onClick, onFocus

screen

Description: Contains properties describing the display screen (monitor) and colors.

What creates it: Automatically created by browser.

How to access it: screen

Properties: availHeight, availLeft, availTop, availWidth, colorDepth, height, pixelDepth, width

Methods: None

Event handlers: None

Select

Description: A selection list included in an HTML form. The user can choose one or more items from a selection list, depending on how the list was created.

What creates it: <FORM NAME="*formName*"><SELECT NAME="*selectName*"></SELECT></FORM>

How to access it: document.*formName*.*selectName* or *formName*.elements[i]

Properties: form, length, name, options, selectedIndex, type

Methods: blur(), focus(), handleEvent()

Event handlers: onBlur, onChange, onFocus

String

Description: An object representing a series of quote-delimited characters.

What creates it: *aString* = new String("*value*") or *aString* = "*value*"

How to access it: *aString*

Properties: constructor, length, prototype

Methods: anchor(), big(), blink(), bold(), charAt(), charCodeAt(), concat(), fixed(), fontcolor(), fontsize(), fromCharCode(), indexOf(), italics(), lastIndexOf(), link(), match(), replace(), search(), slice(), small(), split(), strike(), sub(), substr(), substring(), sup(), toLowerCase(), toSource(), toString(), toUpperCase(), valueOf()

Event handlers: None

Style

Description: An object that specifies the style of HTML elements.

What creates it:

document.classes.*className*.*tagName*

document.contextual(. , .)

document.ids.*elementName*

document.**tags**.*tagName*

How to access it: See the following page:

```
http://developer.netscape.com/docs/manuals/communicator/dynht
            ml/index.htm
```

Properties (Netscape Navigator only): backgroundColor, backgroundImage, borderBottomWidth, borderColor, borderLeftWidth, borderRightWidth, borderStyle, borderTopWidth, clear, color, display, fontFamily, fontSize, fontStyle, fontWeight, lineHeight, listStyleType, marginBottom, marginLeft, marginRight, marginTop, paddingBottom, paddingLeft, paddingRight, paddingTop, textAlign, textDecoration, textIndent, textTransform, whiteSpace

Properties(Internet Explorer only) : background, background-Attachment, backgroundColor, backgroundImage, backgroundPosition, backgroundPositionX, backgroundPositionY, backgroundRepeat, border, borderBottom, borderBottomColor, borderBottomStyle, borderBottomWidth, borderColor, borderLeft, borderLeftColor, borderLeftStyle, borderLeftWidth, borderRight, borderRightColor, borderRightStyle, borderRightWidth, borderStyle, borderTop, borderTopColor, borderTopStyle, borderTopWidth, borderWidth, clear,

clip, color, cssText, cursor, display, filter, font, fontFamily,
fontSize, fontStyle, fontVariant, fontWeight, height, left,
letterSpacing, lineHeight, listStyle, listStyleImage,
listStylePosition, listStyleType, margin, marginBottom, marginLeft,
marginRight, marginTop, overflow, paddingBottom, paddingLeft,
paddingRight, paddingTop, pageBreakAfter, pageBreakBefore,
pixelHeight, pixelLeft, pixelTop, pixelWidth, posHeight, position,
posLeft, posTop, posWidth, styleFloat, textAlign, text Decoration,
textIndent, textTransform, top, verticalAlign, visibility, width,
zIndex

Methods: borderWidths(), margins(), paddings()

Event handlers: None

Submit

Description: A submit button included in an HTML form. This button sends the form information to be processed.

What creates it: <FORM NAME="*formName*"> . . . <INPUT
TYPE="*submit*" NAME="*submitName*" . . . ></FORM>

How to access it: document.*formName*.*submitName* or *formName*.
elements[i]

Properties: form, name, type, value

Methods: blur(), click(), focus(), handleEvent()

Event handlers: onBlur, onClick, onFocus

sun

Description: A top-level object used to access any Java class in the package
sun.*.

What creates it: Automatically created by Java-supporting browsers.

How to access it: Packages.sun

(See Packages)

Text

Description: A text field included in an HTML form.

What creates it: `<FORM NAME="`*formName*`">` . . . `<INPUT TYPE="text"` `NAME="`*textName*`"` . . . `></FORM>`

How to access it: `document.`*formName*`.`*textName* or *formName*`.elements[i]`

Properties: `defaultValue`, `form`, `name`, `type`, `value`

Methods: `blur()`, `focus()`, `handleEvent()`, `select()`

Event handlers: `onBlur`, `onChange`, `onFocus`, `onSelect`

Textarea

Description: A text area element (multi-line text input field) included in an HTML form.

What creates it: `<FORM NAME="`*formName*`"><TEXTAREA` `NAME="`*textareaName*`">` . . . `</TEXTAREA></FORM>`

How to access it: *document*`.`*formName*`.`*textareaName* or *formName*`.` *elements*`[i]`

Properties: `defaultValue`, `form`, `name`, `type`, `value`

Methods: `blur()`, `focus()`, `handleEvent()`, `select()`

Event handlers: `onBlur`, `onChange`, `onFocus`, `onSelect`

window

Description: A browser window or frame.

What creates it:

`<BODY>`

`<FRAMESET>`

```
<FRAME NAME="frameName">
```

```
window.open("windowName")
```

How to access it:

```
self
```

```
window
```

```
window.frames[i]
```

```
window.frameName
```

Properties: closed, defaultStatus, document, frames[], history, length, location, Math, name, navigator, offscreenBuffering, opener, parent, screen, self, status, top, window

Properties (Netscape Navigator only): crypto, innerHeight, innerWidth, jav, locationbar, menubar, netscape, outerHeight, outerWidth, Packages, pageXOffset, pageYOffset, personalbar, screenX, screenY, scrollbars, statusbar, sun, toolbar

Properties (Internet Explorer only) : clientInformation, event

Methods: alert(), blur(), clearInterval(), clearTimeout(), close(), confirm(), focus(), moveBy(), moveTo(), oen(), prompt(), resizeBy(), resizeTo(), scroll(), scrollBy(), scrollTo(), setInterval(), setTimeout()

Netscape Navigator only: atob(), back(), btoa(), captureEvents(), disableExternalCapture(), enableExternalCapture(), find(), forward(), handleEvent(), home(), print(), releaseEvents(), routeEvent(), setHotkeys(), setResizable(), setZOptions(), stop()

Internet Explorer only: navigate()

Event handlers: onBlur, onDragDrop, onError, onFocus, onLoad, onMove, onResize, onUnload

Global Properties

Infinity

NaN (not a number)

Undefined

Built-in JavaScript Functions

escape ( )

Description: Returns the hexadecimal encoding of an argument in the ISO-Latin-1 character set. escape() and it's reverse function, unescape(), are typically used to send special characters safely from a JavaScript script to another program, such as a Java applet. For example, you can encode a special character using the escape() function and send the resulting value to another program that can then decode that character using the equivalent of the unescape() function — and vice versa. (Sending special characters without using this encoding process can result in errors. You can think of the ISO-Latin-1 character set as a lowest-common-denominator language that many programmer languages understand.)

Syntax: escape("*valueToBeEncoded*")

Example: escape("&") // returns the hexadecimal equivalent of & which is "%26"

eval ( )

Description: Evaluates a string of JavaScript code without reference to a particular object.

Syntax: eval("*value*") where *value* is a string representing a JavaScript expression, statement, or sequence of statements. The expression can include variables and properties of existing objects.

Example: eval(new String("2+2")) // returns a String object containing "2+2"

isFinite ( )

Description: Evaluates an argument to determine whether it is a finite number. If the argument is NaN, positive infinity or negative infinity, this method returns false; otherwise it returns true.

Syntax: isFinite(*value*)

Example: isFinite(123) // returns true

isNaN()

Description: Evaluates an argument to determine if it is not a number. Returns `true` if passed `NaN` and `false` otherwise.

Syntax: `isNaN(value)`

Example: `isNaN(123) // returns false`

Number()

Description: Converts the specified object to a number.

Syntax: `Number(anObject)`

Example: `aDate = new Date ("December 17, 1995 03:24:00")`

  `alert (Number(d)) // Displays a dialog box containing` `"819199440000."`

parseFloat()

Description: Parses a string argument and returns a floating point number.

Syntax: `parseFloat("value")`

Example: `var x = "3.14" // returns 3.14`

parseInt()

Description: Parses a string argument and returns an integer of the specified radix or base. (Base 10 is assumed if no radix is supplied.)

Syntax: `parseInt(string[, radix])`

Example: `parseInt("1111", 2) // returns 15`

  `parseInt("15", 10) // returns 15`

String ( )

Description: Converts the specified object to a string.

Syntax: string(an*Object*)

Example:

```
aDate = new Date (430054663215)
alert (String(aDate)) // displays "Thu Aug 18 04:37:43 GMT-
         0700 (Pacific Daylight Time) 1983."
```

taint ( )

Description: Adds tainting to a data element or script. (*Tainting* a JavaScript element prevents that element from being passed to a server without the end user's permission.)

Syntax: taint([*dataElementName*]) where *dataElementName* is the property, variable, function, or object to taint. If omitted, taint is added to the script itself.

Example: taintedStatus=taint(window.defaultStatus)

unescape ( )

Description: Returns the ASCII string for the specified hexadecimal encoding value.

Syntax: unescape("*value*") where *value* is a string containing characters in the form "%xx", xx being a 2-digit hexadecimal number.

Example: unescape("%26") // returns "&"

untaint ( )

Description: Removes tainting from a data element or script. (*Tainting* a JavaScript element prevents that element from being passed to a server without the end user's permission.)

Syntax: untaint([*dataElementName*]) where *dataElementName* is the property, variable, function, or object from which to remove tainting.

Example: untaintedStatus=untaint(window.defaultStatus)

Appendix D

Special Characters

●●●

Sometimes you need to represent special characters in JavaScript strings. Common examples of special characters include white space, currency symbols, and non-English characters.

When you represent special characters in JavaScript, you have a choice: you can use escape characters, octal or hexadecimal representations of the Web-standard character set Latin-1 (ISO 8859-1), or — for versions of Netscape Navigator including 6.0 and later — Unicode.

Together, the ISO 8859 and Unicode standards allow for literally tens of thousands of special characters: enough to represent most of the known human languages! While I couldn't fit all of them in this appendix, the table below should cover most of your special character needs. It lists the most commonly used special characters, along with both the hexadecimal and octal representations JavaScript supports.

Character sets are evolving standards. To get the very latest scoop on JavaScript internationalization and supported character sets — as well as to find representations for special characters not listed in this appendix — check out the section of Netscape's JavaScript manual that describes support for special characters at

```
http://developer.netscape.com/docs/manuals/js/client/jsguide/
            ident.htm.
```

For more information on the Unicode standard, check out the Unicode home page at

```
http://www.unicode.org.
```

The following is example of how you use special characters in JavaScript code:

```
alert("\'JavaScript For Dummies\u00A9\' costs $29.99 in the
            U.S., 195\xA5 in Japan, and \24316 in Britain.")
```

Figure D-1:
Unicode
symbols
translate
into nice
readable
characters.

Microsoft Internet Explorer

⚠ 'JavaScript For Dummies©' costs $29.99 in the
U.S., 195¥ in Japan, and £16 in Britain.

OK

Here are the most commonly used special characters:

Character	JavaScript escape characters	Unicode
backspace	\b	\u000b
form feed	\f	\u000C
new line	\n	\u000A
carriage return	\r	\u000D
tab	\t	\u0009
apostrophe	\'	\u0027
double quote	\"	\u0022
backslash	\\	\u005C

Octal, hexadecimal, and Unicode representations of other common special
characters appear in the following lists:

Octal	Hex	Unicode	Description	Character
\240	\xA0	\u00A0	Non-breaking space	
\241	\xA1	\u00A1	Inverted exclamation mark	¡
\242	\xA2	\u00A2	Cent sign	¢
\243	\xA3	\u00A3	Pound sign	£
\244	\xA4	\u00A4	General currency sign	
\245	\xA5	\u00A5	Yen sign	¥
\246	\xA6	\u00A6	Broken vertical line	¦
\247	\xA7	\u00A7	Section sign	§
\250	\xA8	\u00A8	Diaeresis or umlaut	¨

Octal	Hex	Unicode	Description	Character
\251	\xA9	\u00A9	Copyright sign	©
\252	\xAA	\u00AA	Feminine ordinal indicator	ª
\253	\xAB	\u00AB	Left-pointing double carets	«
\254	\xAC	\u00AC	Logical not-sign	¬
\255	\xAD	\u00AD	Soft hyphen	-
\256	\xAE	\u00AE	Registered sign	®
\257	\xAF	\u00AF	Macron	¯
\260	\xB0	\u00B0	Degree sign	°
\261	\xB1	\u00B1	Plus-or-minus sign	±
\262	\xB2	\u00B2	Superscript two	^{2}
\263	\xB3	\u00B3	Superscript three	^{3}
\264	\xB4	\u00B4	Acute accent	´
\265	\xB5	\u00B5	Micro sign	µ
\266	\xB6	\u00B6	Pilcrow	¶
\267	\xB7	\u00B7	Middle dot	·
\270	\xB8	\u00B8	Cedilla	¸
\271	\xB9	\u00B9	Superscript-one	^{1}
\272	\xBA	\u00BA	Masculine ordinal indicator	º
\273	\xBB	\u00BB	Angle quotation mark (right)	»
\274	\xBC	\u00BC	Fraction-one-quarter	¼
\275	\xBD	\u00BD	Fraction-one-half	½
\276	\xBE	\u00BE	Fraction-three-quarters	¾
\277	\xBF	\u00BF	Inverted question mark	¿

Upper-case letters

Octal	Hex	Unicode	Description	Character
\300	\xC0	\u00C0	A-grave À	
\301	\xC1	\u00C1	A-acute Á	
\302	\xC2	\u00C2	A-circumflex Â	

(continued)

Upper-case letters

\303	\xC3	\u00C3	A-tilde Ã
\304	\xC4	\u00C4	A-umlaut Ä
\305	\xC5	\u00C5	A-ring Å
\306	\xC6	\u00C6	AE Æ
\307	\xC7	\u00C7	C-cedilla Ç
\310	\xC8	\u00C8	E-grave È
\311	\xC9	\u00C9	E-acute É
\312	\xCA	\u00CA	E-circumflex Ê
\313	\xCB	\u00CB	E-umlaut Ë
\314	\xCC	\u00CC	I-grave Ì
\315	\xCD	\u00CD	I-acute Í
\316	\xCE	\u00CE	I-circumflex Î
\317	\xCF	\u00CF	I-umlaut Ï
\320	\xD0	\u00D0	D-stroke Đ
\321	\xD1	\u00D1	N-tilde Ñ
\322	\xD2	\u00D2	O-grave Ò
\323	\xD3	\u00D3	O-acute Ó
\324	\xD4	\u00D4	O-circumflex Ô
\325	\xD5	\u00D5	O-tilde Õ
\326	\xD6	\u00D6	O-umlaut Ö
\327	\xD7	\u00D7	multiplication-sign ×
\330	\xD8	\u00D8	O-slash Ø
\331	\xD9	\u00D9	U-grave Ù
\332	\xDA	\u00DA	U-acute Ú
\333	\xDB	\u00DB	U-circumflex Û
\334	\xDC	\u00DC	U-umlaut Ü
\335	\xDD	\u00DD	Y-acute Ý
\336	\xDE	\u00DE	THORN Þ
\337	\xDF	\u00DF	small sharp s β

Lower-case letters

\340	\xE0	\u00E0	a-grave à
\341	\xE1	\u00E1	a-acute á
\342	\xE2	\u00E2	a-circumflex â
\343	\xE3	\u00E3	a-tilde ã
\344	\xE4	\u00E4	a-umlaut ä
\345	\xE5	\u00E5	a-ring å
\346	\xE6	\u00E6	ae æ
\347	\xE7	\u00E7	c-cedilla ç
\350	\xE8	\u00E8	e-grave è
\351	\xE9	\u00E9	e-acute é
\352	\xEA	\u00EA	e-circumflex ê
\353	\xEB	\u00EB	e-umlaut ë
\354	\xEC	\u00EC	i-grave ì
\355	\xED	\u00ED	i-acute í
\356	\xEE	\u00EE	i-circumflex î
\357	\xEF	\u00EF	i-umlaut ï
\360	\xF0	\u00F0	d-stroke ð
\361	\xF1	\u00F1	n-tilde ñ
\362	\xF2	\u00F2	o-grave ò
\363	\xF3	\u00F3	o-acute ó
\364	\xF4	\u00F4	o-circumflex ô
\365	\xF5	\u00F5	o-tilde õ
\366	\xF6	\u00F6	o-umlaut ö
\367	\xF7	\u00F7	division-sign ÷
\370	\xF8	\u00F8	o-slash ø
\371	\xF9	\u00F9	u-grave ù
\372	\xFA	\u00FA	u-acute ú

(continued)

Lower-case letters

\373	\xFB	\u00FB	u-circumflex û
\374	\xFC	\u00FC	u-umlaut ü
\375	\xFD	\u00FD	y-acute ý
\376	\xFE	\u00FE	thorn þ
\377	\xFF	\u00FF	y-umlaut ÿ

Appendix E

About the CD

● ●

*T*his appendix explains what's on the CD-ROM that accompanies this book, as well as how to install the contents and run each of the examples. Here's a sneak-peek at the contents for those of you who just can't wait:

- ✔ Full working copies of each of the HTML/JavaScript listings that appear in the book
- ✔ A wealth of useful JavaScript development tools
- ✔ Sound and image files used in the examples

Getting the Most from This CD

The best way to get familiar with JavaScript is to load scripts and interact with them as you read through each chapter. If it's feasible for you, I suggest installing the contents of the CD before you pick up the book (or at least before you're more than about a quarter of the way through). Then, when you come across a listing in the book, you can double-click on the corresponding HTML file you've already installed and bingo! Interactive learning.

If you really want to make sure that you understand a concept, be sure you take time not just to run each file, but to play around with it, too. Change a line of JavaScript code and see what happens. You can't go wrong because you can just reinstall from the CD.

The examples are also referenced throughout the text. Some were designed to reinforce the concepts you're discovering; others, to be real, live, workable scripts that you can incorporate into your own Web pages. Enjoy!

System Requirements

Make sure that your computer meets the minimum system requirements listed here. If your computer doesn't match up to most of these requirements, you may have problems in using the contents of the CD.

- A Pentium-based PC, or a Mac OS computer with a Power PC-based processor.
- Microsoft Windows 95 or later, Windows NT4 or later, or Mac OS system software 8.5 or later.
- A copy of either Netscape Navigator 6.0 or Microsoft Internet Explorer 5.5. (Chapter 1 tells you how to get a copy and install it, if you haven't already.)
- At least 16MB of total RAM installed on your computer. For best performance, I recommend that Windows-equipped PCs and Mac OS computers with PowerPC processors have at least 32 MB of RAM installed.
- At least 25MB of hard drive space on a Windows PC or at least 10MB of hard drive space available on a Mac OS computer to install all the software from this CD. (You'll need less space if you don't install every program.)
- A CD-ROM drive — double-speed (2x) or faster.
- A sound card for PCs. (Mac OS computers have built-in sound support.)
- A monitor capable of displaying at least 256 colors or grayscale.
- A modem with a speed of at least 14,400 Kbps and an Internet connection (to connect to the World Wide Web).

If you need more information on the basics, check out *PCs For Dummies,* 7th Edition, by Dan Gookin, or *Macs For Dummies,* 6th Edition, by David Pogue (both published by IDG Books Worldwide, Inc.).

Using the CD with Microsoft Windows

To install the items from the CD to your hard drive, follow these steps:

1. **Insert the CD into your computer's CD-ROM drive and close the drive door.**

2. **Windows users: Click the Start button and click Run.**

3. **In the dialog box that appears, type** D:\SETUP.EXE.

    Most of you probably have your CD-ROM drive listed as drive D under My Computer in Windows. If your CD-ROM drive uses a different letter, type that letter instead of D.

4. **Click on OK in the Run dialog box.**

   A license agreement window appears.

5. **Read through the license agreement, nod your head wisely, and then click on the Accept button.**

   After you click on Accept, you'll never be bothered by the License Agreement window again. The CD interface appears.

6. **Click on a category button to see a list of products in that category.**

7. **Click once on the product name, and click on the Info button at the top of the window for more information about that product.**

   The interface opens a text file (for most of you, the text file pops up in the Notepad text editor, which comes free with Windows) that gives a brief description of what the program does and any special information you might need to know about installing it. When you have finished reading the information, be sure to close Notepad.

8. **To install the product, just click on the Install button and follow the on-screen setup instructions.**

   When the installation is complete, the interface usually reappears in front of other opened windows. Sometimes the installation will confuse Windows and leave the interface in the background. To bring the interface forward, just click once anywhere in the interface's window.

9. **To install other items, repeat Steps 6 through 8.**

10. **When you've finished installing the software you chose, click on the Quit button to close the interface. You can eject the CD now. Carefully place it back in the plastic jacket of the book for safekeeping.**

Using the CD with a Mac OS Computer

To install the items from the CD to your hard drive, follow these steps:

1. **Insert the CD into your computer's CD-ROM drive and close the drive door.**

   In a moment, an icon representing the CD you just inserted appears on your Mac desktop. Chances are, the icon looks like a CD-ROM.

2. **Double-click on the Read Me First icon.**

   This text file contains information about the CD's programs and any last-minute instructions you need to know (that we don't cover in this appendix) about installing the programs on the CD.

3. **Double-click on the CD icon to show the CD's contents.**

4. **To install BBEdit Lite, BBEdit 4.0 Demo, the Ant Demo, or the Chapters' sample JavaScript files, just drag the item's folder from the CD window and drop it on your hard drive icon.**

5. **To install StuffIt Expander, HTML Web Weaver, and W4 Demo, double-click on the appropriate icon with the words "Install" or "Installer."**

6. **To run the demo for ArtBeats WebTools, open the WebTools 1.41 folder and double-click on the Start Demo! icon.**

   This demo runs from the CD. You don't need to install anything to use it.

7. **After you've finished installing the software you chose, eject the CD and carefully place it back in the plastic jacket of the book for safekeeping.**

JavaScript For Dummies Chapter Files

Each of the chapter listings that appear in the book is contained on the companion CD in the CHAPTERS folder. The naming convention used is list####.htm, where # corresponds to each specific chapter and listing number. For example, you can find Listing 8-1 in the file named list0801.htm.

In addition to the chapter listings, the CD contains multimedia files and additional files for your review. To see a list and description of these items, please see the text file LISTINGS.TXT, located in the CHAPTERS folder.

You may find it more convenient to copy the CHAPTERS folder to your hard drive. To install the files, see "Using the CD with Microsoft Windows" or "Using the CD with a Mac OS Computer" section of this appendix.

What You'll Find

In addition to HTML files containing the JavaScript chapter listings, the following development tools are on the companion CD. Many of the tools are either trial versions or shareware, which means if you like the product and use it regularly, you need to contact the company directly and arrange to purchase a copy of your very own.

Allaire HomeSite 30-day evaluation version. HomeSite, from Allaire, is an HTML editor for Windows 95 with many features that make Web programming a breeze. You can add and check tags, anchors, and formatting quickly. You can find updates at

`http://www.allaire.com.`

BBEdit (Demo) and BBEdit Lite (Freeware). From Bare Bones Software, BBEdit Lite is a freeware text editor available for the Macintosh that makes a great HTML editor, too. Get the skinny on Bare Bones by visiting

```
http://www.barebones.com/products/bbedit/bbedit.html.
```

Dreamweaver Trial Version. Dreamweaver is an industrial-strength Web development tool that runs on both Windows and Power Mac; it also works hand-in-glove with Macromedia's Web-graphics development tool, Fireworks. To purchase a copy of your very own — or just to get more information on Dreamweaver — visit

```
http://www.macromedia.com/software/dreamweaver/
```

NetObjects ScriptBuilder Trial Version. This Windows-only product has just one goal in life: to help developers build client- and server-side scripts. Features include a syntax checker, a point-and-click object model, and an automatic cross-browser code inspector. Product information can be found at

```
http://www.notobjects.com/products/html/nsb3.html
```

Paint Shop Pro Evaluation Version. JASC Inc.'s Paint Shop Pro is a shareware graphics viewing and editing tool available for Windows. You can find updates at `http://www.jasc.com`.

StyleMaker Shareware. Danere's StyleMaker helps you create scriptable cascading style sheets. You choose from basic styles and then configure to your heart's content; built-in preview capability is built right in. For more information, visit

```
http://www.danere.com/StyleMaker/try.htm
```

SurfMap JavaScrip Trial Version. This visual editing tool for Windows lets you create customized, collapsible navigation maps for your site. Find updates and product information at `http://www.surfmap.com`.

Web Weaver Demo Version. McWeb Software's Web Weaver is a professional HTML editor for Windows platforms. The "gold" version offers spell checking and a few other features not found in the evaluation version. For details, visit

```
http://www.mcwebsoftware.com/webweav.asp.
```

If You Have Problems (Of the CD Kind)

I tried my best to compile programs that work on most computers with the minimum system requirements. Alas, your computer may differ, and some programs may not work properly for some reason.

The two likeliest problems are that you don't have enough memory (RAM) for the programs you want to use, or you have other programs running that are affecting the installation or running of a program. If you get error messages such as Not enough memory or Setup cannot continue, try one or more of these methods and then try using the software again:

- Turn off any antivirus software you have on your computer. Installers sometimes mimic virus activity and may make your computer incorrectly believe it is being infected by a virus.

- Close all running programs. The more programs you're running, the less memory is available to other programs. Installers also typically update files and programs. So if you keep other programs running, the installation may not work properly.

- Have your local computer store add more RAM to your computer. This is, admittedly, a drastic and somewhat expensive step. If you have a Windows 95 PC or a Mac OS computer with a PowerPC chip, however, adding more memory can really help the speed of your computer and allow more programs to run at the same time.

If you still have trouble installing the items from the CD, please call the Hungry Minds Customer Care phone number: 800-762-2974 (outside the U.S.: 317-572-3993).

Index

• A •

About.com Web site, 285
ActiveX objects, 271
agt variable, 98
alert display statement, 302–304
alert method, 38–39, 72
Allaire HomeSite 4.5, 356
America Online browser, 298
Anchor object, 322
angle brackets, 291
animated GIF, 236
animated GIF Web site, 89
animation
  hiding and showing image, 244–246
  on/off type, 237–239
  overview of, 17, 236
  slide show, 240, 242–243
Applet object, 322
APPLET tag, 271
Area object, 323
AREA tag, 66
areas, defining for image, 171
arguments, 323
Array object, 323
assigning results of JavaScript
    statements to HTML attributes, 279
assignment operator, 61
attaching external script, 120
atttribute, 68
auto-scrolling, 276–277

• B •

BBEdit Lite 5.5.1, 357
binary operator, 59
Boolean object, 324
Boolean value, 62
break statement, 51–52
browser. *See also* Microsoft Internet
    Explorer; Netscape Navigator
  animation and, 237
  cookies and, 125
  debugging problems, 306
  designing Web page and, 89
  document object model and, 87
  documentation Web sites, 19
  event handling and, 145
  Event object and, 154
  hiding code from non-JavaScript-
      enabled type, 32, 34
  image and, 162
  JavaScript and, 12
  plug-ins and, 270–271
  querying document object model,
      88–89
  Submit button and, 159
  testing page in, 297–298
  turning off JavaScript support, 30
  version-specific code and, 33
Browser icon, 6
browser "sniffer" script
  code for, 89–90, 92–94
  generating page based on, 106–107
  indexOf method, 105
  order of statements, 94
  parseInt function, 104–105
  purpose of, 88
  string code, 102
  strings in, 101
  toLowerCase method, 103
  variables, defining, 98–100
bugs. *See also* debugging
bugs in JavaScript 1.2, 121

built-in functions
    list of, 343–345
    overview of, 249
button elements
    event handlers for, 144
    onClick event handler for, 149–151
    overview of, 143, 147
Button object, 324

• *C* •

calling function
    code for, 35–36, 57, 75–76
    description of, 35
calling Java applet methods, 262–263
cascading style sheets, 247–248
case-sensitivity of interpreter, 290, 321
catch block, 309–311
CD
    system requirements for, 354
    troubleshooting, 357
CD contents
    CHAPTERS folder, 356
    development tools, 356–357
    installing with Mac OS, 355–356
    installing with Microsoft Windows,
        354–355
    overview of, 1
    text editing utilities, 18
    uses of, 353
CGI (Common Gateway Interface), 16
CGI (Common Gateway Interface)
        program, 123
changeColor function, 248
Checkbox object, 324
clearInterval method, 255
clearTimeout method, 257
click event, 166
click method, 72
clientInformation object, 325
client-side JavaScript, 14

client-side JavaScript language reference,
        302, 347
client-side objects that support event
        handlers, 145–147
CNET Builder.com Web site, 284
code
    copying, 286
    typing, 3
code library. *See* library
collapsible table of contents
    code for, 229–230
    example of, 227
color, changing with mouse rollover, 194
comment
    code for, 37
    debugging and, 301
    overview of, 36
    types of, 44
commercialism of Internet, 283
Common Gateway Interface (CGI), 16
    program, 123
comparison operator, 62
compiled language, 13
condition, 47
conditional ? operator, 137
conditional expression
    if...then statement, 37–38
    if...else, 45
configuring level of support for cookies,
        126–127
connecting frames, 224, 226
content frames
    creating, 221, 223–224
    index links, connecting to, 224, 226
content, refreshing
    automatic interval, 253, 255
    on demand, 256–257
continue statement, 51–52
conventions in book, 2–3
cookie property of document object, 136
cookies
    attributes for, 136–137
    CGI script and, 130

configuring level of support for, 126, 127
creating, 136
deleting, 140
description of, 123
expiration date for, 131, 140
exploring files, 127, 129
repeat visitor script, 130–131, 133–135, 137–139
security issues, 124–125
uses of, 124
visiting sites with, 127
copying code, 286
copyright, 286
counting months, 111
creating
  cookies, 136
  function that expects number but accepts string, 290
  image links for navigation bar, 172–174
  index and content frames, 221, 223–224
  mouse rollover, 181, 187, 189–190, 192
  simple mouse rollover, 194
crypto object, 325
curly braces, 45, 76
custom greeting code, 137–139
customizing page appearance, 277–279

• D •

data types for Netscape Navigator, 78–80
data validation
  code for, 197–198
  existence validation script, 201–202
  field types, 200
  form-level validation script, 208–209, 211–215, 217
  individual input fields, 199
  numeric validation script, 203–205
  overview of, 196
  phone number validation script, 205–206
  tutorial Web site, 196

date formatting script, 118–120
Date function, 249, 251–252
Date object
  constructing using no information, 112
  constructing using specific information, 110–111
  date formatting script, 118–120
  display variations, 115
  methods for, 112, 114–115
  methods Web site, 115
  overview of, 109, 326
  syntax for, 110
  time formatting script, 116–117
debugging. *See also* errors
  browser problems, 306
  checking documentation, 302
  comments and, 301
  displaying variable values, 302–304
  exception handling, 308–311
  HTML code, 306
  JavaScript 1.2, 121
  JavaScript code, 307
  limiting function size, 305
  newsgroup help with, 307
  overview of, 299
  process of elimination approach, 305–306
  pseudo-code and, 300
  trial-and-error approach, 308
  working backward from clues, 301–302
declaring
  function, 57
  variable, 55
defining
  areas for image, 171
  function, 35–36, 75–76
  variable, 98–100
deleting cookies, 140
dependent field validation, 200, 208–209, 211–215, 217
detecting plug-ins, 271–274, 276
development cycle, 22

DHTML
  Microsoft Internet Explorer and, 81
  overview of, 235
displaying property values of object, 49
displayProperties function, 48–49
displayProverb function, 35–36
do while loop, 51
document object
  cookie property of, 136
  description of, 71
  event handlers and, 74
  overview of, 326
document object model (DOM)
  animation and, 237
  browser and, 87
  description of, 11, 14, 43
  event handlers, 73–74
  functions, 74, 76
  methods, 71–74
  Netscape Navigator, 77, 81
  object, 68–69
  overview of, 67, 321
  properties, 69–70
  querying, 88–89
  resources for, 104
  Web sites, 321
DOM. *See* document object model
Dreamweaver 3, 357
dumping, 49
Dynamic HTML. *See* DHTML

• E •

e-mail address pattern validation script,
    197–198
e-mail address validation script, 199
e-mail, linking to, 176
ECMA standard
  cross-browser compatibility and, 87
  overview of, 86
elements[] object, 327
EMBED tag, 270

embedding function, 58
end-of-statement operator, 100
endless loop, 47
equal sign operator, 63
errors. *See also* debugging
  browser incompatibility, 297–298
  equal sign use, 63
  HTML mistakes, 290
  JavaScript reserved words and, 315
  logic type, 297
  nesting quotes, 294
  overview of, 289
  placement of scripting statement,
      293–294
  spelling, 289
  treating numbers as strings, 294–296
  unmatched pairs, 291–292
escape function, 136, 343
European Computer Manufacturers
    Association (ECMA), 86
eval function, 343
event
  description of, 143
  logging time elapsed between, 250
  triggering, 11
event handler
  assigning value to, 41
  blur-related, 200
  browser and, 145
  button elements and, 143–144, 147
  client-side objects that support,
      145–147
  description of, 67–68, 143
  onBlur, 199–200
  onChange, 200
  onClick, 73, 149–151, 166, 251–252
  onFocus, 200
  onLoad, 73, 251–252
  onMouseOut, 167
  onMouseOver, 166, 184, 186–187
  onReset, 159
  onSelect, 200

onSubmit, 158
onSubmit and onReset, 152–154
order form script, 154–155, 157–158
overview of, 40, 73–74
radio elements and, 147
reset and submit elements and, 151
Event object, 154, 327
exception handling, 308–311
existence validation script, 201–202
exists function, 202
expiration date for cookies, 131, 140
expression
  break statement, 51–52
  comments and, 44
  conditional type, 45
  continue statement, 51–52
  description of, 44
  do while loop, 51
  for loop, 46–48
  for...in loop, 48–49
  label statement, 53
  legal type, 55
  overview of, 44
  switch statement, 53–54
  while loop, 50
  with statement, 54
external script
  attaching to HTML file, 120
  description of, 118
  formatting date, 119–120

● F ●

feedback to users, 217
files
  cookies, viewing, 127, 129
  naming, 184
  saving in plain text format, 23
  storing, 120
FileUpload object, 328
firewall, 265
flow chart, 300

focus method, 74
for loop, 46–48
form. See also HTML forms
  preventing automatic reset of; order
    form script
Form object, 328
form object, event handlers for, 152–154
FORM tag, 159
form-level validation script, 208–209,
  211–215, 217
forms
  data validation, 196–200
  existence validation script, 201–202
  form-level validation script, 208–209,
    211–215, 217
  JavaScript features and, 195
  numeric validation script, 203–205
  phone number validation script,
    205–206
  preventing automatic reset of, 159
  testing, 217
for...in loop, 48–49
Frame object, 328
frames
  collapsible table of contents, 227
  collapsible table of contents, code for,
    229–230
  connecting, 224, 226
  index and content, creating, 221,
    223–224
  loading two on one click, 226
  overview of, 219
  preventing display of site in, 222
  table of contents example, 220
FTP (file transfer protocol), 19
fully-qualified name, 39
fully qualified property, 71
function
  advantage of using, 57
  built-in, list of, 343–345
  built-in, overview of, 249
  calling, 57

function *(continued)*
  defining and calling, 35–36, 75–76
  description of, 44
  embedding, 58
  limiting size of, 305
  overview of, 35, 74, 76
  returning value from, 58
  syntax for, 57
  testing code with, 302
function call, 58
function keyword, 57
Function object, 329

• G •

Gamelan Web site, 285
generating tools, 176
generating Web page based on type of
    browser, 106–107
GIF, animated type, 236
global properties, 342
global variable, 100
GoGraph Web site, 181
graphics interchange format (GIF),
    animated type, 236

• H •

halting scheduled execution, 257
hardware requirements
  for CD, 354
  overview of, 1, 18
HEAD tag, 279
Hidden object, 329
hiding SCRIPT tag, 32, 34
History object, 329
hot spot
  description of, 168
  designating, 170–171
HREF attribute, 176
HTML
  button elements, 143–144, 147
  debugging, 306

errors in, 290
JavaScript and, 14
radio elements, 147
reset and submit elements, 151
uses of, 259
HTML file, creating, 22–25
HTML forms
  JavaScript features and, 195
  password element, 268
HTML-generating Web development
    tools, 193

• I •

identifying visitors, 124
IDG Books Worldwide Customer
    Service, 358
if...else statement, 45
if...then statement, 37–38
image
  adding to Web page, 161–163
  browser and, 162
  changing with onMouseOver event
    handler, 184, 186–187
  hiding and showing, 244–246
  interactive, 161
  navigation bar and, 172–174, 176
  onClick event handler and, 166
  onMouseOut event handler and, 167
  onMouseOver event handler and, 166
  pre-loading, 181–182, 184
  rollover, creating, 187, 189–190, 192
  sources for, 181
  splash page redux script, 168, 170–171
  splash page script, 164
Image object
  event handlers for, 167
  overview of, 330
  Web sites for, 163
image object, properties of, 69–70
IMG tag, 161–163, 243
in scope variable, 56
incremental operator, 60

independent field validation, 200
index frames
  connecting to content headings, 224, 226
  creating, 221, 223–224
indexOf method, 105
initial expression, 47
initializing variable, 55
inserting script, 31–32
intelligence, adding, 16
interacting with users, 217
interactive features, 9, 16
interactive image, 161
interim browser release, 12
Internet Explorer. *See* Microsoft Internet
  Explorer
Internet resources. *See* newsgroups;
  Web sites
interpreted language, 13
intranet, 265
isANumber function, 205
isAPhoneNumber function, 206–208
isAValidEmail function, 198–199
isFinite function, 343
isNaN function, 203, 344
iterating, 48–49

• J •

Java applet
  calling methods from, 262–263
  description of, 236
Java compared to JavaScript, 12
Java execution environment, 262
java object, 330
JavaArray object, 330
JavaClass object, 331
JavaClock example, 262–263
JavaObject object, 331
JavaPackage object, 331
JavaScript
  advantages of, 15
  animations, creating with, 17

browsers and, 11–13, 15
client-side type, 14
customizing pages with, 17
debugging code, 307
description of, 10
features of, 11
hardware requirements for, 1, 18
HTML and, 14
intelligence, adding with, 16
interactive features, 16
interpreted language of, 13
Java compared to, 12
limitations of, 259
reserved words in, 315
software requirements for, 1, 18
version-specific code and, 33
versions of, 121
JavaScript application
  clarifying ideas for, 22
  description of, 21
  HTML file, creating, 22–25
  script, creating and attaching, 26–27, 29
  script, testing, 29–30
  tools for creating, 21
JavaScript Authoring Guide Web site, 19
JavaScript entity, 279
JavaScript interpreter, 67
JavaSoft Web site, 264
JScript, 11, 86

• L •

label statement, 53
legal expression, 55
library
  benefits of, 228
  collapsible list example from, 229–230
  description of, 227
limiting size of function, 305
Link object, 332
linking to e-mail, 176
literals, 56

load event, 250–252
loading
  frames, 226
  URL into new browser window, 268–270
loadTwoFrames function, 226
local variable, 100
locateImage function, 186
Location object, 332
logging time elapsed between events,
  250–252
logic errors, 297
logical operator, 62
loosely-typed language, 78

• M •

Mac OS, installing CD contents using,
  355–356
manipulating
  cascading style sheet properties,
  247–248
  definition of, 101
MAP tag, 66
MARQUEE tag, 88, 276
Math object
  Netscape Navigator and, 80
  overview of, 332
META tag, 255
method. *See also* event handler
  adding to object, 64–65
  built-in, overview of, 249
  calling, 39
  code for, 38–39
  description of, 38, 67–68
  information Web site, 277
  overview of, 71
  referring to, 72–73
  time-related for Window object, 249,
  253, 255–257
  uses of, 74
Microsoft
  exception handling information, 311
  JScript, 86, 284, 298

proprietary features, 87
  script debugger Web site, 299
Microsoft Internet Explorer
  clientInformation object, 325
  configuring cookie support, 127
  cookie files, viewing in, 129
  document object model information
  Web site, 321
  documentation for, 19
  downloading and installing, 19
  JavaScript and, 11, 13, 15
  plug-ins and, 271
Microsoft Windows, installing CD
  contents using, 354–355
MIME (Multipurpose Internet Mail
  Extension), 271
MimeType object, 333
modifying user input, 217
months, counting, 111
mouse events, responding to, 164
mouse rollover. *See also* onMouseOver
  event handler
  code for, 166
  creating, 181, 187, 189–190, 192
  description of, 16, 179
  pre-loading images for, 182, 184
  simple, creating, 194
multiple-line comment, 45
Multipurpose Internet Mail Extension
  (MIME), 271

• N •

naming
  files, 184
  function, 57
navigation bar
  image links, creating, 172–174
  linking to e-mail, 176
  onMouseOver event handler, 184,
  186–187
  overview of, 172
  pre-loading images, 182, 184
  rollover, creating, 187, 189–190, 192, 194

navigator object
  information on, 104
  overview of, 333
nesting quotes, 294
NetObjects ScriptBuilder 3, 357
Netscape
  browser "sniffer" script, 88
  client-side JavaScript language
    reference, 298, 347
  code library Web site, 230
  data validation tutorial Web site, 196
  DevEdge FAQ Web site, 285
  exception handling information, 311
  JavaScript and, 86
  proprietary features, 87
  script debugger Web site, 300
Netscape Navigator
  configuring cookie support, 126
  cookie files, viewing in, 127, 129
  crypto object, 325
  Detect Plug-Ins button, 271
  detecting plug-ins, 276
  document object model, 77, 81
  document object model information
    Web site, 322
  documentation for, 19
  downloading and installing, 19
  JavaScript and, 11, 13, 15
  JavaScript data types, 78–80
  Math object, 80
  plug-ins and, 270–271
netscape object, 334
new operator, 63–65
newsgroups
  debugging and, 307
  JavaScript-related development, 287
  overview of, 286
Notepad text editor, 23
number
  creating function that expects number
    but accepts string, 296
  treating as string, 294–295
  treating string as, 296

Number function, 344
Number object, 334
numeric validation script, 203–205

• *O* •

object
  definitions of, 68–69
  description of, 67
  methods of, 68, 71–74
  properties of, 68–70
  types of, 68
object model, 66–67. *See also* document
    object model
Object object, 322, 334
OBJECT tag, 271
object-based compared to object-
    oriented language, 67
onBlur event handler, 199–200
onChange event handler, 200
onClick event handler, 73, 149–151, 166,
    251–252
onFocus event handler, 200
onLoad event handler, 73, 251–252
onMouseOut event handler, 167
onMouseOver event handler, 166, 184,
    186–187
onReset event handler, 152–154, 159
onSelect event handler, 200
onSubmit event handler, 152–154, 158
OnTheCD icon, 6
OnTheWeb icon, 6
open method, 270
operand, 44
operators
  assignment type, 61
  comparison type, 62
  conditional ?, 137
  description of, 44, 59–60
  end-of-statement, 100
  equal sign, 63
  expressions and, 44
  list of, 59

operators *(continued)*
  logical type, 62
  new, 63–65
  precedence of, 60–61
  typeof, 65
  void, 66
Option object, 335
order form script
  code for, 155, 157–158
  overview of, 154
order of statements, 94

• *P* •

Packages object, 335
page. *See* Web page
Paint Shop Pro, 357
parameter, 72
parentheses, unmatched, 292
parseFloat function, 203, 205, 344
parseInt function, 104–105, 203, 344
password element for HTML form, 268
Password object, 335
password protection scheme,
  265–266, 268
pattern matching, 206–208
phone number validation script, 205–206
picture. *See* image
placement
  of cookies, 125
  of script, 97, 293–294
plain text format, 23
plug-in
  browser and, 270
  description of, 236
  detecting, 271–274, 276
Plugin object, 336
preloadImages function, 182, 184
pre-loading image, 181–182, 184
preventing
  automatic reset of form, 159
  framed site display, 222

print method, 74
Project Cool JavaScript Zone Web
  site, 284
prompt method, 266, 277–279
property
  description of, 67–68
  fully qualified type, 71
  overview of, 69–70
proprietary features, 87
proverb generator application
  HTML and JavaScript code for, 27, 29
  HTML code for, 24–25
pseudo-code, 300

• *Q* •

quotation marks
  nesting incorrectly, 294
  unmatched, 292

• *R* •

radio elements
  onClick event handler for, 149–151
  overview of, 147
Radio object, 336
refreshing content
  automatic interval, 253, 255
  on demand, 256–257
RegExp object, 336–337
registration form code, 131, 133–135
reload method, 256–257
repeat visitor script
  custom greeting, 137–139
  overview of, 130–131
  registration form, 131, 133–135
requirements phase, 22
reserved words, 315
reset elements
  onReset event handler for, 152–154
  overview of, 151
Reset object, 337

return statement, 58
returning value from function, 58
reusing code, 305
rollover, 179. *See also* mouse rollover

• S •

saving
  files in plain text format, 23
  transaction state, 124
scope of variable, 100
screen object, 338
script
  creating and attaching, 26–27, 29
  inserting, 31–32
  placement of, 97, 293–294
  testing, 29–30
SCRIPT tag
  attaching external script, 120
  functions and, 76
  hiding, 32, 34
  LANGUAGE attribute, 33
  overview of, 31–32
  SOURCE attribute, 227
scripting language
  counting months in, 111
  description of, 10
  loosely-typed type, 78
  object-based compared to object-
    oriented, 67
ScriptSearch.com Web site, 22, 285
scrolling text effect, creating, 276–277
scrollTo method, 276
security issues
  cookies, 124–125
  HTML forms, 268
  password protection, 265–266, 268
Select object, 338
semi-colon end-of-statement operator,
  46, 100
server-side JavaScript Web site, 14

setInterval method, 253, 255
setTimeout function, 237–239
setTimeout method, 253, 256–257
shouting, 217
showEvent function, 151
single-line comment, 45
Site Last Updated message, 260–261
slide show, creating, 240, 242–243
software requirements, 1, 18
source code
  viewing, 11
  viewing and copying, 286
special characters, 347–349, 351–352
spelling errors, 289
splash page redux script
  designating hot spots, 170–171
  overview of, 168
splash page script
  onClick event handler and, 166
  onMouseOut event handler and, 167
  onMouseOver event handler and, 166
  overview of, 164
  responding to mouse events, 164
square brackets, 45
standards for special characters, 347
stateless, 123
statements, order of, 94
stop method, 74
storing files, 120
string
  code for, 102
  creating function that expects number
    but accepts string, 296
  description of, 44
  indexOf method, 105
  overview of, 101
  parseInt function, 104–105
  special characters for, 347–349, 351–352
  toLowerCase method, 103
  treating as number, 296
  treating number as, 294–295

String function, 345
string manipulation statements
  adding strings, 102
  creating strings, 102
  methods for, 102
  overview of, 101
String object, 338
style object, 194, 339
StyleMaker 1.4, 357
Submit button, 159
submit elements
  onSubmit event handler for, 152–154
  overview of, 151
Submit object, 340
substring method, 206–208
sun object, 340
SurfMap JavaScript, 357
swap function
  calling, 187
  overview of, 186
  slide show and, 243
switch statement, 53–54
syntax. *See also* expression; operators
  description of, 43
  expressions and, 44
  function declaration, 57
  overview of, 43
  return statement, 58
  semi-colon end-of-statement
    operator, 46
  variable, 55–56

• T •

table of contents
  collapsible example, 227
  collapsible example, code for, 229–230
  frames and, 220
tags, unmatched, 291
taint function, 345
tainting, 345
TARGET attribute, 225–226

target platform, 85
TechnicalStuff icon, 3, 6
test case, 306
testing
  code with special function, 302
  color of Web page, 317
  form, 217
  page in browser, 297–298
  script, 29–30
text, scrolling effect, creating, 276–277
text editor, 23
Text object, 341
Textarea object, 341
this keyword, 100
time formatting script, 116–117
time-related method and Window object,
    249, 253, 255–257
Tip icon, 6
toggle function, 245
toLowerCase method, 103
tools
  generating, 176
  HTML-generating Web development, 193
transaction state, saving, 124
transient cookies, 131
triggering event, 11
try block, 309–311
turning off
  image loading, 162
  JavaScript support, 30
typeof operator, 65
typing code, 3
typing errors, 289

• U •

unary operator, 59
unescape function, 136, 345
Unicode standard, 347
unmatched pair errors
  angle brackets, 291
  overview of, 291

parentheses, 292
quotation marks, 292
tags, 291
untaint function, 345
update expression, 47
URL
  loading into new browser window,
    268–270
  viewing in frames, 219
Usenet, 286
user-activated slide show, creating, 240,
  242–243
users. *See also* visitor
  interacting with, 217
  modifying input from, 217

• *V* •

validateForm function, 209, 211–215, 217
value of object property, 70
var keyword, 55, 99
variable
  declaring and initializing, 55
  defining, 98–100
  description of, 44, 97
  displaying values, 302–304
  in scope, 56
  scope of, 100
viewing
  cookie files, 127, 129
  source code, 11, 286
  URLs in frames, 219
visibility property, 244–246
visiting sites with cookies, 127
visitor. *See also* users
  identifying, 124
  keeping at site, 268–270
void operator, 66

• *W* •

Warning icon, 6
Web client. *See* browser
Web page
  browser compatibility and, 89
  customizing appearance of, 17, 277–279
  generating based on type of browser,
    106–107
  keeping visitor at, 268–270
  Site Last Updated message, 260–261
  testing, 317
  testing in browser, 297–298
  tracking time user spends on, 250
Web sites
  About.com, 285
  America Online browser, 208
  animated GIFs, 89
  BBEdit Lite, 357
  browser documentation and support, 19
  client-side JavaScript language
    reference, 298, 302, 347
  CNET Builder.com, 284
  Date object methods information, 115
  document object model information,
    104, 321
  Dreamweaver (Macromedia), 357
  Event object information, 154
  exception handling information, 311
  Gamelan, 285
  GoGraph, 181
  Image object information, 163
  JavaScript Authoring Guide, 19
  JavaScript data validation tutorial, 196
  JavaSoft, 264
  methods information, 277
  Microsoft Internet Explorer, 19
  Microsoft JScript, 284
  navigator object information, 104
  NetObjects ScriptBuilder, 357
  Netscape browser "sniffer" script, 88

Web sites *(continued)*
  Netscape code library, 230
  Netscape DevEdge FAQ, 285
  Netscape JavaScript Developer
    Central, 284
  Netscape Navigator, 19
  open method information, 270
  Paint Shop Pro (JASC Inc.), 357
  Project Cool JavaScript Zone, 284
  RegExp object information, 337
  script debuggers, 299
  ScriptSearch.com, 22, 285
  server-side JavaScript, 14
  special character information, 347
  string manipulation statements, 101
  Style object information, 339
  StyleMaker 1.4 (Danere), 357
  SurfMap JavaScript, 357
  Usenet, 286
  Web Weaver (McWeb Software), 357
  WebReverence.com, 285
  ZDNet, 284
Web Weaver, 357
WebReference.com Web site, 285
wetware, definition of, 85
while loop, 50
window object
  alert method, 72
  clearTimeout method, 257
  Netscape Navigator, 77
  overview of, 341–342
  setInterval method, 253, 255
  setTimeout method, 256–257
  time-related methods for, 249
window, loading URL into new, 268–270
with statement, 54
word processor and HTML files, 23

• Z •

ZDNet Web site, 284

Notes

Notes

Notes

Notes

Notes

Notes

Notes

Notes

Notes

Hungry Minds, Inc.,
End-User License Agreement

READ THIS. You should carefully read these terms and conditions before opening the software packet(s) included with this book ("Book"). This is a license agreement ("Agreement") between you and Hungry Minds, Inc. ("HMI"). By opening the accompanying software packet(s), you acknowledge that you have read and accept the following terms and conditions. If you do not agree and do not want to be bound by such terms and conditions, promptly return the Book and the unopened software packet(s) to the place you obtained them for a full refund.

1. **License Grant.** HMI grants to you (either an individual or entity) a nonexclusive license to use one copy of the enclosed software program(s) (collectively, the "Software") solely for your own personal or business purposes on a single computer (whether a standard computer or a workstation component of a multi-user network). The Software is in use on a computer when it is loaded into temporary memory (RAM) or installed into permanent memory (hard disk, CD-ROM, or other storage device). HMI reserves all rights not expressly granted herein.

2. **Ownership.** HMI is the owner of all right, title, and interest, including copyright, in and to the compilation of the Software recorded on the disk(s) or CD-ROM ("Software Media"). Copyright to the individual programs recorded on the Software Media is owned by the author or other authorized copyright owner of each program. Ownership of the Software and all proprietary rights relating thereto remain with HMI and its licensers.

3. **Restrictions On Use and Transfer.**

   (a) You may only (i) make one copy of the Software for backup or archival purposes, or (ii) transfer the Software to a single hard disk, provided that you keep the original for backup or archival purposes. You may not (i) rent or lease the Software, (ii) copy or reproduce the Software through a LAN or other network system or through any computer subscriber system or bulletin-board system, or (iii) modify, adapt, or create derivative works based on the Software.

   (b) You may not reverse engineer, decompile, or disassemble the Software. You may transfer the Software and user documentation on a permanent basis, provided that the transferee agrees to accept the terms and conditions of this Agreement and you retain no copies. If the Software is an update or has been updated, any transfer must include the most recent update and all prior versions.

4. **Restrictions on Use of Individual Programs.** You must follow the individual requirements and restrictions detailed for each individual program in Appendix E of this Book. These limitations are also contained in the individual license agreements recorded on the Software Media. These limitations may include a requirement that after using the program for a specified period of time, the user must pay a registration fee or discontinue use. By opening the Software packet(s), you will be agreeing to abide by the licenses and restrictions for these individual programs that are detailed in Appendix E and on the Software Media. None of the material on this Software Media or listed in this Book may ever be redistributed, in original or modified form, for commercial purposes.

5. **Limited Warranty.**

   (a) HMI warrants that the Software and Software Media are free from defects in materials and workmanship under normal use for a period of sixty (60) days from the date of purchase of this Book. If HMI receives notification within the warranty period of defects in materials or workmanship, HMI will replace the defective Software Media.

   (b) HMI AND THE AUTHOR OF THE BOOK DISCLAIM ALL OTHER WARRANTIES, EXPRESS OR IMPLIED, INCLUDING WITHOUT LIMITATION IMPLIED WARRANTIES OF MERCHANTABILITY AND FITNESS FOR A PARTICULAR PURPOSE, WITH RESPECT TO THE SOFTWARE, THE PROGRAMS, THE SOURCE CODE CONTAINED THEREIN, AND/OR THE TECHNIQUES DESCRIBED IN THIS BOOK. HMI DOES NOT WARRANT THAT THE FUNCTIONS CONTAINED IN THE SOFTWARE WILL MEET YOUR REQUIREMENTS OR THAT THE OPERATION OF THE SOFTWARE WILL BE ERROR FREE.

   (c) This limited warranty gives you specific legal rights, and you may have other rights that vary from jurisdiction to jurisdiction.

6. **Remedies.**

   (a) HMI's entire liability and your exclusive remedy for defects in materials and workmanship shall be limited to replacement of the Software Media, which may be returned to HMI with a copy of your receipt at the following address: Software Media Fulfillment Department, Attn.: *JavaScript For Dummies,* 3rd Edition, Hungry Minds, Inc., 10475 Crosspoint Blvd., Indianapolis, IN 46256, or call 1-800-762-2974. Please allow four to six weeks for delivery. This Limited Warranty is void if failure of the Software Media has resulted from accident, abuse, or misapplication. Any replacement Software Media will be warranted for the remainder of the original warranty period or thirty (30) days, whichever is longer.

   (b) In no event shall HMI or the author be liable for any damages whatsoever (including without limitation damages for loss of business profits, business interruption, loss of business information, or any other pecuniary loss) arising from the use of or inability to use the Book or the Software, even if HMI has been advised of the possibility of such damages.

   (c) Because some jurisdictions do not allow the exclusion or limitation of liability for consequential or incidental damages, the above limitation or exclusion may not apply to you.

7. **U.S. Government Restricted Rights.** Use, duplication, or disclosure of the Software for or on behalf of the United States of America, its agencies and/or instrumentalities (the "U.S. Government") is subject to restrictions as stated in paragraph (c)(1)(ii) of the Rights in Technical Data and Computer Software clause of DFARS 252.227-7013, or subparagraphs (c) (1) and (2) of the Commercial Computer–Restricted Rights clause at FAR 52.227-19, and in similar clauses in the NASA FAR supplement, as applicable.

8. **General.** This Agreement constitutes the entire understanding of the parties and revokes and supersedes all prior agreements, oral or written, between them and may not be modified or amended except in a writing signed by both parties hereto that specifically refers to this Agreement. This Agreement shall take precedence over any other documents that may be in conflict herewith. If any one or more provisions contained in this Agreement are held by any court or tribunal to be invalid, illegal, or otherwise unenforceable, each and every other provision shall remain in full force and effect.

Installation Instructions

To install the items from the CD to your hard drive, follow these steps:

1. **Insert the CD into your computer's CD-ROM drive and close the drive door.**

2. **Windows users: Click the Start button and click Run.**

3. **In the dialog box that appears, type** *D*:\SETUP.EXE, **where** *D* **is your CD-ROM drive.**

4. **Click on OK in the Run dialog box.**

   A license agreement window appears.

5. **Read through the license agreement, nod your head wisely, and then click on the Accept button, and the CD interface appears.**

   The CD interface has three general regions: the category buttons on the left side of the window, the product window (it's shaped like the ...*For Dummies* signboard), and the Install, Info, and Exit buttons at the top of the interface screen.

   When you first open the interface, the product window displays instructions on using the CD. The category buttons list the categories of software available on the CD.

6. **Click on a category button to see a list of products in that category.**

7. **Click once on the product name, and, if you want to view the program's notes, click on the Info button at the top of the window for more information about that product.**

8. **To install the product, just click on the Install button and follow the on-screen setup instructions.**

9. **To install other items, repeat Steps 6 through 8.**

10. **When you've finished installing the software you chose, click on the Quit button to close the interface. You can eject the CD now. Carefully place it back in the plastic jacket of the book for safekeeping.**

For more information, see the "About the CD" appendix.

Notes

Notes